YOU'RE NOT STUPID!

GET THE TRUTH

A BRIEF ON THE
BUSH PRESIDENCY

BY WILLIAM JOHN COX

PROGRESSIVE PRESS
JOSHUA TREE, CALIFORNIA

You're Not Stupid!
Get the Truth:
A Brief on the Bush Presidency

A Progressive Press Book
Published by Tree of Life Publications,
PO Box 126, Joshua Tree CA 92252
www.progressivepress.com

Library of Congress
Cataloging-in-Publication
data has been applied for
ISBN 0-930852-32-X

First Printing June 2004

Printed in Canada by
Friesens Corp., Altona, Manitoba

DEDICATION

For Thomas Paine,

An American Patriot with Common Sense

and

For Helen,

An Uncommon Wife

CONTENTS

This book is written for you, a busy person, as a useful compilation of political information and opinion drawn from diverse published sources.

The Bush administration has been running on lies in the belief that we are too stupid to figure it out. The business of exaggeration in politics has gone beyond the usual. It has become a culture of nastiness and downright lies. Is this acceptable?

How much do we really know about our president's life, his background and his character? To understand George W. Bush's administration better, it helps to become better acquainted with the well-smoothed path he has followed to the top.

Republican Senator McCain was tortured for five years in Vietnam as a POW. Democrat Vice President Gore was a man of vision and integrity. Yet Bush managed to destroy the character of each of these men using twisted lies, setting himself up to become president by judicial appointment.

Beyond the philosophical question of whether George W. Bush represents the voters, there are very real questions that linger about the legitimacy, the constitutionality, even the legality of his election.

Once having been established as president, no matter how questionably, Bush set about thanking the corporate wealthy, his peers who paid the contributions that elected (or selected) him, by putting "his" executive branch at their service.

Bush claims a successful record on education both as governor of Texas and as president, but a closer examination reveals it to be largely a public relations smokescreen. His policies, once the smoke has been blown aside, are revealed to be hostile to public education and to the democratic values on which it rests.

It's been observed that to find who has the most power in a society, you need only look to see who does not pay taxes. The touted Bush tax breaks, once the window dressing is removed, are exposed as a public giveaway to those who already have the most.

The terrorist attacks on September 11, 2001, shocked the nation. But what may be nearly as shocking is how much information the government had beforehand, and how stupendous were the incompetence and chicanery that attended its failure to prevent that catastrophe.

The saga of the midterm elections in 2002 is not a shining hour for American politics. Rather, it's a tale of new lows in dirty tricks and a corrupt politicization of the war on terrorism.

Blood for oil? A closer look at the history of Iraqi-American relations can tell what is really at stake. Just how much have the interests of U.S. oil corporations influenced the government's policies and actions, including the invasion of Iraq? To whose benefit are we risking our soldiers, our national treasury, and our traditional alliances with other nations?

Washington Crossing the Delaware
By Emanuel G. Leutze (1816-1868)

IN SELF DEFENSE

Some of the things you will read in this book are painful truths, and it will be difficult and distressing to acknowledge the reality they portray.

As an intelligent, reading public, we must keep our minds open and face these depressing facts, even while supporting our troops in Afghanistan and Iraq and responding to the realistic threat of terrorism in our own land. Americans have done this before and we can do it again. Although we sometimes feel powerless, we are not. By joining to support one another, and doing what is good for people, for ourselves, we will take back our country and assure that freedom continues to ring throughout the land!

This book is not an attack on our flag and the freedoms it represents; it is, in fact, an alarm bell calling us to rally to its defense by making us aware of how our common interests are being ignored and our human rights violated. Not just the human rights of a few minorities, but all of us. The truth may appear to be an attack on the Republican Party, but it is not. It just happens that a particular group of people who represent the special interests of international corporations have taken over the Republican Party and have overshadowed the millions of Republicans who operate with honesty and integrity, many of whom have themselves been victimized. This is not about Democrats versus Republicans, because there are also Democratic politicians who have sold out and who have ceased to represent the people in their own party. This is about you and me, the ordinary hard-working people in this country, who need to look truth in the face, take a deep breath, draw a line, and take a stand for our own interests, our families, our communities, and our nation.

ACKNOWLEDGMENTS

This book is written for you, a busy person, as a useful compilation of political information and opinion drawn from diverse published sources.

After my mother died when I was four, my father took me to his bed, where each night he would read dime western novels. After I quickly became bored with the pictures on the covers, he taught me to read. Since I was the youngest in the family and my siblings were all in school, there was no one to watch me during the day, so I rode on the tractor beside my father as he plowed the fields. One night, as I listened from another room, he and the school principal conspired at the kitchen table to use my father's birthday in August, instead of mine in February, to enroll me in the first grade a year early.

There was no mandatory kindergarten in Texas back then; there still isn't. My teachers gave me new books to read and taught me to comprehend the meaning of words. Lubbock County established an extension library in the back room behind Roy's Café across the highway from the school in Wolfforth, a refuge of knowledge and a window to the world in a barren land for a lonely little boy. Ever since, I have lived in a garden of abundant literature, the bounty of a free society. For those who taught me to read and think, and for those who have shared their labor and creativity, I am indebted beyond words.

Back before the 2000 presidential election, Molly Ivins and Lou Dubose tried to warn us in *Shrub* that George W. Bush was "a fixin" (as we say in Lubbock) to mess with us. This year, Ivins and Dubose are back again with *Bushwhacked*, telling us how he's pulled it off and the hurt he's causing.

Al Franken made me laugh in *Lies and the Lying Liars Who Tell Them*, and Greg Palast depressed me with *The Best Democracy Money Can Buy*. Both were sources, but the two books that put most of it together were *The Lies of George W. Bush* by David Corn and *The Book on Bush* by Eric Alterman and Mark Green. For those of you who want an excellent in-depth report of Bush's politics of deception, stop: go pick up one or both of these books. You'll be glad you did.

The problem is not that there is not enough information.   It's out there in dozens of excellent books and in hundreds of articles, both in mainstream publications and on the Internet. This is an attempt to synthesize and compile this information into a brief overview of the Bush administration and its gross deceptions.   In addition to those authors named above, I have specifically relied upon the works of others identified in the bibliography as primary sources and who are entitled to individual recognition for their substantial contributions: Paul Begala; Noam Chomsky; Richard A. Clark, Joe Conason; Jim Hightower;   Douglas   Kellner;   Mark   Crispin   Miller;   Bill Minutaglio; James Moore and Wayne Slater; Kevin Phillips; William Rivers Pitt and Scott Ritter; Sheldon Rampton and John C. Stauber;   Christopher   and   Robert   Scheer   and   Lakshmi Chaudhry; Norman Solomon and Reese Erlich; and Jennifer Van Bergen.   Heroes are defined by their courage in spite of the dangers they face, using the weapons at hand.   If we are to take back our country and make the world a safer place, all of these who wielded the pen must be counted among the warriors.

David Levinson was a great journalist and an even better friend, who passed along to the great newsroom in the sky a few years ago, where there are no deadlines and every hour is happy.   He would have said that this book was a "marvelous idea," as he always did about my projects, and, as always, I talked to him in my head as I slaved through the prose. Thanks, David; I couldn't have done it without you.

An author couldn't have asked for an easier book deal or for a more sensitive, knowledgeable and understanding publisher. John Paul Leonard has been a godsend.

Finally, thank God for the Internet (and whoever invented it) and Google.com. Our new "Fifth Estate" has been homesteaded in the midst of our free society, and it is here to stay.   With it and the Fourth to protect us and as a balance against the power of the other three, democracy will survive, and the voters of America will again rule.

INTRODUCTION

I decided to prepare this book because I became convinced it was needed. Back in 1980, I represented a survivor of Auschwitz and filed a lawsuit against some radical right-wing organizations that feed upon fear and hatred and who deny the Holocaust as a publicity ploy. These were marginal groups largely composed of kooks and nuts, some of whom celebrate the birthday of Adolph Hitler and dream of a new Imperium. Although they were actively seeking to mislead young people through the establishment of a phony "institute" and the publication of a "scholarly journal," I didn't believe they were an imminent threat to our freedoms. The matter was resolved when a wise Superior Court judge took judicial notice of the fact that Jews were gassed to death in Auschwitz in the summer of 1944.

However, in the past three years I have watched our government being taken over by another group of far more sophisticated zealots, who have seized extraordinary power and who appear to have engaged us in an unlawful war. It is not terrorism that I fear most, it is the unbridled power that has been assumed by our own government, to our detriment.

Next, I decided that I could write the book. One of the skills I have acquired is the ability to absorb and compile large amounts of information into brief, comprehensive documents written in a simple language. Perhaps it's because I never learned a whole lot of fancy words, but following the ABCs got me by as I wrote the "Policy Manual" of the Los Angeles Police Department and the "Role of the Police in America" for President Nixon's National Advisory Commission on Criminal Justice Standards and Goals. This skill has since served me well in drafting legal briefs over the years.

Finally, once I concluded that the danger was real and present, I had no choice. As Albert Camus once wrote, "And henceforth, the only honorable course will be to stake everything on a formidable gamble: that words are more powerful than munitions."

Thousands of our young women and men are fighting in Iraq and, whether or not we agree with their being there, we must give credit to the bravery of our sons and daughters who are being maimed and who are dying. They are the best, the bravest, and the brightest the world has ever seen. They deserve better than to be cynically used to promote selfish corporate and corrupt political interests. They certainly deserve better than to be sneaked back into the country in the middle of the night, once they have given their lives and limbs in Bush's War.

Our soldiers deserve to come home to a country which recognizes and honors their sacrifice by providing them with adequate medical care and veterans' benefits to compensate them for their losses. Finally, they deserve to come home to a country where the Bill of Rights, which they allegedly fought to defend, has been preserved for them and their descendants. They are dying for us; we have to have the courage to fight for them, though we risk being called unpatriotic and labeled as traitors.

The ultimate conclusion of this book was not lightly arrived at. It is not an easy thing to accuse our president of having failed to protect us and to wonder if the failure was intentional or negligent. It is not easy to accuse him of intentionally lying to Congress and the American people and thereby committing felony offenses. It is not easy to accuse him of violating international laws against humanity, the laws of war, the Charter of the United Nations, and the supreme law of the land. It is not easy to accuse him of a wholesale violation of our constitutional rights. It is not easy to question whether he should be impeached and stand trial or be left to the mercy of the voters. However, these things must be said.

We can no longer remain silent and hope for a better day. Our freedom is too precious. It is as Thomas Paine wrote, "These are the times that try men's souls. The summer soldier and the sunshine patriot will, in this crisis, shrink from the service of their country; but he that stands it now, deserves the love and thanks of man and woman." It is time to hear the evidence and if sufficient, to take action.

In view of the primitive simplicity of their minds, they [the masses] more easily fall victim to a big lie than to a little one, since they themselves lie in little things, but would be ashamed of lies that were too big.

— Adolf Hitler, *Mein Kampf*

Dynasty. In a dynasty, you don't have to earn anything.

— George W. Bush, *New York Times*, November 4, 1998

The President is merely the most important among a large number of public servants. He should be supported or opposed exactly to the degree which is warranted by his good conduct or bad conduct, his efficiency or inefficiency in rendering loyal, able, and disinterested service to the nation as a whole. Therefore it is absolutely necessary that there should be full liberty to tell the truth about his acts, and this means that it is exactly as necessary to blame him when he does wrong as to praise him when he does right. Any other attitude in an American citizen is both base and servile. To announce that there must be no criticism of the President, or that we are to stand by the President, right or wrong, is not only unpatriotic and servile, but is morally treasonable to the American public. Nothing but the truth should be spoken about him or any one else. But it is even more important to tell the truth, pleasant or unpleasant, about him than about any one else."

— Theodore Roosevelt, *The Works of Theodore Roosevelt*, 1926

PREFACE

The Bush administration has been running on lies in the belief that we are too stupid to figure it out. The business of exaggeration in politics has gone beyond the usual. It has become a culture of nastiness and downright lies. Is this acceptable?

We're Not As Stupid As *They* Think We Are

There's *something* going on, and *we* have to do something about it. Otherwise, *they're* going to pull it off.

• *Something* is a movement to shift the burden of taxation from corporations and the wealthy to the middle and working class.

• *Something* is a movement to put business in control of governments and to privatize all public services, including education.

• *Something* is the surrender of individual freedoms in response to cultivated fear.

They are getting away with it because *they* lie about what *they* are doing, and *we*, you and me, seem to be swallowing it, hook, line and sinker.

This is about the lies we're being told. Not about the usual political puffing, exaggerations or spinning. It is about lies, plain and simple. It's about who's telling the whoppers and about who's being duped. It's about you and me, and about those who are trying to take advantage of us and our trusting nature.

They believe that they can tell us *they're* going to do one thing and that we're too stupid to see that they do something entirely different. *They* believe that they can tell us something, and then later say the opposite and that we're too stupid to notice. *They* believe we are ignorant and are too lazy to become informed. None of this is true.

America *is* the Promised Land. Our population comprises the greatest genetic pool of humanity on earth. For over 500 years, the best the world has to offer have struggled to get here and there's a reason why people line up at our embassies and consulates in every country to legally immigrate here, and to sneak across our borders when they can't. We have freedom, and we have the intelligence and courage to defend it. We have only to recognize the danger. The time is now. Read on. You're not stupid! Get the truth.

Nasty Political Lies

Perhaps one way to define politics is the art of not telling the truth. To be elected, politicians must avoid telling the truth at all costs, because if they told the truth about everything all the time, everyone would find something to disagree with, and no one would ever get elected. So politicians learn to not tell the truth. They avoid taking positions; they hedge their comments, speak in ambiguities, abstain, hide and deny, dissemble, and otherwise torture the true meaning of words. Perhaps it's always been that way, and perhaps it'll always be that way. But, right now, there's a new game in town.

In 1995, Representative Newt Gingrich said, "I think one of the great problems we have in the Republican Party is that we don't encourage you to be nasty." To overcome this character defect, his advice was to "go negative early" and to "never back off."[1] He published a political handbook entitled *Language, a Key Mechanism of Control*, in which he encouraged Republicans to paste labels on Democrats such as "corrupt," "sick," "pathetic," "greedy," "anti-flag," "traitors," "decay," "permissive attitude," "anti-family," "bizarre," and worst of all "liberals."[2] Throw it on the wall and see if it sticks, who cares whether or not it's true? Of course, Gingrich advised Republicans to refer to their own party values using words and labels such as, "moral," "crusade," and "family."[3]

Frank Luntz, who collaborated with Gingrich in drafting the "Contract with America," advised "Republicans to call themselves 'conservationists,' not 'environmentalists'; to talk of 'climate change' instead of the more alarming 'global warming'; and to foster skepticism about the science of environmental problems." In a later memo to the Bush administration, Luntz advised, "A compelling story, even if factually inaccurate, can be more emotionally compelling than a dry recitation of the truth."[4]

Since then, Gingrich's students have learned their lessons well, and the nastiest lesson they have learned is how to tell lies, how to deny their lies, and how to make it seem that others, who are telling the truth, are lying.

Gingrich, who claims to be an historian, may have borrowed some of his insights from Adolf Hitler, who taught, "By means of shrewd lies, unremittingly repeated, it is possible to make people believe that heaven is hell–and hell, heaven. The greater the lie, the more readily it will be believed."

Today, in the United States, our president, George W. Bush, has abandoned the principles of the proud party of Lincoln and has advanced the political art of avoiding the truth to the high science of flat out lying. This book will show how he has institutionalized falsehood as a matter of policy, and how frightening his success is. More than scary, his practice absolutely threatens our freedoms and undermines our democracy.

Do you believe it is acceptable for politicians to lie to us? Have you given up hope on hearing the truth from politicians? You're not stupid! Get the truth.*

1. Franken, Al, *Lies and The Lying Liars Who Tell Them: A Fair and Balanced Look at The Right* (New York: Dutton Penguin Group, 2003), p. 139.

2. Conason, Joe, *Big Lies: The Right-Wing Propaganda Machine and How It Distorts the Truth* (New York: Thomas Dunne Books, 2003), p. 60.

3. Ibid., pp. 117, 118.

4. Alterman, Eric and Mark Green, *The Book on Bush: How George W. (Mis)leads America* (New York: Viking, 2004), pp. 17, 20.

* Note to reader: Many of the following references are to articles and materials that were located on the Internet. Every attempt has been made to provide accurate and current URLs; however, they are often changed. The best solution, should you be unable to connect to a site, is to copy the entire title in quotation marks, along with the author's name, into your search engine. You should find either the correct URL or an alternative source.

WHO'S BUSH?

How much do we really know about our president's life, his background and his character? To understand George W. Bush's administration better, it helps to become better acquainted with the well-smoothed path he has followed to the top.

How is it that a lying and denying alcoholic, with arrests for theft and disturbing the peace and a conviction for drunk driving; one born with a silver spoon in his mouth, with no empathy for the plight of ordinary people; an inarticulate spoiled brat who just didn't get the lessons of a good education; a chronically failed businessman who's never earned anything on his own; and a high school cheerleader who avoided military service in Viet Nam by joining the National Guard and then going AWOL–gets himself elected as President of the United States? Well, you can be darn sure he didn't exactly tell us the truth about his background.

To the Manner Born

George W. Bush (Bush Jr.) was born to privilege, high finance, and intrigue. His great-grandfathers, Samuel Bush and George Herbert Walker, were among the founders of the "military-industrial complex,"* making millions profiteering off of World War I, thanks to their close connections with the Rockefellers, Remingtons and the War Industries Board.

Bush's paternal grandfather, Prescott Bush, Sr., was a wealthy banker involved in financing Hitler's war machine, and a United States Senator instrumental in originally recruiting Richard Nixon into politics. Prescott Bush served in military intelligence during World War I, and later acted as a high-level "confidant, 'asset,' or counselor" to the intelligence community. All of these ancestors were graduates of Yale University and

---

*Defined by President Eisenhower in 1961 as a "conjunction of an immense Military Establishment and a large arms industry." He warned that "we must not fail to comprehend its grave implications."

members of its secret society, Skull and Bones, whose members have been at the forefront of America's intelligence services.[5]

In 1942, George Herbert Walker Bush (Bush Sr.) may have been inducted into the Office of Strategic Services (OSS) as early as age 18, upon his graduation from Phillips Academy-Andover. Without any college and contrary to military regulations, he was commissioned, trained as a Navy pilot, and assigned to the South Pacific. During a patrol, his aircraft was struck by anti-aircraft fire and the young pilot bailed out. In his panic, he abandoned his two crewmen to their deaths, even though the aircraft was designed to be crash landed on the ocean.[6]

Bush Sr. returned from the war and attended Yale, where he was initiated into Skull and Bones. If he was not already a CIA "asset," it is probable that his athletic coach, Allen "Skip" Waltz, who was the CIA's full-time headhunter at Yale, recruited him at that time. Upon graduation, Bush Sr. was employed by Dresser Industries, which had long-term connections with the intelligence community. He subsequently moved to Texas and incorporated Zapata Petroleum, which through its many subsidiaries likely served as a conduit for money and supplies to CIA operations in the Caribbean, including Guatemala and the Bay of Pigs invasion.[7]

With the support of Presidents Nixon and Ford, Bush Sr. became a Congressman, the Chairman of the Republican National Committee, and the Director of the CIA. Although Ronald Reagan personally disliked Bush Sr., Reagan reluctantly picked him as Vice President to unify the Republican Party.[8] Following Reagan's second term, Bush Sr. was elected President of the United States and served one term before being defeated for reelection by Bill Clinton in 1992. As president, Bush Sr. was described as "remorselessly deceitful when it served his purpose."[9]

Bush Jr.'s mother, Barbara Pierce, is a descendant of President Franklin Pierce, and her father was president of McCall Publishing Company.[10]

George and Barbara Bush were raised in wealthy households attended by servants. Their marriage in 1945 brought together two aristocratic lineages, and on July 6, 1946, the young prince, George Jr., was born in New Haven, Connecticut.

In 1948, the Bushes moved to Odessa, Texas, where George Sr. went into the oil business. He was frequently away from home, and his wife, Barbara, primarily raised George Jr. It was she who attended his Little League games and disciplined him. When twelve-year-old George Jr. would get in a fight with Jeb, his five-year-old little brother, "Bar would always get in the middle of those fights and bust them up and slap them around," according to Uncle Jonathan Bush. Barbara Bush was "the one who instills fear."[11] George Jr. describes her as "a very outspoken person who vents very well–she'll just let it rip if she's got something on her mind."[12] Jeb Bush recalls, "Mom was always the one to hand out the goodies and the discipline. In a sense, it was a matriarchal family."[13]

The Bush family maid, Otha Taylor, said, "They would squabble a lot. You know how kids and parents that are just alike will get? He was definitely like his mother, they were exactly alike, even their humor was alike."[14] When his mother's favorite dog died, George Jr. mocked her distress, yelling out, "Doggone it!"[15] He also inherited her sharp tongue.[16]

Once after Barbara Bush allowed Otha Taylor to go home an hour early because she didn't have any work to do, George Sr. reprimanded Barbara, "Where's Otha? She's supposed to stay here until her hour is up, regardless if she has anything to do or not." Otha remembers, "He's a really mean man." According to her, the Bushes believed in "teaching lessons."[17]

Bush's younger brother Neil recalls when he was seven years old and his little brother Marvin six, George Jr., age 16, would give them ten seconds to start running down the hall before he began shooting BB pellets at them.[18]

Bush's boyhood friend Terry Throckmorton remembers how he and Bush would capture frogs that would gather in the water at a low spot behind Bush's house: "We'd put firecrackers in the frogs and throw them and blow them up."[19]

Bush Jr. followed his father's footsteps to Andover and Yale; however, instead of graduating Phi Beta Kappa and being captain of the baseball team like his daddy, Bush Jr. was a cheerleader with a C average. Sponsored by his father, Bush was initiated into Skull and Bones.

At Yale, Bush was elected president (like his father) of the Delta Kappa Epsilon (DKE) fraternity at a time when new pledges had to undergo physical and psychological abuse. The *Yale Daily News* said that fraternity hazing at Yale was a "degrading, sadistic and obscene process" and that the DKE hazing ended with the burning of a half-inch-long Delta sign on the pledge's back.

The New York Times reported on the hazing and quoted Bush Jr. as saying the wound was "only a cigarette burn." Bush was also quoted in the campus newspaper that there "was no scarring mark, physically or mentally. I can't understand how the authors ... can assume that Yale has to be so haughty not to allow this type of pledging to go on at Yale." [20]

In addition to a fully paid education at Andover, Yale, and later at Harvard Business School, Bush has gone through life never having to worry about paying the rent, where the next meal was coming from, or if he could afford medical care for his children.

Do you think Bush has any clue about our lives and the difficulties we face? Do you think he has the ability to empathize with ordinary working people? You're not stupid! Get the truth.

"I do not have a perfect record as a youth."

That much is true. Not only was George W. Bush arrested in 1968 for stealing a Christmas wreath and again for disorderly conduct at a football game while he was in college, but in December 1972, after a Christmas drinking spree with his teenage brother, Marvin, the 26 year-old Bush ran over a neighbor's trash can as he drove home. When his father sought to reprimand him about his drunken driving, Bush challenged him to fight, "I hear you're looking for me. You want to go mano a mano right here?"[21]

At about the same time, Bush was probably arrested for possession of cocaine in Houston, Texas. It appears that as part of a deal with the judge, Bush Sr. arranged for Bush Jr. to serve a few months of community service at Professionals United for Leadership League, a youth organization chaired by Bush Sr.[22]

Bush attended Harvard Business School between 1973 and 1975 and, according to him, spent his time "drinking and carousing and fumbling around."[23]

Then, in the early morning hours of September 4, 1976, a Kennebunkport, Maine police officer saw 30-year-old Bush driving erratically and swerving off the road into a hedge, with his teenage sister, Dorothy, in the car.[24] Bush failed a sobriety test, then was handcuffed and taken to the police station. He pled guilty at a court hearing a month later, paid a fine, and his Maine driver's license was suspended. In 1978, even though he had not completed a required driver rehabilitation course, Bush returned to court to get the suspension lifted, and denied having a drinking problem.

Given an ultimatum by his wife, Bush says he swore off drinking alcohol after a drunken 40th birthday celebration on July 6, 1986.[25] However, he wasn't fully weaned from the bottle, and in April of 1987, he was out drinking in a Mexican restaurant in Dallas when he spotted Al Hunt, the *Wall Street Journal*'s Washington bureau chief, with his wife and four-year-old son. Hunt had contributed to a story that questioned whether Bush Sr. would be elected president, and the drunk and disorderly Bush yelled, "You no good f***ing son of a bitch. I will never f***ing forget what you wrote"[26]

When Bush ran for governor in 1994, he stated, "What I did as a kid? I don't think it's relevant."[27] Only seven years before, the drunken "kid" was stumbling around out of control. Not relevant? One of his first acts as governor was to get a new driver's license number and to purge his driving record.

In 1996, when then Governor Bush was called to jury duty, he left blank the written questionnaire about prior arrests and trials. When he was called to be on the jury in a drunk driving case, his general counsel, Alberto Gonzales, met with the defense attorney and judge in chambers and asked that Bush be excused before the more difficult *voir dire* (Old French–"to speak the truth") of jurors began.[28] In 1998, a reporter directly asked Bush if he had ever been arrested. Bush lied, "After 1968? No."[29]

During the 2000 presidential campaign, Bush's press spokesperson, Karen Hughes, repeatedly denied that Bush had ever been convicted. In 1999, Bush personally stated during one television interview that there were no "smoking guns" and during another that if there were any damaging information, "you'd have heard about it by now." However, the truth caught up with Bush just four days before the election when a Fox television reporter was able to confirm Bush's drunk driving conviction through the Maine Secretary of State.

When confronted, Bush said he had been driving "too slow" and, after being arrested, had simply paid a fine and gone home. He denied ever going to court in the matter.[30] He stated that he did not disclose the conviction in order to be a good role model for his twin daughters—who have been cited multiple times by the police for underage alcohol-related criminal offenses.[31]

Has Bush truly recovered? He denies that he was ever a "clinical" alcoholic, and apparently he has never sought professional help. Whether or not he has really stayed on the wagon, his loud, foul-mouthed and rude behavior has continued, such as his calling a *New York Times* reporter a "major league asshole" over an open microphone during the 2000 campaign.

More bizarre, during a March 2002 briefing of three U.S. Senators by his National Security Advisor, Condoleezza Rice, President Bush stuck his head in the room and yelled, "F**k Saddam. We're taking him out!"

Equally suspicious is the strange "pretzel" incident in which he fell on his face in his White House bedroom while watching a ball game on television. He blamed his passing out on having failed to properly chew a pretzel.

Do you believe Bush has successfully overcome his alcohol addiction? You're not stupid! Get the truth.

Over the Hill

In 1968, 296,406 American boys were drafted into the military service. Most of them were sent to Vietnam, many of them were wounded, maimed, and crippled for life, and 6,332 came home in body bags. George W. Bush was not one of them. Even though Bush lost his draft deferment upon graduation from Yale, even though there was a waiting list of 500 to get into the Texas Air National Guard, and even though he could only answer 25 out of 100 questions on the pilot aptitude test,[32] strings were pulled, calls were made, and Bush was allowed to sign up for a six-year hitch in one of the coveted slots.[33]   In his application, he was asked if he was willing to volunteer for overseas duty (i.e., Vietnam).   He checked the box, "do not volunteer."[34]

When Bush was asked in 1990 if he had joined the National Guard to avoid service in Vietnam, he said, "I was not prepared to shoot my eardrum out with a shotgun in order to get a deferment. Nor was I willing to go to Canada. So I chose to better myself by learning how to fly airplanes." When the same question was asked during the governor's race in 1994, he said, "Hell no. Do you think I'm going to admit that?" By 1999, he had decided that a better answer was, "At the time I wanted to fight."[35]

In 1969, 283,586 American boys were drafted into the military service, and 6,249 came home from Vietnam in body bags. George W. Bush was not one of them. He was home learning to fly an old F-102 fighter that was being phased out of military service.[36]

In 1970, 162,746 American boys were drafted into the military service, and 4,911 came home from Vietnam in body bags. George W. Bush was not one of them. In his ghostwritten autobiography, *A Charge to Keep*, Bush says that he completed flight training in 1970 and "continued flying with my unit for the next several years." Well, let's see if that was true.

In 1971, 94,092 American boys were drafted into the military service, and 2,867 came home from Vietnam in body bags. And, in 1972, 49,514 American boys were drafted into the military service, and 2,609 came home in body bags. George W. Bush was not one of them. On August 1, 1972, he lost his flight status for failing to submit to an annual physical examination, a few months after the Air Force instituted a rigorous random drug testing policy.[37] He was grounded, never to fly again. A month later, Major James R. Bath, one of Bush's "lot of fun" buddies, was also suspended for the same reason.[38] (Remember this name.)

Bush received permission in May 1972 to do his training in Alabama, where he was working on the political campaign of a family friend, Winston Blount. He was specifically ordered to report to "Lt. Col. William Turnipseed, DCO, to perform equivalent training." At this point, it appears that Bush went AWOL for the next year, as Retired General Turnipseed later stated he was certain that Bush never reported for duty.[39] Nor does it appear that he did anything of significance in the campaign. A full-time senior staffer reports that Bush was "worthless" and "not dependable." He was "rarely available" to work on the campaign, but he never requested any time off to attend National Guard meetings. The staffer said "the guard was the last thing on Bush's mind."[40]

After the Alabama election in November, Bush didn't return to his Houston assignment. He didn't come back from "over the hill" until after May 1973, when two of his superior officers noted that they could not perform his annual evaluation because he had "not been observed at this unit" during the preceding 12 months. But, what the heck, the war was winding down anyway, and Bush was no longer needed to defend the Homeland. When later asked about being AWOL, Bush said, "I did the duty necessary. ... Any allegations other than that are simply not true."* 9,087,000 military personnel really did do their "duty" during the Vietnam era, and over 58,000 died.

---

*On February 14, 2004, faced with a likely race against Democratic Senator John Kerry, a Vietnam War hero, Bush released his military records in which the only evidence that he ever appeared at the Alabama National Guard was a dental examination performed there on

When Bush went off to study at the Harvard Business School, he continued to wear his National Guard flight jacket to classes, creating a perception that he had served in the military. As we will see, perceptions are very important to Bush.[41]

Do you think Bush did his duty? You're not stupid! Get the truth.

What an MBA Can Do for You

After the University of Texas turned down Bush's application to attend its law school, he decided to get a graduate business administration degree from Harvard instead. The legal profession's loss turned out to be the business profession's gain, as Bush over and over showed the rest of us how to make lemonade out of lemons. Where anyone else would have crashed and burned, Bush's golden parachute floated him safely through the financial storms that continued to buffet his business career.

In 1978, again following in his daddy's footsteps, Bush decided to go into the oil business in Texas. He started up an oil-drilling operation, Arbusto (Spanish–"bush, shrub") Energy with the help of his uncle, Wall Street banker Jonathan Bush.[42] Even though the price of Texas crude quickly went into the toilet, and Bush Jr. may have spent more time in barrooms and on the golf course than in the oil patch, he was able to keep his company afloat with continuing investments by family members and international businessmen seeking to maintain favor with Bush Sr., who was fortuitously elected Vice President in 1980.

In 1979, Bush sold five percent of Arbusto to his old buddy, James Bath (remember) for $50,000. At the time, Bath was operating as the U.S. front man for Salem bin Laden, the brother

---

January 6, 1973. He explained that he did not bother to report for medical examinations after May 15, 1971 because he felt there was no reason to take one because the Alabama National Guard did not fly the type of jet he was trained on. (Bumiller, Elisabeth and Philip Shenon, "Bush Acts Against Critics on Guard Records and 9/11," *The New York Times*, February 14, 2004, http://www.nytimes.com/2004/02/14/politics/14BUSH.html?th.)

of Osama bin Laden.* Given the fact that Bath was personally without funds at the time, it is considered highly likely that the money came from bin Laden.[43]

When Salem bin Laden died in a Texas airplane crash in 1988, a powerful Saudi banker, Khalid bin Mahfouz, took over bin Laden's financial interests in Houston, Texas. Mahfouz's sister is married to Osama bin Laden, and Bath continued as Mahfouz's U.S. front man.[44] Bath was later investigated by the FBI for funneling Saudi money through Houston business relationships to influence the foreign policies of Presidents Reagan and Bush Sr.[45]

In 1982, with his company worth less than its debt of $400,000 and with only $48,000 in the bank, Bush decided that he needed to take his corporation public to raise some money. To improve the balance sheet, an investor friend of James Baker III, later Bush Sr.'s Secretary of State, stepped forward and purchased ten percent of the company for $1,000,000. The investor later called the purchase a "losing wicket."[46]

Since his oil patch buddies were calling his company "are busted," Bush renamed the company Bush Exploration and went public. He wanted to issue $6 million in stock, but only raised $1.14 million. Bush Exploration continued to lose money and two years later was again on the verge of bankruptcy.[47]

This time the bailout came from two investors from Cincinnati who owned a company known as Spectrum 7. They merged with Bush Exploration, and Bush ended up with 16.3 percent of Spectrum 7 and a salary of $75,000 a year. Since thus far, all Bush had done was to drill dry holes and lose money, the question is what did Bush bring to the table? Spectrum 7's president, Paul Rea, reported that Bush's name was a "drawing card" for investors.[48]

By 1986, having lost another $400,000, more than $3,000,000 in debt, and with Spectrum 7's shares just about worthless, another bailout was in order. This time the savior was Harken Energy Corporation, which was operated by a Republican fund

---

* James Bath was "an asset of the CIA, reportedly recruited by George Bush [Sr.] himself" in 1976. (Phillips, Kevin, *American Dynasty*, p. 269.)

raiser. Harken traded one each of its publicly traded shares for every five of Spectrum 7's, and Bush ended up with stock worth about half a million. He became a member of Harken's Board, was given $600,000 in stock options and a consulting contract paying him $120,000 a year.

What did Bush bring to the deal? One of Harken's major investors stated that "he was supposed to bring in the Gulf connection. But it didn't come to anything. We were buying political influence. That was it. He was not much of a businessman."[49]   Equally candid was one of Harken's co-founders, Phil Kendrick, who was smart enough to sell his stock three years before Bush Jr. came aboard, and who said, "His name was George Bush. That was worth the money they paid him."[50]

In 1987, Harken sold 17.6 percent of the company to Saudi Sheik Abdullah Taha Bakhsh, whose banker was bin Mahfouz, who, if you recall, also served as the bin Laden's banker.

In 1989, after Bush Sr. was elected President and with an introduction from the new ambassador, Harken was able to obtain exclusive drilling rights for 35 years from Bahrain in the Persian Gulf, and Harken's stock price began to rise. However, Harken was actually losing money, and to hide 1989 losses of $12.6 million, Harken engaged in a sham sale of a subsidiary to a partnership of Harken insiders, allowing it to claim a profit of $8 million. Harken's accountant was Arthur Andersen, and this was the same kind of "aggressive accounting" that later sank Enron–and Andersen with it.

Bush chaired a special committee of Harken directors convened to review Harken's $11 million loan to the insiders that they used to finance the purchase. The next year, after the SEC began to look into the phony sale, Harken had to restate its actual 1989 losses, plus report additional millions in losses for the first quarter of 1990. With this bad news, Harken stock took a nosedive. In the meantime, instead of the usual bailout by his daddy's friends, Bush had already bailed out.[51]

Bush had attended a Harken Board of Directors meeting in May 1990 where the crisis was discussed, and he served on the

Board's Fairness Committee concerned with the effect bankruptcy would have on the small shareholders. By late May 1990, a cash crunch was only days away and the repayment of loans was questionable. Bush was an "insider," and he was a member of the Audit Committee. On June 15, 1990, all members of the Board, including Bush, were advised in writing that under the circumstances, it would be illegal for them to sell any stock.[52]

Undeterred, Bush sold two-thirds of his Harken stock for $848,560 to an unidentified private purchaser on June 22, 1990, but delayed reporting the sale to the SEC for eight months after the filing deadline. The SEC (headed by a Bush Sr. appointee, and whose General Counsel was Bush Jr.'s former attorney) investigated and, surprise-surprise, failed to find sufficient evidence of insider information. Nevertheless, the SEC letter sent to Bush stated that the investigation "must in no way be construed as indicating that the party has been exonerated or that no action may ultimately result."[53]

After the matter became public, Bush first stated in 1994 that he was "absolutely certain" that he had complied with the law in reporting the insider sale. Then his campaign for governor claimed that he had filed the required report and that the SEC had lost it. Bush personally claimed, "I was exonerated." Later (as President), his press secretary claimed that Harken's lawyers had mixed up the reporting, even though Harken's lawyers had informed Bush in writing that reporting was his responsibility. Regarding the phony sale of the Harken subsidiary that allowed him to dump his stock without a loss, Bush himself stated, "All I can tell you is – is in the corporate world, sometimes things aren't exactly black and white when it comes to accounting procedures."[54]

Harken's small shareholders saw their stocks precipitously drop from $4 a share (ultimately to forty-one cents); however, Bush was able to sneak away with enough money to pay off a half-million-dollar loan he had taken out the year before to purchase a two-percent interest in the Texas Rangers, Dallas's baseball franchise. Although Bush was named as one of two managing partners, he was restricted from having anything to do with the actual management of the franchise.

After the city of Arlington, Texas raised local taxes and condemned private property to build a new $190 million stadium, the partnership sold the franchise for $250 million.⁵⁵ Because of financial bonuses in the agreement for the two "managing" partners, Bush ended up with almost $15 million (more than the real managing partner), even though he had done little or nothing to earn it except appear at the games and cheer the players.

Thus it came to be that George W. Bush, who had never held down a real job and whose only marketable asset was his family name and his father's influence, became convinced he had succeeded on his own and that he was ready for bigger and better things. During the 1994 campaign for governor, he stated that his success was due to "hard work, skillful investments, the ability to read an environment that was ever-changing at times and react quickly." He insisted that he had never profited from his family connections.

Perhaps Bush's success really was the result of his Harvard Business School training, but do you believe it? Do you think Bush has any idea how hard ordinary people have to work just to make ends meet? You're not stupid! Get the truth.

Let Them Eat Cake!

When he ran for president in 1999, Bush held himself out as a "compassionate conservative." His campaign website reported that he had led the nation in adopting a strong Patients' Bill of Rights, and he claimed that he had signed legislation to improve health care for children in Texas.⁵⁶ But was he telling the truth?

In 1995, the Texas legislature passed an HMO reform act to improve patient protections. Bush vetoed the measure. Two years later, the legislature passed a similar measure that included a provision to allow patients to sue their HMO for medical malpractice. Bush again threatened to veto the measure unless the legislature "gutted" its protections. However, when it appeared the legislature would be able to override his veto, Bush allowed the measure to become law *without* his signature. Not only did *he not* lead the nation in health care reform, *he* did everything in his power to *defeat* health care reform in Texas.⁵⁷

During the election, Bush promised, "If I'm president... people will be able to take their HMO insurance company to court. That's what I've done in Texas and that's the kind of leadership style I'll bring to Washington." However, when insurance companies later sued Texas to void the Texas law and block state lawsuits against HMO's for denying rights, the Bush presidential administration joined with the insurance companies and urged the Supreme Court to find that such state claims "are subject to complete" preemption by federal law and must be dismissed. Bush's lawyers claimed that allowing "patients to sue their HMO will increase the cost of healthcare and add an extra burden on employers."[58]

Bush also bragged that *"we"* had passed legislation creating the Children's Health Insurance Program. At the time, Texas had the highest number of uninsured children per capita in the United States. The legislature wanted to make the program available to all uninsured children whose families earned up to twice the poverty level, or $33,000. Bush fought to lower the standard to $25,000 a year. Under his plan, almost half, or 220,000, of these 500,000 uninsured children would not have qualified for the coverage. After a five-year battle, during which 500,000 children went without adequate health care, the legislature finally prevailed, and Bush ungraciously told one of the measure's proponents, "Congratulations. You crammed it down our throats."[59] The truth is that *he* was not a part of the *we* who fought for children's medical care in Texas.

When television commentator Dan Rather questioned Bush about the abysmal level of medical coverage in Texas, he parried, "I think you can find all kinds of statistics to make all kinds of cases. ... I don't know the statistics."[60] While Bush didn't directly deny that the statistics were wrong, and while he did not outright admit that he didn't know what he was talking about, he certainly did not show any compassion for the health of poor Texas children.

Do you believe Bush truly cares about the health and well being of you and your family? You're not stupid! Get the truth.

5. Phillips, Kevin, *American Dynasty: Aristocracy, Fortune, and the Politics of Deceit in the House of Bush* (New York: Viking, 2004), 178-185, 195-199, Appendix A, pp. 335-341.

6. Sampley, Ted, "George Bush Parachutes Again to Exorcize Demons of Past Betrayal, March-May 1997, www.usvetdsp.com/story46.htm.

7. Phillips, op. cit., pp. 200-208.

8. Ibid., p. 32.

9. Ibid., p. 148.

10. Minutaglio, Bill, *First Son: George W. Bush and the Bush Family Dynasty* (New York: Three Rivers Press, 2001), p. 23.

11. Ibid., p. 49.

12. Ibid.

13. Ibid., p. 57.

14. Ibid., p. 48.

15. Ibid., p. 98.

16. Ibid., p. 100.

17. Ibid., pp. 48, 49.

18. Miller, Mark Crispin, *The Bush Dyslexicon: Observations on a National Disorder* (New York: W.W. Norton & Company, 2002), p. 338.

19. Hightower, Jim, *Thieves in High Places: They've Stolen Our Country–And It's Time To Take It Back* (New York: Viking Press, 2003), p. 14.

20. Minutaglio, op. cit., pp. 111-113.

21. Ibid., pp. 99, 147-148.

22. Phillips, op. cit., p. 45.

23. Begala, Paul, *Is Our Children Learning?: The Case Against George W. Bush* (New York: Simon & Schuster, 2000), p. 27.

24. Franken, op. cit., p. 46.

25. Minutaglio, op. cit., p. 210.

26. Miller, op. cit., p. 50.

27. Corn, David, *The Lies of George W. Bush: Mastering The Politics of Deception* (New York: Crown Publishers, 2003), p. 28.

28. Moore, James and Wayne Slater, *Bush's Brain: How Karl Rove Made George W. Bush Presidential* (Hoboken: John Wiley & Sons, 2003), p. 278.

29. Corn, op. cit., pp. 29, 30; see also "Busted," November 3, 2000, http://dir.salon.com/politics/feature.

30. "Bush Jr.'s Skeleton Closet," www.realchange.org/bushjr.html.

31. "Family Ties," www.thedubyareport.com/family.html.

32. Palast, Greg, *The Best Democracy Money Can Buy: The Truth About Corporate Cons, Globalization, and High-Finance Fraudsters* (New York: Plume, Penguin Group, 2002), p. 107.

33. Minutaglio, op. cit., p. 121.

34. Corn, op. cit., p. 25.

35. Ibid., pp. 24, 25.

36. Minutaglio, op. cit., p. 125.

37. Conason, op. cit., p. 65.

38. Moore, James, *Bush's War for Reelection: Iraq, The White House, and the People.* (Hoboken, New Jersey: John Wiley & Sons, Inc., 2004), p. 177; see also Miller, Roger, "Bush & Bin Laden – George W. Bush Had Ties to Billionaire bin Laden Brood," October 7, 2001, American Free Press, www.americanfreepress.net/10_07_01/Bush_Bin_Laden_-_George_W_B/bush.

39. Conason, op. cit., p. 64.

40. Moore, *Bush's War for Reelection*, op. cit., p. 154.

41. Minutaglio, op. cit., p. 156.

42. Ibid., p. 198.

43. Wiles, Rick, "Bush's Former Oil Company Linked to bin Laden Family," October 3, 2001, http://www.rense.com/general14/bushformer.htm.

44. Palast, op. cit., p. 104; see also Kellner, Douglas, *From 9/11 to Terror War: The Dangers of the Bush Legacy* (Lanham, Maryland: Rowman & Littlefield, 2003), p. 35; see also Ahmed, Nafeez Mosaddeq and John Leonard *The War on Freedom: How and Why America was Attacked, September 11, 2001* (Joshua Tree, California: Tree of Life Publications. 2002), pp.194-197.

45. Ahmed, op. cit., p. 194.

46. Ivins, Molly and Lou Dubose, *Bushwhacked: Life in George W. Bush's America* (New York: Random House, 2003), p. 7.

47. Ibid.

48. Ibid., p. 8.

49. Corn, op. cit., p. 191.

50. Ivins, op. cit., p. 8.

51. Ivins, op. cit., p. 9.

52. Corn, op. cit., pp. 193, 196-197.

53. Ivins, op. cit., pp. 11-14; see also Alterman and Green, op. cit., pp 70, 71.

54. Ibid., p. 12; see also Corn, op. cit., pp. 193, 195.

55. Minutaglio, op. cit., p. 322.

56. Corn, op. cit., p. 17.

57. Ibid.

58. Savage, David G., "Patients' Right to Sue HMOs Before High Court," *Los Angeles Times*, March 24, 2004, p. A12.

59. Corn, op. cit., pp. 17, 18.

60. Ibid., p. 18.

THE PREVARICATOR* I:
THE PRESIDENTIAL CAMPAIGN

Republican Senator McCain was tortured for five years in Vietnam as a POW. Democrat Vice President Gore was a man of vision and integrity. Yet Bush managed to destroy the character of each of these men using twisted lies, setting himself up to become president by judicial appointment.

When George W. Bush announced his candidacy for president in 1999, he promised, "We will prove that someone who is conservative and compassionate can win without sacrificing principle. We will show that politics, after a time of tarnished ideals, can be higher and better. We will give our country a fresh start after a season of cynicism."[61] But did he? The truth is quite to the contrary.

Throughout the campaign, Bush misrepresented his accomplishments as governor of Texas, taking credit for things he had nothing to do with and misrepresenting the benefit of the things he did. It turns out that the tax cuts he claimed to have made really didn't reduce the tax burden of the ordinary people; the size of government in Texas increased rather than decreased as he asserted it had; the "improvement" in student test scores was jiggered; and the quality of air in Texas got worse rather than better during his stewardship. However, these are complicated matters subject to multiple interpretations. What about basic political principles, shiny ideals, and the absence of cynicism?

"John. It's politics."

In 1967, while Bush Jr. was drinking himself through Yale, another son of an illustrious family was actually flying A-4E Skyhawks over North Vietnam. John McCain, whose father and

---

* To prevaricate—to be deliberately ambiguous or unclear in order to mislead or withhold information; to evade; equivocate; quibble; shuffle.

grandfather were four-star admirals in the Navy, graduated from the Naval Academy in 1958. McCain was shot down in 1967, and for the next 5½ years, while Bush was *using* his family's influence to avoid the draft, McCain was being tortured *because* of his family connections.

In 1973, while Lieutenant Bush was still AWOL, Captain McCain was released from prison, and for his heroism was awarded the Silver Star, Bronze Star, Legion of Merit, Purple Heart and Distinguished Flying Cross. McCain went on to represent the people of Arizona during two terms in the House of Representatives and three terms in the U.S. Senate. Senator McCain was an outspoken opponent of wasteful government spending and an advocate for reform of the campaign finance system. He was an expert on telecommunications and aviation issues, and promoted business competition and government deregulation.[62] A formidable candidate, Senator McCain ran in the primaries in 1999 against Bush for the Republican presidential nomination.

At the beginning of the campaign, Governor Bush and Senator McCain shook hands and promised not to run negative campaigns against each other. The promise held until McCain won the primary in New Hampshire by a wide margin, and the South Carolina primary became a must-win situation for the Bush campaign.[63] Bush was overheard on an open microphone speaking to South Carolina State Senator Mike Fair, who said, "Y'all haven't even hit his soft spots." Bush replied, "We're going to." And he added that he was "not going to do it on TV."[64]

On another platform, Bush stood silently by while the head of the so-called "National Vietnam and Gulf War Veterans Coalition" accused McCain of having always opposed Agent Orange and Gulf War compensation measures. All of which were absolute lies. McCain actually sponsored the Agent Orange Act and testified in favor of compensation for Gulf War Syndrome veterans. Did Bush stand up and correct these malicious lies? Nope. He said, "Thank you, buddy." Even after five senators (including two Republicans) who had also fought in Vietnam defended Senator McCain, Bush refused to apologize.[65]

This diatribe was only the shot across the bow of the McCain campaign. What followed was a full broadside of nasty tactics, including spreading rumors that McCain had been brainwashed while a POW, and that he had infected his "mob-connected" wife with a venereal disease. Perhaps more effectively in the South, thousands of voters began receiving telephone calls in so-called "push polls" pioneered by Bush's political advisor, Karl Rove. In a real live caricature of *Pinky and the Brain*, Rove has been called the "evil genius" behind Bush's political career.* Pretending to represent a polling company, voters were asked such questions as, "If you knew that Senator McCain had fathered an illegitimate black child, would you be more likely or less likely to vote for him?" Duh! How different the result, if the voter had been asked if they were more or less likely to vote for McCain if they knew that he and his wife had adopted a dark-skinned orphan child from Bangladesh and rescued her from poverty. But the truth would not have worked nearly so well.

Perhaps Bush's slickest trick was accusing Senator McCain, who had sponsored campaign finance reform legislation, of soliciting money from lobbyists who had special interests, and pressuring "agencies on behalf of contributors," when in fact, lobbyists had contributed five times as much to Bush as to McCain. There was also the direct mail to Republicans accusing Senator McCain of trying to remove the anti-abortion plank from the Republican platform.[66] All lies. But it worked. Bush won the South Carolina primary 53 to 42 percent.

After it became public that Bush had given a speech at Bob Jones University (a fundamentalist Christian institution that prohibits its students from interracial dating), Bush stated that he "did denounce. I de–I denounced it. I denounced interracial dating. I denounced anti-Catholic bigacy–bigotry. ... No, I-I-I-I spoke out against interracial dating. I mean, I support inter–the policy of interracial dating."[67] Whatever it was that he finally

---

*Bush Jr.'s nickname for Rove is "Turd Blossom," because whenever he was around, something was sure to pop up.

spit out, Bush lied, because he had said nothing about the University's racist policy during his speech.[68]

A remarkable quote in the *New York Times* on March 15, 2000 clearly illustrates that perceptions are far more important to Bush than the truth: "I readily concede I missed an opportunity at Bob Jones; I'd have been a hero. If I had gone down there and said, 'We're all God's children; we can receive redemption in all different kinds of ways; the Catholic religion is a great religion. Judaism is a great religion.' It's all I would have needed to have said. One sentence."[69]

When McCain sponsored an ad during the Michigan primary revealing Bush's speech at the University, where it is taught that the Pope is the "anti-Christ" and the Catholic Church is a "satanic cult," Bush whined that McCain had called him "an anti-Catholic bigot."[70] True or not, that's not what the ad said.

Just before a debate in the South Carolina primary, Bush and Senator McCain stood next to each other. McCain looked sadly at Bush and shook his head, saying, "George." Bush wimped, "John. It's politics." McCain answered, "George, everything isn't politics."[71]

Do you think Bush ran an honest, "untarnished" campaign? Do you think the best candidate became the Republican nominee? Would you feel more secure if McCain had been elected president? You're not stupid! Get the truth.

The Goring of Gore

Once Bush was able to wrest the nomination from McCain, he turned his weapons of deception on Vice President Al Gore, the candidate of the Democratic Party. A Karl Rove poll had revealed a weakness–that voters had questions about Gore's integrity. Therefore, Bush began to say repeatedly that Gore would say anything to get elected, and the big lie of the Bush campaign became that Gore was the liar. Bush said, "I have always been concerned about Vice President Gore's willingness to exaggerate in order to become elected. ... America had better beware of a candidate who is willing to stretch reality in order to win points." The Bush campaign ran an ad accusing Gore of "reinventing himself."[72]   What was the truth?   Who reinvented whom?

Early in the campaign, after a three-city tour of Texas, Gore was casually discussing movies late at night with several reporters aboard Air Force Two.   He mentioned a story in the *Nashville Tennessean* newspaper that had apparently misquoted *Love Story* author Erich Segal as saying that Al Gore and his wife, Tipper, were the models for the lead characters in his book. When *Time* magazine carried a story about Gore and included the comment, Segal issued a correction to the effect that, while he *had* combined Gore and his college roommate, actor Tommy Lee Jones, to form the character of the male lead, the female lead was based upon someone other than Tipper.

The *Time* reporter who wrote the story later said that what Gore actually said was, "all I know is that's what he [Segal] told reporters in Tennessee."   Was this a lie?   The *Tennessean* had in fact quoted Segal (albeit wrongly) as saying that both were models for the story.[73]   Gore did not lie, but once the snowball started rolling down the hill it sure got big before it crashed at the bottom.

During a television interview in March 1999, Gore said, "During my service in the United States Congress, I took the initiative in creating the Internet."   This is essentially a true statement.   Gore *was* a co-sponsor of the legislation that created defensenet, a project that linked military computers and later became the Worldwide Web.   In the 1980's, after the Pentagon stopped funding a number of civilian projects that weren't directly related to military applications, Gore *was* instrumental in arranging for the National Science Foundation to create nsfnet, which ultimately became today's Internet.

In 1989, Gore *introduced* the National High-Performance Computer Technology Act, a five-year, $1.7 billion program to expand the capacity of the Internet and to support research and development for an improved national computer system, and to assist colleges and libraries to connect to the new network. Speaking in 1989, Gore told a House committee, "I genuinely believe that the creation of this nationwide network will create an environment where work stations are common in homes and even small businesses." President Bush Sr. signed the bill in 1991. However, Republican Congressman Dick Armey *created* the story that Gore claimed to have "invented" the Internet. It was Armey's creative words that got picked up and misreported by the media during the 2000 campaign.[74]

In November 1999, Gore was speaking to a group of high school students in Concord, New Hampshire. To encourage them to get involved, he told about a young high school girl in Toone, Tennessee, who reported a problem to him in the late 1970's about toxic waste in her hometown. Gore had called for a congressional investigation and held hearings, and, as he told the students, "I looked around the country for other sites like that. I found a little place in upstate New York called Love Canal. Had the first hearing on that issue, and Toone, Tennessee–that was the one you didn't hear of. But *that was the one that started it all.* (emphasis added)" Gore went on to say, "We passed a major national law to clean up hazardous dump sites. And we had new efforts to stop the practices that ended up poisoning water around the country. We've still got work to do. But we made a huge difference. And it all happened because one high school student got involved."

All this was totally true; however, the next day in reporting the talk, the *Washington Post* ignored the context and twisted Gore's words to ridicule him. The article said Gore had bragged in saying, "'I found a little place in upstate New York called Love Canal,' he said, referring to the Niagara homes evacuated in August 1978 because of chemical contamination. 'I had the first hearing on this issue.'... Gore said his efforts made a lasting impact. '*I was the one that started it all,*' he said. (emphasis added)"[75]

The Republican National Committee seized upon the story, stating, "Al Gore is simply unbelievable–in the most literal sense of that term. ... It's a pattern of phoniness." The RNC then edited the *Post*'s misquotes even more to misrepresent Gore as saying, "*I was the one who started it all.* (emphasis added)" As the news media went wild over the story, the Concord students did everything in their power to correct the record, finally issuing a press release entitled, "Top 10 Reasons Why Many Concord

High Students Feel Betrayed by Some of the Media Coverage of Al Gore's Visit to their School." But who listens to children?

During the first presidential debate with Bush on October 3, 2000, Gore mistakenly mentioned that he had accompanied FEMA director James Lee Witt on a trip to Texas after major fires in the state. This was not quite true; Gore had actually traveled to Texas with one of Witt's deputies, although he had accompanied Witt on many such trips to other states. Karen Hughes, Bush's spokesperson, immediately crowed, "He made up the story." But what was the truth and what were the lies in the debate? In refusing to accept an invitation from Gore to endorse a campaign finance reform bill, Bush lied, "this man has outspent me."[76] At that point, Bush had spent more than $121 million, more than double Gore's $60 million.

Bush also lied in saying that "all seniors are covered under prescription drugs in my plan." However, according to Bush's website, only seniors with incomes below $11,300 would receive full coverage. Those with incomes below $14,600 would receive partial coverage, and those above would only receive approximately 25 percent of the premium costs for a drug plan. When Bush and Gore differed over whose plan would provide the greatest benefit to a senior earning $25,000 a year, and when Gore seemed to be scoring points for accuracy, Bush took a cheap shot saying Gore "is a man who's got great numbers. He talks about numbers. I'm beginning to think not only did he invent the Internet but he invented the calculator."[77]

In the second debate on October 11, 2000, Bush claimed that with his tax plan, "by far the vast majority of the help goes to the people at the bottom end of the economic ladder." Actually, under the proposed plan, the bottom half of the economic "ladder," those earning less than $40,000, would only get ten percent of the tax cut. If Bush's proposed elimination of the estate tax were figured in, less than 13 percent would go to the bottom 60 percent, and 51 percent would go to the top five percent of the households.[78]

Was Bush successful in his attack on Gore's credibility? As they say, "The proof of the pudding is in the eating." Voters were asked in exit polling "Which one candidate quality mattered most in deciding how you voted?" The most frequent answer, by 24 percent of voters, was "honesty." Of those, 80 percent said they voted for Bush; only 15 percent voted for Gore.[79] Go figure? Beginning to see the light? You're not stupid! Get the truth.

---

61. Corn, op. cit., pp. 12, 13.

62. "Senator John McCain Biography," www.vietnamwar.com/JohnMcCainBio.html.

63. Corn, op. cit., p. 33.

64. Moore, op. cit., p. 257.

65. Corn, op. cit., p. 34.

66. Ibid., pp. 35, 36.

67. Miller, op. cit., p. 189.

68. Corn, op. cit., pp. 36, 37.

69. Miller, op. cit., p. 248.

70. Corn, op. cit., p. 37.

71. Moore, op. cit., p. 257.

72. Corn, op. cit., pp. 38, 46.

73. Franken, op. cit., p. 41.

74. "Did Al Gore Invent the Internet?" August 18, 2000, http://www.issues2000.org/askme.

75. "A Chronology of Media and GOP Distortions Re Gore's Love Canal Statement," GoreWatch.net 2000, http://www.bushwatch.com/goremarch.

76. Miller, op. cit., p. 163.

77. Corn, op. cit., p. 49.

78. Ibid., p. 40.

79. Ibid., p. 52.

THE THEFT OF THE PRESIDENCY

Beyond the philosophical question of whether George W. Bush represents the voters, there are very real questions that linger about the legitimacy, the constitutionality, even the legality of his election.

On November 7, 2000, a total of 105,405,100 Americans went to the polls and voted in the 2000 general election for president. Of these, 50,999,897 cast a vote for Al Gore, and 50,456,002 voted for George W. Bush. Thus, by a plurality of over a half million, more Americans thought that Vice President Gore would make a better president than Texas Governor Bush. As to which way the voters were leaning, if we add the 2,882,955 votes cast for Ralph Nader to Gore's and the 448,895 cast for Patrick J. Buchanan to Bush's, we find the balance well to the left, with almost three million voters preferring a more liberal approach to the country's problems.*

However, the people do not directly vote for their leader. If they had, Al Gore would have been elected. The president of the United States is the executive of the government formed by the several states, united. Because of the Electoral College system established by the Constitution, each state first determines which candidate won a plurality of votes by the people in that state, then that candidate's electors cast their votes in the Electoral College. Since the number of electoral votes in each state depends upon the number of representatives and senators that state has in Congress, it is possible for a majority of the people to vote for one candidate and for the states to vote for another. This has happened before and it happened in 2000.

At the end of Election Day, it was close, awfully close, and it all came down to Florida, where Bush's little brother, Jeb, was governor. To win, 270 electoral votes are required. Except for

---

* If Nader and Buchanan had not run, and adding those votes to the totals for Gore and Bush, Gore would have won New Hampshire with four electoral votes and Florida with 25 for a total of 295. Winning either state would have given Gore a majority in the Electoral College.

Florida, Gore was ahead in the states with 266 votes; Bush had 246 votes. Gore was ahead by 20 electoral votes, but if Bush got Florida's 25 votes, he would win 271 to 266 in the Electoral College. Which he did. But how it came to be is a sad and sorry tale.

Casing the Joint

It all started innocently enough. Following allegations of wide-spread fraud in Miami's mayoral election in 1997, in which the deceased voted early and often (as they used to say in Chicago), the Florida legislature passed a law in 1998 to eliminate registrants not entitled to vote because they were deceased, mentally incompetent or had been convicted of a felony. Clearly those pushing up daises or in the slammer shouldn't vote, but what about those "felons" who have successfully completed probation, their jail time, and parole? Only 13 states, including Florida, prohibit such rehabilitated felons from voting. In the remaining 37 states, they automatically regain their rights.[80] Therein lay fertile ground for sowing mischief.

The reform law required that a list of ineligible voters be compiled and maintained by a private firm. Florida was the only state ever to do this. The Division of Elections under the Republican Secretary of State contracted with Database Technologies, which, following a merger, became the DBT Online subsidiary of Atlanta-based ChoicePoint Inc. (ChoicePoint DBT). One problem with privatization of the process is that the formulas and data involved are commercial secrets, and are not a matter of public record.[81]

In Florida, a more fundamental problem with private preparation of the list is that once the state's Elections Division sends the ineligible voter "list" to the county elections supervisors, a presumption of guilt requires the elections supervisors to eliminate these names from their registered voter rolls, unless they "determine that the information provided by the [state elections] division is incorrect."[82]

Early indications that something was wrong came in a memorandum from the Florida State Association of Supervisors of Elections in August 1998, warning the Secretary of State that eligible voters were being "capriciously" removed from the rolls.[83]

In November 1998, Republican Jeb Bush was elected as Governor of Florida and a political crony, Katherine Harris, became the Secretary of State and head of the Division of Elections. The plot thickens. While no smoking gun has ever been found to provide direct evidence of specific intent, there is abundant circumstantial evidence that *someone* must have noticed that felons tend to vote for liberal Democrats more often than for conservative Republicans.

One study estimated that 93 percent of felons of *all races* supported President Clinton in 1996.[84] Moreover, it has been estimated that 46 percent of convicted felons are African-American, and while it can't be proven that *anyone* in the Jeb Bush administration foresaw the outcome, in fact over 80 percent of registered African-American voters voted in the 2000 Florida election, and 93 percent of them voted for Vice President Gore.[85] So, it didn't take a genius for *somebody* to figure out that eliminating African-Americans and people with felony convictions would substantially reduce the number of registered Democrats in Florida.

Given this opportunity for mischief, the Florida election was rigged every way from Sunday right from the get-go, resulting in the elimination of thousands of eligible voters and the legitimate votes they should have been able to cast. First the obvious, later the more insidious. Since the voting rights of convicted felons in 37 states are automatically restored, the Full Faith and Credit Clause of the U.S. Constitution requires Florida to allow those who move to Florida to vote without interference, as the Florida Court of Appeals ordered in the case of *Schlenther v. Florida Department of State* in June 1998. However, when Governor Jeb Bush took office until as late as September 18, 2000, his Office of Executive Clemency gave the following orders to the Division of Elections: "Any individual whose civil rights were restored automatically by statute in the state of conviction and does not have a written certificate or order, would be required to make application for restoration of civil rights in the State of Florida."

Since civil rights are *automatically* restored in the majority of states, there are no "written certificates or orders." Thus, all rehabilitated felons moving into the State had to apply for executive clemency from, guess who, Bush's little brother, Jeb. Given the large number of persons moving into Florida and basic demographics, it has been estimated that this scheme denied thousands of eligible citizens their opportunity to ever register to vote in the first place.[86]

The Division of Elections provided ChoicePoint DBT with a list of registered Florida voters, and selected which states to include in its research to identify registered voters as convicted felons. Following Florida's criteria, ChoicePoint DBT computers generated a list of ineligible Florida voters that erroneously included the names of 2,000 persons, convicted in Ohio and Illinois, whose civil rights had been restored.

Then, in May 2000, 8,000 names were erroneously added to the list from another state. These Florida voters were not even felons; they had only been convicted of misdemeanors. Guess which state provided those names? You got it. Texas, governed by Jeb's big brother, George.[87] After an outcry, there was some attempt to correct these blatant errors before the election, but nonetheless, hundreds, if not thousands, of eligible voters were illegally prevented from voting.

Now for the more insidious gaming of the system. Remember that Florida was the only state that contracted privately for the list to be prepared. The $2,317,800 bid submitted by ChoicePoint DBT was the highest (the company that initially had the contract had only charged $5,700).[88] For this, ChoicePoint DBT promised to rely upon its 1,200 data bases to process and cross reference a total of 273,318,667 records. More importantly, the contract required ChoicePoint DBT to conduct "manual verification using telephone calls and statistical sampling."

Since any grown-up computer can crunch the numbers, it appears that what the people of Florida were paying all this extra money for was a hands-on follow-up effort to make sure that innocents were not included on the list of ineligible voters. However, *somebody* in the Jeb Bush administration made the decision that all these extra efforts were not really necessary. On the State's copy of the contract is the notation *"don't need,"* and ChoicePoint DBT confirms that it never made any telephone calls to verify the accuracy of the list of ineligible voters it produced.

Even though ChoicePoint DBT later notified the State (as required by the contract) that its statistician had certified the list as 99.9 percent accurate, the reality was far different. Depending upon the criteria, it *is* possible to reduce the error rate to approximately one percent. For example, if the name, date of birth, address and social security number all had to be exactly the same, the error factor would be quite low. However, Florida first requested only a 10 percent error factor. Thus, a hypothetical "Alex Smyth" was deemed to be the same as "Alex Smith," etc. Then, Florida upped the allowable error factor to 20 percent and instructed ChoicePoint DBT to ignore identifiers such as middle names, initials, and "Jr." and "Sr." The company later confirmed that Florida actually wanted the list to include "more names than were actually verified as being a convicted felon."[89]

Now, it really gets slimy. Florida is one of the few states that require voters to provide their race when registering. Even though ChoicePoint DBT did not use race as a factor in its search criteria, it did provide race on its list, and the county election supervisors could use it as a match criteria in trying to determine if a person on the list was the same as someone in their registration files. In other words, if the other data was less than a perfect match (such as John vs. Johnny), but they were both black?[90] Well, you get the picture.

Some county election supervisors made telephone calls, sent certified letters and published the names in the newspapers trying to make sure the right individual was targeted. In at least one county, the election supervisor herself got a letter notifying her that she was not entitled to vote because she was a felon. Another county that includes Tallahassee went to some effort to verify that the 694 individuals named on the list as felons were the same as on its rolls. It could only verify that 34 were the same. Applying the percentage of error in this sample to the state as a whole, it is estimated that as many as 52,000 of the 66,000 names provided by ChoicePoint DBT may have been wrongly included on the list and were denied their legitimate right to vote.[91]

What does this mean in an election won by Jeb's big brother, George, by 537 votes, one in which thousands and thousands of eligible voters were kept from voting? It means that *somebody* in Jeb's administration gamed the system in advance, and it certainly appears *they* got away with it. How would you feel if your name coincidentally showed up on such a list? You're not stupid! Get the truth.

The Heist

On November 7, 2000, the votes of 5,963,110 individuals for president were counted in Florida. However, 179,855 votes were not counted, and the reason these votes were not counted depended, in large measure, upon the race of the voter. In those counties that used optically scanned paper ballots, the machines could be programmed to either reject or retain ballots that were erroneously marked. For example, if someone voted for both Bush and Gore, the reject mechanism, *if activated*, would return the ballot to the voter to correct his or her error. However, in those counties with the greatest percentage of African-American voters, the reject mechanism *was not activated* and the voting machine retained the erroneously-marked ballot and it was not counted. In those counties with the greatest percentage of white voters, the reject mechanism *was activated*, and the ballot was returned to the voters to correct their errors.

Thus, 12 percent of the votes in Gadsden County with 52 percent African-Americans were not counted, while only one percent of the votes in Citrus County with two percent African-Americans were not counted.[92] Since it is statistically certain that a substantial majority of these 179,855 voters wanted to, intended to, and thought they had cast a vote for Vice President Gore, what would have been the result if all the machines had been set the same? But, what the hey, a miss is as good as a mile, and close only counts in horseshoes. The only votes that could be counted were the ones that made it through all the hoops.

On November 7, 2000, 2,912,790 Florida citizens' votes were counted for Bush and 2,912,253 for Gore, a difference of 537 votes. Because the count was so close, the Division of Elections ordered a recount on November 8, 2000, as mandated by Florida law. Most counties ran the ballots through the machines again; however, 18 counties only verified their tallies and did not reprocess the ballots. The partial recount lowered Bush's margin to 327 votes.[93]

Several major problems with the election quickly became apparent. In Palm Beach, the use of a strange "butterfly" ballot resulted in thousands of voters casting erroneous votes. Because of the design of the ballot, many ended up voting for both Gore and Buchanan, and others voted for Buchanan when they thought they were voting for Gore. In a county where his own Florida coordinator reported that Buchanan only had 300 to 500 supporters, Buchanan received 3,407 votes. Bush, speaking through his later Press Secretary, Ari Fleischer, claimed that Palm Beach was a Buchanan stronghold.

Using the reverse lie perfected in the campaign, Fleischer said, "It's important that no party to this election act in a precipitous manner to distort an existing voting pattern in an effort to misinform the public." Even Buchanan himself said, "I do believe a number of those votes cast for me were clearly intended for Al Gore." Several major news outlets later concluded that the "butterfly" ballots probably deprived Gore of between 6,000 and 9,000 votes.[94] However, once the errors were made, the intent of anonymous voters marking "butterfly" ballots could not be reconstructed, and we can only wonder how it could have been different.

But there were "rejected" ballots, thousands and thousands, that could be manually examined to determine the voter's intent. Approximately 60 percent of Florida counties used punch-card ballots that required the voters to use a stylus to punch out a perforation in the ballot for machine counting. The voter's intent could be determined by visually examining the ballots to determine if there was a "dimple" in the perforation or if the "chad" was incompletely pushed out. These became known as the "undercounted" ballots. To compel a manual recount in four counties where he had the greatest support, Gore filed a lawsuit against Katherine Harris, the Florida Secretary of State (who also co-chaired Bush's Florida campaign). Bush could have done the same thing in counties where he had the greatest support, but he decided to stand pat.[95]

On November 15, 2000, Bush stated, "We have a responsibility to make sure that those who speak for us do not poison our politics. And we have a responsibility to respect the law, and not seek to undermine it when we do not like its outcome."[96] Let us see if his deeds follow his words.

On December 8, 2000, the Florida Supreme Court ruled that the totals certified by the Secretary of State should include between 168 and 176 votes picked up for Gore in the Miami-Dade County recount and 215 votes for Gore picked up in the Palm Beach recount, even though it was not completed until after the November 26th statutory cutoff date. Moreover, the Court ruled that the approximately 9,000 votes remaining to be examined when Miami-Dade County suspended its recount should be tabulated and included in the certified tally, and that all other Florida counties should recount all undervoted ballots to identify any uncounted legal ballots. The court directed that a vote was legal if there is a "clear indication of the intent of the voter."[97]

How did those who "spoke" for Bush respond to this very sensible ruling to let the clear intent of the voters govern the result? They lied, naturally. Fleischer said, "What's happening in Palm Beach is exactly why our nation switched from hand counting ballots to the more precise, less subjective counts done by precision machines."[98] True? Not at all. Experts at the very companies that manufacture voting machines conceded that, "It is totally reasonable that the most accurate way to do it is a carefully run recount," and that "a manual recount can be extremely accurate." Two officials of the Association for Computing Machinery recommended that all the Florida votes be recounted manually as being "the only fair course."[99]

Did Bush gracefully accept the Florida decision and avoid "undermining it when [he] didn't like the outcome?" Of course not. He immediately filed a lawsuit in federal court to stop the true will of the Florida voters from being determined. Bush's complaint alleged that the manual recount would be less accurate and more subjective, resulting in a dilution of the votes in the rest of the state. He complained that the standards used in determining the validity or intent of the ballots were arbitrary and could result in an inconsistent treatment of identical ballots from two different counties.[100] Is this true?

In 1997, Governor George W. Bush signed a Texas law requiring manual reviews in close elections. It stated "A manual recount shall be conducted in preference to an electronic recount." The law required a vote to be counted if "an indentation on the chad from the stylus or other object is present and indicates a clearly ascertainable intent of the voter to vote."[101] How is this different from what the Florida Supreme Court ordered?

No matter the well-reasoned opinion by the Florida Supreme Court or the rights of the Florida voters to express their clear intent, the United States Supreme Court in a *"per curiam"* and highly curious opinion joined in by Chief Justice Rehnquist (appointed by Reagan) and Justices Scalia (appointed by Reagan), Thomas (appointed by Bush Sr.), Kennedy (appointed by Reagan), and O'Connor (appointed by Reagan) ruled in *Bush v. Gore* on December 12, 2000, in favor of the Republican candidate George W. Bush.* Surprise? The Court found that the "intent of the voter" standard may sound good in principle, but it lacked specific standards to ensure equal application. The final lie of the campaign.

Do you agree that the will of the people prevailed in the 2000 presidential election? You're not stupid! Get the truth.

---

* Remember this lineup of justices later when you read about their association with the Federalist Society.

80. Palast, op. cit., p. 31.

81. Ibid., p. 23.

82. Ibid., p. 27.

83. Ibid., p. 38.

84. Ibid., p. 37.

85. Ibid., pp. 23, 32.

86. Ibid., pp. 35, 40, 41, 43, 69-71.

87. Ibid., pp. 30, 31.

88. Ibid., p. 44.

89. Ibid., pp. 57, 58.

90. Ibid., p. 60.

91. Ibid., p. 46.

92. Ibid., pp. 62, 63.

93. Corn, op. cit., p. 54.

94. Ibid., p. 55.

95. Ibid., p. 56.

96. Ibid., p. 60.

97. Tony Sutin, ed., "Presidential Election Law/The Recount," http://jurist.law.pitt.edu/election/electiontime.htm

98. Corn, op. cit., p. 57.

99. Ibid., pp. 57, 58.

100. Sutin, op. cit.

101. Corn, op. cit., pp. 58, 59.

A BUSINESS ADMINISTRATION

Once having been established as president, no matter how questionably, Bush set about thanking the corporate wealthy, his peers who paid the contributions that elected (or selected) him, by putting "his" executive branch at their service.

If you do something often enough and long enough, it can become a habit, so we shouldn't have been surprised when the incoming Bush administration accused the outgoing Clinton staff of trashing the White House. A flood of leaks to the media reported file cabinets with the drawers glued shut, obscene graffiti scrawled on walls, cut telephone and computer lines, viruses and pornographic images in computers, missing keyboard keys, and piles of trash. True? Not a bit. Over a year later the General Accounting Office reported to Congress that there was no evidence of damage deliberately caused in the White House by employees of the Clinton administration. So, why the lies? Addictive behavior? It's hard to stop once you get used to something that gets you high, and Bush and his gang, who stole the presidency, were flying high indeed.

If It's Bad for Business, It's Too Bad for the Rest of Us

There's an analogy following, but first you've got to get the setup. Remember when many of the states adopted lotteries to raise money for the schools? Well, the first thing that happened is that the legislatures reduced the budgets previously earmarked for the schools by the amount brought in by the lotteries, and the ones who really made out are the companies that operate the lotteries, which is why they lobbied for them in the first place. But, wait a second, how about the big winners, the ones we see on television every month or so jumping up and down, the instant millionaires who quit their jobs the next morning? Yeah, someone wins every once in a while, but the odds against it are millions and millions to one, a sucker bet at best. The net effect of the lotteries is to impose an indirect tax on the poor and working class, who buy into the pipe dream and purchase most of the tickets.

Now for the analogy. There are millions and millions of Americans raised in the "me" generation, who are convinced they are going to make it to the top. Well, it's true that we all have the opportunity to start a business, work hard and, perhaps, to get rich. That *is* the American Dream, but we're not all named George Bush and it's more difficult for some than others. While some of us may work our way to the top of a corporation and get rich, many, if not most of us, will have to continue working harder every day for a salary with ever declining benefits. However, we continue to dream as we work, and we accept onerous working conditions because we don't want to kill the goose that lays the golden eggs.

Corporations count upon us to follow our fantasies, rather than our logic. To keep the dream alive, average working people have been brainwashed into believing that what's good for business is good for them (in the long run). The truth is that corporations simply consider labor as a factor in their economic formulas, and they could care less about the aspirations of workers and the dangers of the workplace, unless it affects the bottom line. Hours worked and overtime become worker "productivity," health care and worker's compensation become "overhead." The number of workers injured or killed on the job is just a cost of doing business, one to be managed like any other element of production.

If you think that corporations have a soul and that any of them give a darn about you and your family, go ahead and put in your overtime without time-and-a-half, and try to squeeze out an extra couple of dollars from your household budget to buy a lottery ticket. It'll give you a better chance of making it to the big time.

The problem is that corporations have just grown too powerful. They, rather than you and me, decide who runs the government, and the government now controls you and me, rather than controlling the corporations. Our strength is no longer in "We the People"; our salvation is in the profitability of "Big Business." Today, 51 of the top 100 economies in the world are corporations; the remaining 49 are governments. Democracies are supposed to protect the rights of *all* citizens and to provide the *people* with voting power to express their desires and define their political expectations. However, it is corporate power that increasingly determines political policies and insulates corporations from government regulation and taxation.

When Eisenhower was president, corporations paid approximately a quarter of federal taxes. By 2000, their share was down to 10 percent, and by 2001, they were only paying out seven percent.[102] However, go down to the local courthouse and see who is using our justice system to enforce their contracts, collect their debts and block enforcement of environmental and consumer protection laws. Look at the daily schedules of our legislators and government executives and see who gets "face time." Write a letter to any of them and see if you get a personal answer; telephone and see if they'll take your call. It's *our* government, we pay the politicians' salaries with our taxes, and they need our votes to get elected, but big money talks and the little guys get squat.

Are we really getting our share of the American pie through our hard work? During the past 30 years, our average annual salary (adjusted for inflation) has only edged up ten percent. At the same time, the income of the top one percent has jumped 157 percent. In 1998, the wealthy in the top one percent earned more than the 100 million workers in the bottom 40 percent. While health benefits and overtime pay of workers *were being cut*, the income of America's top ten corporate CEO's went from 39 times that of the average worker's to more than 1,000 times. The Bureau of Labor Statistics tells us that between 1989 and 1999, the average American worker clocked an additional 184 hours per year,* which was 550 hours more than the average European worker.[103] That's called "productivity," and American workers are the most productive on earth. However, management gets

---

* If we assume a two-week vacation and five holidays, the additional 184 hours calculates out to almost 9.5 percent longer we had to work to earn the addition 10 percent increase in wages. Wow! Things really are getting better. Maybe we should put in even more hours; we might get another raise.

the credit for baking the pie, and the ones who tend the ovens don't even get a sniff, much less a crumb.

The median income for a family of four is $44,000 a year, and 70 percent of Americans earn less than $50,000; however, when asked in polls, approximately 90 percent of Americans claim to be in the middle class. The truth is that during 2001, for the first time since 1993, an additional million and a half Americans fell below the federal poverty line drawn at $18,100 a year for a family of four. That means that 33 million Americans, almost 12 percent of the population, including 13 million children, are at risk. Almost three million of these children actually suffer from hunger, having to skip meals and go without food. The gap between the rich and the poor is greater in America than in any other industrialized nation, and it is growing.[104]

A free enterprise system can only operate effectively in the long run if there is a balance of power between business and labor, and a capitalist economy can only continue to exist in a free and democratic society when there are well-conceived government regulations to rein in the power generated by and associated with the accumulation of money. In 2000, there was a new honcho in the White House, bought and paid for by big business. What did he do? Well, one of the first things Bush did was to get rid of some troublesome worker protection regulations left over from the Clinton administration that interfered with the profits of his constituency.

Reversal of Ergonomic Standards

In 1988, Bush Sr.'s Labor Secretary, Elizabeth Dole, ordered the drafting of regulations to protect workers from injuries, such as carpal tunnel syndrome, caused by repetitive motions. It took 12 years and two administrations to complete these ergonomics standards. One reason it took so long was that Big Business fought them tooth and toenail, and their guy with the pliers was attorney Eugene Scalia, the son of Supreme Court Justice Antonin Scalia, who gave Bush Jr. the deciding vote for president. (Eugene works for the same law firm that convinced his father to give the presidency to Bush.) During hearings, Scalia claimed that healthy workers milk the system by claiming "that they are injured in order to avoid work and obtain benefits," and that one of the biggest risks in the workplace is boredom. He claimed that ergonomics was founded on "junk science," that increases in reported injuries were caused by a form of hysteria, that complaining workers were "simply unhappy or malingerers," and that they should buy their own protective gear.[105] Do you know anyone who has suffered these injuries? Ask them if their disabilities are caused by hysteria!

After the testimony of over a thousand witnesses and seven thousand written comments, the proposed regulations were drafted and, in the last days of his administration, President Clinton ordered them to be published in the *Federal Register* in order to become binding on employers.[106]

However, as soon as Bush was installed in the White House, he issued a press release in which he complained that the ergonomics regulations "would cost employers, large and small, billions of dollars annually while providing uncertain benefits." They would require businesses to "provide compensation for an extremely broad class of injuries, whose cause is subject to considerable dispute." Thereby encouraged, Republican Senator Tom DeLay was able to bring the regulations before the Senate for a vote. After Bush's new Secretary of Labor, Elaine Chao, wrote a letter promising to work on new and better ergonomics standards, the Senate voted to kill the proposed regulations.[107]

In a demonstration of his compassion for injured workers, Bush then nominated Eugene Scalia as the Solicitor of Labor in April 2001 to represent them, since individual workers cannot hire their own attorneys to enforce the federal regulations. A conflict of interest? Senate Democrats expressed grave doubts about his objectivity, and it appeared that Scalia's nomination might not be approved. However, Bush made a "recess appointment" in January 2002, which allowed Scalia to temporarily take the job. The temporary appointment expired when the Senate went into recess in November 2002, and Bush designated Scalia as the Acting Solicitor. Scalia stepped down two months later citing among his accomplishments an improvement in the "Department's enforcement and regulatory programs."[108]

In lieu of the mandatory standards, the Labor Department circulated voluntary industry guidelines, and it rewards companies who voluntarily comply by presenting them with a flag to run up their company flagpole! In a speech on June 5, 2002, Deputy Labor Secretary D. Cameron Findlay proudly reported that the Department of Labor had reduced its regulatory agenda by 40 percent in less than one year, and that the Department was focusing more on voluntary compliance with the laws on the books, rather than on "heavy-handed" enforcement.[109]

When Bush signed the bill repealing the ergonomics standards, he stated, "I was pleased to sign a bill that got rid of needless regulations." The AFL-CIO estimates that U.S. workers suffer a workplace ergonomic injury every 18 seconds, and the National Academy of Sciences estimates that one million workers a year lose work due to "work-related musculoskeletal pain or impairment of function" and that these injuries drain between $45 and $54 billion a year from the economy.[110]

How many of you have suffered repetitive motion injuries? How many of you have received adequate compensation? Do you think Bush feels your pain? You're not stupid! Get the truth.

Elimination of Overtime Pay

Once the Bush administration had adequately secured corporate protection against on-the-job injuries, it set out to ensure that millions of other workers were allowed to work as long as they wanted without having to burden their employers with overtime pay. One of the ways that American workers have been sucked into pipe dreams of untold riches has been to make them all managers of one sort or another. In convenience stores across the nation, every clerk is an assistant manager, and virtually every position in corporate America carries a title. Often, all the worker gets *is* the title; the salary that's left over after payroll taxes isn't enough to live on. In the past, notwithstanding the title, managers really had to supervise someone to be exempt, and administrative, technical, or professional employees could not spend more than 20 percent of their time performing non-exempt duties; otherwise, they had to be paid overtime.[111] No longer.

On March 27, 2003, the Department of Labor announced new regulations governing enforcement of the Fair Labor Standards Act. The 20-percent standard was eliminated and exemptions from overtime were expanded to include thousands, if not millions, of "white collar" workers, such as administrative personnel, police officers, firefighters, and nurses, who formerly had to be paid overtime. However, you would think that the Department was doing these workers a favor. The news release announcing this "modernization" stated, "By recognizing the professional status of skilled employees, the proposed regulation will provide them a guaranteed salary and flexible hours."[112]

After both houses of Congress voted in 2003 to block implementation of the new overtime rules, Democrats inserted a provision in the 2004 omnibus- spending bill to prevent the Labor Department from using government funds to put the new rules into effect. However, after Bush threatened to veto the bill if the provision was left in, the Republican leadership stripped it from the bill. The bill was passed on January 22, 2004, and the rules denying overtime pay to over eight million workers became effective.[113]

There was the expected outcry, and in April 2004, the administration increased the ceiling where workers are almost automatically disqualified for overtime pay from $65,000 to $100,000.[114] However, the administration has been giving tips to employers on how to avoid legitimate overtime pay. Business have been told they can "cut workers' hourly wages and add the overtime to equal the original salary, or raise salaries to the new $22,100 annual minimum threshold, making [workers] ineligible."[115]

Are you losing your overtime rights? Do you think President Bush cares about how many hours you have to work to put food on the table, or whether you have any time to spend with your children?

Bush is convinced that President Calvin Coolidge was right when he said, "the chief business of the American people is business." According to Randall Roden, Bush's best friend as they were growing up, "Midland [Texas] is probably where he first got the mistaken idea that doing well in business is the solution to America's problems, that is, what's good for business is good for America. 'Opportunity and business fortune for all' isn't really true for everyone."[116]

Do you believe that what is best for business is always best for you and your family? You're not stupid! Get the truth.

The Energy Companies' Crisis

With the election of Bush in 2000, the energy industry was faced with a crisis. Having fronted millions of dollars in political contributions during the 1999-2000 election cycle, with approximately 75 percent, or more than $48.3 million, going to Republicans and nearly $3 million to Bush alone, it was in a rush to seal the deal. It wasn't enough that the industry had installed its man in the White House, the industry wanted it all. And darn near got it. The Vice President, Dick Cheney, had been the CEO of Halliburton Company, an oil industry service company. The Secretary of the Interior, Gale Norton, had represented the mining industry and received nearly $800,000 from energy industries during her race for the U.S. Senate in 1996. The Secretary of Commerce, Don Evans, came from the oil and gas industry. The Secretary of Energy, Spencer Abraham, was an opponent of stricter fuel economy standards in the Senate, and as a candidate, he received over $700,000 from the auto industry. Bush's Chief of Staff, Andrew Card, served as a lobbyist against stricter fuel economy standards. And Condoleezza Rice, Bush's National Security Advisor, served for ten years on Chevron's board of directors, which gave $758,588 to Republican candidates and committees in the 1999-2000 election. In addition, the energy industry supplied numerous deputy secretaries, special assistants, and other senior administrators to serve in the Bush administration.[117] Where is the balance? Who represents our interests?

The takeover actually started before the inauguration when Bush selected 31 representatives from the energy industry to serve on his energy transition team. Then, within days of taking the oath, he created the National Energy Policy Development Group, chaired by Vice President Cheney, to formulate energy policy. For the next three months, working in secret, the Group conferred with numerous representatives of the energy industry to draft a recommended policy. Altogether, the task force had 714 direct contacts from energy company representatives and only 29 with identified nonindustry groups.[118] Cheney said that he was personally too busy to meet with representatives of environmental groups, but he found time to meet with a number of energy company executives. Among those he met with was Ken Lay, the CEO of Enron, a Texas energy company that had donated $563,000 to Bush's campaigns over the years and was the energy industry's top contributor during the 1999-2000 election, giving more than $2.3 million, mostly to Republicans.[119]

Bush and Lay go way back. Lay supported Bush Sr. as early as 1980, when he unsuccessfully ran for president. In 1986, Bush Jr.'s company, Spectrum 7, had a ten-percent piece of a producing oil and natural gas well in Martin County, Texas, operated by a subsidiary of Enron.[120] In 1988, Bush Jr. telephoned Argentina's public works minister, identified himself as the son of the U.S. vice president, about to become president, and urged that Argentina award a pipeline contract to Enron that could be worth hundreds of millions of dollars.[121] According to Lay, he spent "quality time" with Bush Jr. in 1989 when Lay was trying to get Bush Sr. to locate his presidential library in Houston.[122]

During the 1992 presidential race, Lay worked closely with Bush Jr. at the Republican nominating convention in Houston. Then, when Bush ran for governor in 1994, Lay and his wife donated $47,500 to Bush Jr. and $12,500 to his opponent, incumbent Ann Richards.[123] In addition, Enron's political action committee and its executives contributed a total of $146,500 to Bush and $19,500 to Richards. During the 2000 election, Lay was a "Pioneer," having raised over $100,000 for Bush, and he gave more than $275,000 to the Republican Party. Enron sent the Republicans more than a million, which helped pay for the national convention.[124] In appreciation, Bush invited Lay to a private lunch on his second day in the White House.

In March 2001, Lay suggested, and Bush Jr. appointed, two commissioners to the Federal Energy Regulatory Commission (FERC) who were in favor of electricity deregulation.[125] Then, on April 17, 2001, Lay met privately with Cheney and gave him Enron's wish list containing eight policy recommendations, seven of which were subsequently adopted by Cheney. He also advised Cheney how the administration should respond to the crisis going on in California, which was suffering daily rolling electrical blackouts, and to pleas for wholesale price caps because of skyrocketing electric bills.[126] Cheney listened carefully, and the next day he parroted the Enron line in speaking out against price caps, confusing retail with wholesale caps. The crisis continued for weeks with the energy companies, including Enron, pumping billions of dollars from the California economy into their coffers as they enjoyed profits of 400 to 600 percent.

Two years later the FERC concluded that "Enron and its affiliates intentionally engaged in a variety of market manipulation schemes that had profound adverse impacts on market outcomes." One Enron division was able to earn over $500 million by manipulating gas and electricity prices.[127]

In December 2003, FERC reached settlements with two other energy companies, Mirant Corporation and Duke Energy Corporation, for a fraction of the claims by California regulators. Mirant agreed to pay $3.7 million and Duke agreed to pay $2.05 million to settle allegations that the companies manipulated the bidding process and intentionally withheld energy during the electricity crisis.* California claimed that Mirant owed $28

---

* In October 2003, investigative reporter Greg Palast obtained 34 pages of Enron memoranda regarding a meeting on May 17, 2001 in Los Angeles involving Ken Lay, convicted stock swindler Mike Milken, and future California Governor Arnold Schwarzenegger. The purpose of the meeting was to find a way to sidetrack a $9 billion lawsuit filed by California Lieutenant Governor Cruz Bustamante against a group of energy companies, including Enron. The solution? Engineer a recall election in which Schwarzenegger is elected governor. Once in office, he can bless whatever sweetheart settlement the FERC comes up with. Any surprise? Except for those of you who may have wondered why

million and that Duke's settlement was far less than it owed. The California Attorney General's spokesman stated, "FERC has little or no credibility with California, and these settlements and proposed settlements are the latest example of why."[128]

Enron was not alone at the trough. The coal barons of West Virginia were there as well as the electrical power industry. All had been very generous during the campaign, and they all had their wish list to manage their energy "crisis." The coal companies wanted to be able to blow off the tops of mountains to expose coal seams and to bulldoze the debris into streambeds. The nuclear power industry wanted more nuclear plants, and the coal-fired power plants wanted protection against enforcement of the Clean Air Act. It was like Christmas when Bush unveiled his energy plan.[129]

When Bush established the Energy Group, he had directed it to "develop a national energy policy designed to help the private sector, State and local governments, promote dependable, affordable, and environmentally sound production and distribution of energy for the future."[130] Notice that he started with helping the private sector and ended with protecting the environment, and that's about the way the policy came down. While there was a wink and a nod in the direction of conservation, such as encouraging federal agencies to turn out the lights, the emphasis in the report issued on May 16, 2001, was to encourage development of fossil fuels and nuclear energy and to ease pollution regulations for power plants, refineries, and pipelines to facilitate increased production. Specifically, while the Clinton EPA had begun to file suits against coal-fired power plants that violated the Clean Air Act, the Bush energy plan directed the Justice Department to consider reversing the "existing enforcement actions" already filed against violators, a blatant interference with law enforcement. Subsequent studies

---

the Terminator suddenly got interested in politics. (Palast, Greg, "Arnold Unplugged: It's Hasta La Vista To $9 billion If The Governator is Selected," October 3, 2003, www.gregpalast.com.detail. cfm?artial+=2838row=1.)

have shown that relaxed enforcement will allow an additional 1.4 million tons of pollutants into the air.[131]

The energy plan went on to encourage the development of more nuclear power plants. The next day, Bush stated, "By renewing and expanding existing nuclear facilities, we can generate tens of thousands of megawatts of electricity at a reasonable cost without pumping a gram of greenhouse gas into the atmosphere." He also called for drilling for oil in Alaska's Arctic National Wildlife Refuge.

Bush opposed a bipartisan Congressional effort to require an increase in the overall automobile fuel efficiency standards, even though the auto industry has the technology to increase the mileage efficiency of SUVs to 25 to 30 miles per gallon and to bring standard vehicles up to 40 mpg. An increase of just 0.4 mpg in the fuel efficiency of the nation's auto fleet would save more oil than drilling in the Alaskan reserve would produce. (Remember that Bush's chief of staff, Andrew Card, formerly lobbied against increased standards.)[132]

Regarding conservation, Cheney stated, "Virtually all of the recommendations for financial incentives and assistance tax credits and so forth are for conservation and increased efficiency and renewables. There are no new financial subsidies of any kind for the oil and gas industry." A complete lie! The Bush Energy Plan provided for $28 billion in subsidies and tax breaks for the oil, gas, coal and nuclear industries, in addition to $33 billion the energy industry was already scheduled to receive. This giveaway cost each one of us about $220.[133]

Cheney and Energy Secretary Spencer Abraham had met privately with over a hundred executives and lobbyists from the energy industry while largely ignoring the environmentalists; however, Cheney refused to provide any names. Congressional Democrats requested the General Accounting Office (GAO) to find out the names. Cheney refused a formal request from the GAO, and for the first time in history, the GAO sued the President for the release of the names. Bush refused, saying confidentiality was necessary to ensure he received unfettered advice. In December 2002, the federal court ruled that the GAO lacked sufficient grounds to compel release of the names and the

GAO dropped the case. However, there were additional suits filed by the Sierra Club and Judicial Watch, but more about that later.[134]

But even Christmas in May was not enough for Enron. It had set out in 1992 to build the world's largest natural gas fired power plant in India in a joint venture with General Electric and Bechtel. However, the next year, the World Bank declined to finance the "Dabhol" project in Maharashtra state because it concluded the plant was "not economically viable." Undeterred, Enron obtained $302 million in loans from the U.S. Export-Import Bank and the Overseas Private Investment Corporation and was able to open the plant in 1999. When the power it produced proved to be more expensive than supplies from domestic producers, Maharashtra state stopped paying the bills and tried to cancel the purchase agreement. Enron then shut down the plant claimed the state owed it millions of dollars, and tried to sell its interest for $2.3 billion.

In April 2001, Secretary of State Powell raised the matter with India's foreign minister, and by June there was an administration interagency working group coordinated by the National Security Council pushing for India to settle. Cheney "mentioned Enron" when he met with Sonia Gandhi, an opposition leader, and the matter was on Bush's agenda for his November 2001 meeting with India's foreign minister. However, the item was hurriedly pulled when Enron imploded on the day before the meeting.[135]

Enron was forced to disclose that it had overstated its profits by $600 million over the previous five years, and Enron's stock lost $26 billion in market value during the next seven weeks. During this period, thousands of its employees lost their life savings when Enron prevented them from selling their Enron stocks out of their retirement plans. While Enron was stiff-arming its employees, its top managers were selling over $1 billion of their own shares, and while Lay was encouraging his employees to keep their money in the company, he personally sneaked away with $50 million.

It turns out that Enron had received some of the same advice regarding phony partnerships that its accountant, Arthur

Andersen, had given Harken when Bush was on its board of directors. Enron had relied upon secret partnerships and unscrupulous trading in derivatives to inflate its profits. Moreover, it came to light that Enron had not paid any income taxes in four of the previous five years, through a variety of schemes.[136] When was the last time you got a free pass on your income taxes?

In November 2001, Lay telephoned both Treasury Secretary Paul O'Neill and Commerce Secretary Don Evans in an attempt to get a last-minute government bailout of Enron.[137]

So what did Bush have to say when asked about his buddy, his most generous supporter? He lied, naturally. What he actually said was, "First of all, Ken Lay is a supporter, and I got to know Ken Lay when he was a head of the–what they call the Governor's Business Council in Texas. He was a supporter of Ann Richards in my run in 1994, and she had named him head of the Governor's Business Council, and I decided to leave him in place, for the sake of continuity. *And, that's when I first got to know Ken* and worked with Ken, and he supported my candidacy for–and–but this is what–anybody's going to find, if–is that this administration will fully investigate issues such as the Enron bankruptcy. (emphasis added)"[138] It's hard to be articulate and to lie at the same time, even if one's had a lot of practice, but even Bush couldn't pull it off. He had been in bed with Lay for a long time before 1994, and they had snuggled a whole lot closer than he was trying to make it seem.

On January 28, 2002, after being asked if Enron had received any special treatment in Cheney's energy plan, Bush again lied, naturally, "If they came to this administration looking for help, they didn't find any."[139]

If Bush and Lay spent "quality time" together in 1989, is Bush telling the truth when he says they did not get to know one another until 1994? Who did Bush support–Enron or the working people who got screwed by Enron? You're not stupid! Get the truth.

102. Ivins, op. cit., p. 41.

103. Ibid., pp. 40-43.

104. Ibid., p. 39.

105. Ibid., pp. 52-55; see also Mirer, Frank, "Eugene Scalia Opposes Making Employers Pay for Protective Equipment," December 2001, (http://www.uaw.org/solidarity/01/1201/front06.html); see also Ratner, David, "Bush's Pick for Nation's Chief Labor Law Enforcer is Drawing Fire From Unions," July 13, 2001, (www.laborresearch.org/story2).

106. Ivins, op. cit., p. 64.

107. Ibid., pp. 65-68.

108. Ibid., pp. 68-70; see also "Eugene Scalia to Step Down as Acting Solicitor of Labor," OPA News Release, January 6, 2003, www.dol.gov/opa/media/press/opa.

109. "U.S. Department of Labor Deputy Secretary Findlay Encourages Electrical Contractors in Speech on 21st Century Workforce," June 5, 2002, www.ieci.org/default.asp.

110. "Bush Worker Safety 'Plan' Fails to Protect Workers," December 5, 2002, www.aflcio.org/yourjobeconomy/safety.

111. "U.S. Department of Labor Proposal Will Secure Overtime for 1.3 Million More Low-Wage Workers," OPA News Release, March 27, 2003, www.dol.gov/opa/media/press/opa.

112. Ibid.

113. Simon, Richard, "Senate OKs $328.5-Billion Spending Bill," *Los Angeles Times*, January 23, 2004, p. A14.

114. Greenhouse, Steven, "Labor Dept. Revises Plans to Cut Overtime Eligibility," *The New York Times*, April 21, 2004, www.nytimes.com/2004/04/21/politics/21WAGE.html.

115. "Bush Stiffs Workers on Overtime," *The Daily Mis-Lead*, April 20, 2004, http://daily.misleader.org/ctt/asp?u=2323986&1=29783.

116. Minutaglio, op. cit., p. 31.

117. "Industry Dream Team," www.nrdc.org/air/energy/aplayers.asp.

118. Alterman and Green, op. cit., p. 84.

119. Corn, op. cit., p. 184.

120. Ibid., p. 179.

121. Ibid., pp. 178, 179; see also Ivins, op. cit., pp. 189, 190.

122. Corn, op. cit., p. 177.

123. Ibid., p. 178.

124. Ivins, op. cit., pp. 188, 189.

125. Ibid., pp. 193-194; see also Corn, op. cit., p. 183.

126. Ivins, op. cit., p. 195.

127. Corn, op. cit., p. 185.

128. Werner, Erica, "Energy firms' fines hit $8M," Associated Press, December 20, 2002.

129. www.nrdc.org/air/energy/aplayers.asp.

130. "National Energy Policy," www.blm.gov/energy/policy.

131. www.nrdc.org/air/energy/aplayers.asp.

132. Alterman and Green, op. cit., p. 22.

133. Ibid., p. 19.

134. "Sierra Club Files Suit Against Cheney's Energy Task Force," January 25, 2002, http://newyork.sierraclub.org/rochester/news!.htm.

135. Ivins, op. cit., pp. 196, 197; see also Corn, op. cit., pp. 186-188.

136. Corn, op. cit., p. 175.

137. Ibid., p. 181.

138. Ibid., pp. 176, 177.

139. Ibid., p. 188.

NO CHILD LEFT UNTESTED

Bush claims a successful record on education both as governor of Texas and as president, but a closer examination reveals it to be largely a public relations smokescreen. His policies, once the smoke has been blown aside, are revealed to be hostile to public education and to the democratic values on which it rests.

The availability of a free public education in the United States has been essential in the development of our free and democratic society. Boston Latin School, the first publicly funded secondary school in America, was founded in 1635, and was attended by at least three founding fathers, Benjamin Franklin, Samuel Adams and John Hancock. Thomas Jefferson, the author of the Declaration of Independence, advocated universal basic education paid for by taxes.

In 1837, Massachusetts became the first state to provide state funds to establish free "common schools" throughout the state, and in 1852, its legislature passed the first compulsory education law covering all children. By the end of the Civil War, most states provided free public education; however, its benefits were not available for all children, most often for reasons of race. In 1905, the California Supreme Court ruled that the state could not exclude Chinese children from its public schools, and in 1954, the U.S. Supreme Court ruled that the segregated educational facilities in the South were inherently unequal and unconstitutional.[140]

Citing national security reasons, Congress passed the National Defense Education Act in 1958 to provide federal funds to improve the science and math curriculum of public schools. In 1965, Congress passed the Elementary and Secondary Education Act as part of the War on Poverty. Title I of the Act provided the first federal aid to schools with large numbers of students living in poverty, and the Act also established the Head Start program to provide health, nutrition, and education for low-income preschoolers. President Carter created a cabinet-level Department of Education in 1979.[141]

According to statistics gathered by the National Association of State Boards of Education, in the 1998-1999 school year 14,883 public school districts employed 2,637,846 teachers in 87,125 schools to educate 45,228,526 students through high school. Nineteen percent of these students lived in poverty, but overall, 85.8 percent of them graduated from high school. We spent a total of $265,839,427,000 per year, or approximately $6,000 per student, to educate them. The local districts raised 43.8 percent of their budgets, the states contributed 46.8 percent, and the federal government chipped in less than seven percent.[142]

Teachers, 56 percent of whom have advanced degrees, are paid, on average, $38,509 before taxes. For this, the average teacher works 50 hours a week, including an average of 12 hours of uncompensated school-related activities such as grading papers, performing bus duty, and advising student clubs. Each year, our teachers spend over $1 billion out of their own pocketbooks for essential classroom supplies not provided by their districts. This direct subsidy compares favorably to the pittance provided by the federal government, and it comes with no strings attached.[143]

America's public schools and its teachers have served as the catalyst for melding its immigrant population into a cohesive society. They have provided our children with a sense of pride in America and its role in world affairs; they have prepared our children to become thoughtful adults in casting the responsible votes essential for the preservation of a free and democratic society; and they have empowered our children to defend their freedoms.

Educating Docile Workers for the Corporate State

Horace Mann, the first secretary of education in Massachusetts, encouraged business owners to contribute to the state's public education system by promising them better workers distinguished by their "docility and quickness in applying themselves to work, personal cleanliness and fidelity in the performance of duties." Today, businesses want useful workers who can read, write and do basic mathematics, but they continue to want them to be competitive, obedient and to show respect for authority.[144]

Professionally trained business leaders obsessed with global competition believe that educational theory should be primarily economic. A former chairman of IBM once described children as human capital, teachers as sellers in a marketplace, and the public school system as a monopoly. According to the business model, educators should become bean counters, weighing inputs and outputs, such as the school budgets and test scores. To encourage the maximum production, teaching failures must be punished by the loss of bonuses and the imposition of sanctions.[145]

Since many of these business leaders believe that schools already have adequate resources, they are convinced that the only way to achieve success is to establish standards and to impose accountability through testing, with sanctions for failure. The Business Roundtable, a meeting of corporate leaders, believes that testing is a "bedrock principle" and that the "leadership and credibility of the business community is needed" to ensure the adoption of universal standardized testing. However, the Roundtable worries about the "voices of opposition" that will "emanate from parents and teachers."[146]

On his first day in office, President Bush gathered a group of "education leaders" to meet with him in the White House. However, the guest list was dominated by Big Business, and the chairman of McGraw-Hill said, "It's a great day for education, because we now have substantial alignment among all the key constituents–the public, the education community, business and political leaders–that results matter." Would it surprise anyone to learn that McGraw-Hill wrote the statement of principles for Bush's Texas Education Agency and designed the state's reading curriculum? Or that McGraw-Hill then got the biggest market share of the state's textbook market?[147] You're not stupid! Get the truth.

Dropouts Don't Count

In 1994, when George W. Bush first campaigned for governor in Texas, he stole the Democrats' playbook in the area of educational reform. Education had always been a Democratic issue, and his opponent, Governor Ann Richards, had already pushed through a reform bill during her tenure. First, Bush called for the abolition of the regulatory power of the Texas Education Agency, saying, "We must fund centrally, and we must govern locally." At the same time, he called for accountability and periodic standardized testing.[148]

In 1995, the Texas legislature passed Senate Bill 1, which rewrote the Texas education code to redirect education efforts from providing students with a broad-based liberal arts education to preparing them for employment. The State Board of Education was required to revise curriculum requirements with the "aid and advice" of Texas employers, and all school districts were urged to adopt a school-to-work program that would integrate vocational competencies commencing in kindergarten, and to require all students to select a career pathway no later than the eighth grade.[149] Next, students were to be tested each year, and every school had to be rated in the areas of dropout rate, attendance rate, and the percentage of students who passed the Texas Assessment of Academic Skills (TAAS) test. The net effect of the law was to move control over the schools from the local school districts to the state, where most curriculum decisions were to be made, a reversal of Bush's campaign promises.

There was little objection to adoption or implementation of the new law, even from the state's teaching professionals. One reason may have been the relative weakness of the state's teachers' unions, which have no rights to collective bargaining or tenure. Teachers either cooperated and became true believers, or else they hit the highway.[150]

The same year Bush was elected governor, the board of the Houston Independent School District (HISD) appointed one of its members, Dr. Roderick Paige, as the superintendent of its schools. HISD is the seventh largest public school district in America, with over 210,000 students.

Dr. Paige wasted no time in eliminating tenure for principals, instituting performance contracts modeled on those in the private sector, in which senior staff members' performance determined their continued employment, and introducing teacher incentive pay. He also formed a political alliance with Governor Bush that was to pay dividends for both of them in the future.[151]

Operating under the shadow of the big stick in Austin, powerless teachers gave up trying to teach students how to think and began to teach to the test. Worried administrators began to pore over their schools' statistics. Principals were pressured to use "any means necessary" to raise test scores, and successful curricula were replaced with practice test drills. Teachers were encouraged to concentrate on the "bubble kids," those just below the passing line, and to ignore those at the bottom who would never pass.[152] And, lo and behold, student scores on the TAAS tests began to increase. By 1996, the number of high school graduates who passed the exit-level TAAS increased to 84.7 percent from 82.8 percent the year before. By then, Bush and Paige were set to be nominated for sainthood for having pulled off the "Texas Miracle." However, some dark clouds were gathering on the horizon, but more about that later. First the parade.

By 1999, after being re-elected governor, Bush decided he was ready to run for the White House as the "education candidate." He promised to do for the rest of the United States what he had done in Texas, and he misled a lot of voters into believing that would be a good thing. Once elected, and because Dr. Paige had done such a "good" job in Houston, Bush nominated him as his Secretary of Education. In January 2001, the two set up shop in Washington, D.C.

One of the rules imposed by bank security is to require all managers to take at least two weeks of uninterrupted vacation a year. Banks do this to discover embezzlements during the enforced absences, when managers are not around to cover their tracks.   Well, after Dr. Paige and Bush left Texas, some interesting information began to come to light.

One of the first things that someone noticed was that while student scores on the tests controlled by the Texas Education Agency were steadily increasing, student scores on the nationally administered Scholastic Aptitude Test (SAT) and the American College Testing Program (ACT) were not. While the Texas authorities were reportedly educating a new generation of future Einsteins, the students' SAT and ACT scores were not improving, and, in fact, they were near the bottom of the barrel. Nationally, Texas students ranked 47th on these entrance exams.[153]

Keep in mind that Texas school administrators receive bonuses of up to $10,000 based upon attendance and dropout rates, as well as improvements in test scores. Well, during the school year 2000-2001, HISD's Sharpstown High School reported no dropouts. None! In November 2002, one of the assistant principals, apparently more concerned about integrity than money, wrote to his principal and informed her that the dropout statistics were being faked. He told her, "We go from 1,000 freshmen to less than 300 seniors with no dropouts? Amazing!"[154] Nothing changed. Sharpstown High continued to claim that it had no dropouts, at least until the state stepped in and conducted an audit of the entire school district. The state found that, while HISD had only reported a 2.5 percent dropout rate overall, in fact over 3,000 students seemed to have disappeared from the rolls; however, none of them were carried as dropouts. The true dropout rate was determined to be approximately 52 percent! **HISD was actually found to have one of the poorest graduation rates in the country, being ranked in the bottom ten school districts, an honor also accorded to Dallas and Fort Worth.**[155]

In some schools, low-performing students were encouraged to drop out to avoid having them perform poorly on the standardized tests and thereby reduce the average scores. Another gaming of the system kept low-performing students from taking the critical tenth grade exit examination. Students who failed only one class in the ninth grade were kept there for up to three years if the state issued a waiver. Some were discouraged from taking the course they needed to advance toward graduation, and many simply dropped out (but not according to the school district). In one HISD high school with 3,000 students, only 296 took the tenth grade test, when statistically there should have been between 700 and 750 students in the tenth grade.[156]

In a different twist, HISD's Jack Yates High School reported that from 1998 to 2002, 100 percent of its graduates intended to attend college. However, in 2002, only one third took the SAT, and they only had a combined average score of 763 out of a possible 1,600. Nationally, the combined average for all students was 1,020.[157] In fact, less than 50 percent of the Yates graduates ever took any classes at state colleges or universities. One graduate commented on the false claims, "It doesn't mean anything, because who cares. But it could mean they lie about a lot more of other things."[158]

Before we re-join Bush's parade to the White House, let's take another look at his campaign promise to Texans, "We must fund centrally, and we must govern locally." We saw how he shifted education decision making from local school boards to the state, but what about school funding? Keep in mind that Texas does not have a state income tax, and that money to operate the state government primarily comes from statewide taxes on sales and real property. Because the regressive sales tax produces 58 percent of the state's income, the poor pay a far higher percentage of their incomes as taxes. People earning less than $14,750 pay 16 percent, and those earning over $74,250 only pay 3.8 percent.[159]

In 1997, Bush called for a $3 billion cut in property taxes, which would substantially benefit businesses, and the legislature approved $1 billion. Two years later, in 1999, the economic picture was looking good and, depending on who was cooking the books, the state was expecting a budget surplus of between $2.6 billion and $5.6 billion. Relying on the unrealistic higher projection to pay for it, Bush proposed a $2.6 billion tax cut. The Texas Legislature was leaning toward a $2 billion cut and was trying to figure out how to balance the books.[160] Even though

Texas ranked near the bottom nationally on spending for education (41ˢᵗ), the Legislature cut proposed increases in teacher pay by half, refused to fund mandatory kindergarten for all students, and refused to reduce the class size of kindergarten to fourth grade classes. These last two proposals would have primarily benefited poor students (of whom Texas had more of than any other state) and were estimated to cost approximately $1.2 billion. When Bush was asked about his position on mandatory kindergarten, he said Texas couldn't afford it and that he would "be happy with the bill if it doesn't have mandatory kindergarten."[161] Bush got his tax cut, and the poor children of Texas largely paid for it.

Who suffered most from the failure of the Texas schools? Does Bush care? Do you think there really was a "Texas Miracle" in education? Do you think Bush was truthful about it? You're not stupid! Get the truth.

Big Brother Knows Best

In the 2000 presidential campaign, George W. Bush ran as the education candidate. He stated, "Rarely is the question asked, is [sic] our children learning?" And he promised that, "My education message will resignate [sic] amongst all parents." (Could this man pass a basic English skills test?) Whatever that means, Rove and Bush hammered together an education platform and managed to stay "on message" throughout the campaign.

During a Republican debate in the primaries, another candidate, Steve Forbes, who accused him of lowering the Texas standards to the extent that "your SAT ranking has gone from 40th in the nation to 46th in the nation", criticized Bush about his record on education. Bush sarcastically replied, "objective analysis after objective analysis has ranked Texas as one of the best education states in the country. ... One reason–our SAT scores have improved since I've been the governor. You need to get your research to do a better job." Are you surprised by this blatant lie? In fact, during the Bush administration, the average verbal/math combined SAT score in Texas had dropped three points, while the national average had improved nine points.[162]

Once Bush won the nomination, he chose Richard B. Cheney as his vice president—who as a congressman voted against the creation of the U.S. Department of Education, opposed the Head Start program, and supported a measure to deny federal aid to any school that restricted prayer.[163] Bush quickly moved to establish his "compassionate conservative" credentials by reassuring folks that he wasn't going to do away with the Department of Education or Head Start. At the same time, he hewed to the conservative line in proposing the expansion of charter schools, tax-exempt education savings accounts, and school vouchers.

In 1998, President Clinton proposed voluntary national testing of all fourth graders in reading and all eighth graders in basic math. Instead of covering specific, detailed curriculum, the tests would be basic, reflecting a common set of expectations. The reading test would include open-ended essay questions as well as multiple-choice questions, and the math test would provide partial credit for wrong answers as long as students demonstrated an understanding of how the problem should be solved. The short 90-minute tests were intended to provide reliable data on how American children were mastering the basics, rather than to punish students, teachers, or schools for failure.[164]

Clinton's Secretary of Education, Richard Riley, stated, "If all of our efforts to raise standards get reduced to one test, we've gotten it wrong. If we force our teachers to teach only to the test, we will lose their creativity. ... If we are so consumed with making sure students pass a multiple-choice test that we throw out the arts and civics then we will be going backwards instead of forward."[165] A quiet voice of reason, yet the Republican response was deafening.

Led by Missouri Senator Ashcroft (more about him later), the Republicans managed to insert language in an essential 1998 appropriations bill that shelved the Clinton voluntary testing plan for the balance of the fiscal year. Senator Ashcroft called it an "important victory for local control," and he warned, "This fight is not over. I am confident that the President and his allies will be back in their effort to take power away from parents, teachers and community school boards, seeking to place more power over our schools in the hands of bureaucrats in Washington."[166]

What did presidential candidate Bush do? He continued to play the education game with the stolen Democratic playbook, but with a new referee and increased penalties. He called for *mandatory* testing of all third through eighth grade students and for a *cut* in federal funding of up to five percent in those states where student performance failed to meet specific standards.

What could Vice President Gore say? He was also determined to aggressively improve school accountability and performance; however, he wanted to provide greater resources to struggling schools, especially with respect to building and renovation needs. However, it just didn't have the resonance of "no child left behind."

As we have seen, Bush, not Gore, "won" the election. So, what did the education candidate have to say after he was inaugurated? "You teach a child to read, and he or her will be able to pass a literacy test." Yes, you her'd right! Thus, Bush set out to impose the "Texas Miracle" on the rest of the United States.

After Vermont Senator Jim Jeffords was driven out of the Republican Party by the arrogance of Bush and his evil brain, Karl Rove, Democrats took control of the Senate, and Senator Ted Kennedy became the Chairman of the Health, Education, Labor and Pensions Committee. Since education had always been a Democratic issue, and after Bush promised that the neediest children would get the benefit of the reforms, Kennedy agreed to work with the Bush administration on revisions of the Elementary and Secondary Education Act, which was up for renewal. Kennedy's goals were to maximize funding and to keep school vouchers out of the Act.

After the House and Senate produced different versions of the "No Child Left Behind Act," it was discovered that under the formulas in both bills for measuring educational achievement, virtually *every* school in North Carolina and Texas would be deemed a failure and be subject to reorganization. Since these two states were considered (at least at that time) as leaders in school improvement efforts, there was a good chance for massive national political embarrassment. To resolve the two bills, the congressional conferees did a major revision, redefined "adequate yearly progress," and finally produced a 1,200-page bill that was signed by President Bush on January 8, 2002.[167]

The Act dramatically increased the role of the federal government in public education by requiring all students in grades 3 through 8 to be tested every year in reading and math and by providing measures to hold schools accountable. The states were given until the 2005-2006 school year to develop and implement tests to show adequate yearly progress towards their statewide objectives. *And* the states had to demonstrate through test scores that they could reach 100 percent proficiency for all groups of students within 12 years.[168]

Although Kennedy had been promised that there would be adequate funding, Bush's budget for fiscal year 2004 eliminated one-third of what he had earlier promised. While Congress later restored some of the cuts, the final bill only pays for a small fraction (seven percent) of the cost of public education. The first-year increases to Title I funds amount to 0.4 percent of total education spending, and even the "flexibility" procedures of the Act only allow a local district to shift around approximately 4.3 percent of the Title I funds it had already been committed. Finally, while the bill did not explicitly include school vouchers, it did include a complicated after-school tutoring mechanism that will move as much as $900 per student from schools "in improvement" into the hands of alternative profit, non-profit, and faith-based "supplemental-service providers."

Unfortunately, it is highly likely that the Act *will* do for the rest of the United States what Bush's "miracle" did in Texas. There is a grave risk that the big stick of being labeled as "low performing" will drive administrators to lose dropouts and for teachers to narrowly teach to the test. Students will still receive a good education in more affluent districts, supplemented through parent donations, but in those districts intended to be aided by the Act, in the absence of any real increase in resources, the poor children will be drilled like recruits in a military boot camp. The emphasis on "accountability" will result in testing being used to sort children and to treat them differently, rather than to use testing to help all children receive a quality education. Finally, there is no way there can be continual annual increases in the percentage of students who score "proficient" or above in testing, when the goals are set higher each year, and states are required to list 20 percent of their schools as failures.[169]

The existing appropriation was $11.3 billion and the Act called for $18 billion for Title I spending; however, Bush only requested $12.3 billion in his next budget, an increase of just $1 billion. It is estimated, conservatively, that the $1 billion increase in Title I funding proposed by Bush would not even pay for the added cost of testing and the other Title I mandates of the law, much less have anything left over to keep poor students from getting left behind. Fortunately, Congress rejected Bush's miserly budget request and provided an additional $5 billion for Title I programs.[170]

William J. Mathis, writing in the Phi Delta Kappan, identified several economic models that can be used to define the financial resources actually needed for each child to meet the standards set forth in the Act. To achieve the Act's mandates, the most conservative estimate is that an additional 20 percent, or $84.5 billion, would be required. A more realistic 35 percent increase would require $148 billion.[171]

The states are faced with a dilemma. They can either come up with $148 billion on their own to avoid losing the miserly federal contribution–a bad bargain–or they can reject the Title I money and the mandates. But if they accept the money and impose the standards on their school districts, they can be sued for the difference between the cost to implement the standards and what they receive from Washington–another bad bargain. Since the states are collectively facing a current deficit of $58 billion, it is unlikely that they can balance their budgets without cutting basic educational funding, much less fund federal mandates.

Several districts in Vermont and Connecticut have refused funds to avoid having to comply with NCLB's mandates, and at least seven states have passed resolutions criticizing the law or asking for federal waivers. Maine is considering a bill to prevent state funding of reforms, and a bill to opt out of NCLB entirely has passed the house education committee in the Utah Legislature. Gary Orfield, a Harvard education professor, notes, "Wealthy districts don't have to do much at all under this law. Other districts face demands that are somewhere between difficult and absurd. It's putting maximum pressure on the most vulnerable districts."[172]

Fourteen states have asked the Bush administration for permission to use alternative methods for showing academic gains. The states wrote that "within a few years, the vast majority of all schools will be identified as in need of improvement. Many of those schools will be given that designation despite having shown steady and significant improvement for all groups of students."[173]

The most likely scenario is that the states will try, educational professionals will try, children will try, but no matter how hard they try, the number of drop-outs will increase, schools will narrow their academic curriculum, and poor students will be drilled 'til they drop. Many good schools will be wrongly labeled as failing, and they and their students will be punished for failing when they never had a fair chance. We will all think less of our educational system and ourselves; we will be less than we could have been.

Would you want your own child's performance to be evaluated on one test score? Would you want your own child to have limited opportunities as a result? You're not stupid! Get the truth.

The Test Revolt

While the states have been busy preparing their plans to comply with the Act, and none has the courage required to reject the mandates and to go it alone, some groups are less reticent to demonstrate their disapproval of the new law. Writing in "High Stakes are for Tomatoes," Peter Schrag reported on some of these demonstrations in *The Atlantic*.[174]

After a majority of students failed the Massachusetts Comprehensive Assessment System tests, the state board of education lowered the passing level. Nonetheless, a group of 300 students, backed by their parents, teachers and community leaders, boycotted the test and demanded to be graduated if they had good records and could demonstrate evidence of achievement. Their slogan: "Be a hero, take a zero."

Middle-class parents in Wisconsin influenced the legislature to refuse to fund the state's exit examination until an agreement was reached to allow the achievement of failing students to be assessed using other criteria and to avoid automatic denial of a diploma.

In Virginia, a legislative bill was introduced to require new members of the state's board of education to "take the eighth grade Standards of Learning assessments in English, mathematics, science, and social sciences" and that the results be reported to the public.

Complaints range from the length of the test, which in Massachusetts can take up to a total of 17 hours, to the fact that they are unfair to poor or English-deficient students, or those who simply cannot do well on tests. There is evidence that the emphasis on testing, beginning as early as kindergarten, reduces the teaching of academics and how to think, and that it destroys the creativity and innovation of teachers.

Rather than, or at least as a supplement to standardized testing, these revolutionists want authentic assessments, such as portfolios of art, science and essay projects, and open-ended exercises. One education official of the Bush administration has labeled these test revolutionists as "crickets," few in number and making a lot of noise. Well, crickets may not bite, but they can sure keep you awake at night.[175]

Maybe the answer is to go back to the voluntary national testing proposed by President Clinton, where the emphasis is on the positive and there are no sanctions. Or, as proposed by Albert Shanker, former president of the American Federation of Teachers, a basic level of competency could be established for all students, low enough to ensure that most graduate from high school, and provide honors diplomas for those students who earn and deserve the recognition.[176]

Do you think that mandatory testing and the withdrawal of funding from schools that need it the most is the best way to ensure academic excellence in America? What's going to happen in a couple of years when two thirds or as many as 85 percent of our schools are declared to be failing? Do you want Bush and his Dr. Paige to take over and run your local school? You're not stupid! Get the truth.

140. "Education History," Good Schools Pennsylvania, http://www.goodschoolspa.org.

141. Ibid.

142. "Education Issues," National Association of State Boards of Education, www.nasbe.org/educational_issues/educational_issues.

143. "Not Just A Job," NEA NOW, Volume 24, No. 1, October 2003.

144. "Public Schools in the United States: Some History," Applied Research Center, http://www.arc.org/erase/history.

145. Ivins, op. cit., p. 83.

146. Ibid., pp. 83, 84.

147. Ibid., p. 95n.

148. Robbins, Mary Alice, "Bush draws fire of education board," *Amarillo Globe-News*, February 8, 2000, http://www.amarillonet.com/stories.

149. Patterson, Chris, "SCHOOL-TO-WORK IMPLEMENTATION IN TEXAS," January 1998, http:www.tppf.org/education/stwky/stwky.

150. "The truth about Texas school reform," www.salon.com/news/feature/1999/11/01/elpaso/index1.html.

151. Dobbs, Michael, "Houston school district's accountability questioned," November 9, 2003, *Star-Telegram*, www.dfw.com/mld/startelegram/2003/11/09/news/state/7221021.html.

152. Ivins, op. cit., pp. 77, 80.

153. Ibid., p. 78.

154. Brauchli, Christopher, "Droppin' Out and Droppin' Lies in Houston," Common Dreams News Center, September 6, 2003, http:www.commondreams.org/views03/0906-06.html.

155. Ibid; see also Schemo, Diana Jean, "Rod Paige Defends Houston Schools," *New York Times*, July 26, 2003, www.interversity.org/lists/arn-1/archives/jul2003/msg00400.html.

156. Ivins, op. cit., pp. 79, 80.

157. http://www.collegeboard.com/prod_downloads/about/
news_info/cbsenior/yr2002/pdf/table2.pdf.

158. Brauchli, op cit.

159. Hall, James, "Tax-Cutting, Texas-Style," 2001, www.american-partisan.com/cols/2001/hall/qtr1/0313.htm.

160. Ibid.

161. Dubose, Louis, "The Education Governor: Will Bush rob school kids to pay for a tax cut?" 1999, www.texasobserver.org.

162. Corn, op. cit., pp. 19, 20.

163. Begala, op. cit., p. 130.

164. Froomkin, Dan, "Tests Are Key to the Clinton Education Agenda," *The Washington Post*, 1998, www.washingtonpost.com/wp-srv/politics/special/testing/testing.

165. Schrag, Peter, "High Stakes Are for Tomatoes," *The Atlantic*, August 2000, http:www.theatlantic.com/issues/2000/08/schrag.html.

166. "Clinton's National Testing Plan Defeated," *Education Reporter*, December 1997, www.eagleforum.org/educate/1997/dec97/test.

167. Broder, David S., "Long Road to Reform," *The Washington Post*, December 17, 2001, http://www.washingtonpost.com.

168. "The New Rules," *Frontline*, http://www.pbs.org/wgbh/pages/frontline/shows/schools/nochild/nclb.html.

169. "Initial FairTest Analysis of ESEA As passed by Congress, Dec. 2001," http://www.fairtest.org/nattest/ESEA.html.

170. Ivins, op. cit., p. 89.

171. Mathis, William J., "No Child Left Behind: Costs and Benefits," *Phi Delta Kappan*, http://www.pdkintl.org/kappan/k0305mat.html.

172. Paulson, Amanda, "Fazed by the rules and reach of 'No Child Left Behind,' more states opt out of the most substantive reform in a generation," *Christian Science Monitor*, February 11, 2004, http://www.csmonitor.com/2004/0211/p01s02-ussc.html.

173. Schemo, Diana Jean, "14 States Ask U.S. to Revise Some Education Law Rules," *The New York Times*, March 25, 2004, www.nytimes.com/2004/03/25/education/25CHIL.html.

174. Schrag, Peter, "High Stakes Are for Tomatoes," *The Atlantic*, August 2000, www.theatlantic.com/issues/2000/08/schrag.html.

175. Ibid.

176. Ibid.

HAVE I GOT A DEAL FOR YOU

It's been observed that to find who has the most power in a society, you need only look to see who does not pay taxes. The touted Bush tax breaks, once the window dressing is removed, are exposed as a public giveaway to those who already have the most.

America's system of federal income taxation is founded upon voluntary compliance with the law, and the only reason it has a chance of working is that all are expected to pay their fair share. At least you and I do, because our taxes are deducted from our paycheck, or we're afraid we'll go to jail if we fudge on our deductions. But what about the big guys?

Well, it all depends on whom you know and how much you pay in political contributions to you-know-who. In 1995, 84 millionaires filed tax returns on which they owed no income tax, and 17 percent of the 7,500 corporations having assets of over $250 million paid no taxes at all.[177]

Things haven't gotten any better. Between 1996 and 1998, 50 of our mega-corporations, including AT&T, Bristol-Myers Squibb, Chase Manhattan, Enron, ExxonMobil, General Electric, Microsoft, Pfizer, Philip Morris, and WorldCom, failed to pay any federal income taxes at all.[178] None! One reason they didn't have to pay taxes was because they received $55 billion in tax breaks during the same period. Their cost? A mere $150 million and change in political contributions between 1991 and 2001. How much income tax do you pay each year?

The Halliburton Corporation, through the use of offshore subsidiaries, evaded paying any income taxes during five of the six years that Dick Cheney was its CEO, even though it received over $2.3 billion in government contracts. For this, Cheney was paid $36 million in salary, bonuses, and stock options during his last year on their payroll.[179] What's your annual income?

Perhaps it all depends on who is in charge of collecting the taxes. Bush's new Treasury Secretary is John Snow, who last worked for CSX Corporation as its CEO.* He apparently did a good job because CSX paid him over $10 million in his last year. Why was he worth so much? Perhaps it's because CSX received $122 million in tax rebates and didn't have to pay any taxes in 2000 or 2001.[180] Perhaps Snow can lend you and me a hand. But don't hold your breath.

In 1995, Congress, under the leadership of Newt Gingrich, passed a "tax reform" act that makes the Internal Revenue Service increasingly concentrate its attention on the working poor, rather than the lazy rich. By 2001, audits of the working poor had increased by 48.6 percent, and those applying for the Earned Income Tax Credit had a one-in-47 chance of being audited. Those earning over $100,000 have only one chance in 208 of getting a call from the taxman, although there are naturally far fewer of them.[181] Between 1993 and 2002, the number of civil fraud penalties against corporations fell by two-thirds, from 555 to 159.[182]

In November 2002, the White House prohibited Charles Rossotti, the head of the IRS, from telling Congress that the IRS needed a major increase in enforcement agents because it was "steadily losing the war with tax cheats, especially the wealthiest and most sophisticated among them." He wanted to alert Congress that by investing an additional $2 billion in enforcement, they could get back more than $70 billion.[183]

It gets worse. Eighty-five percent of us lost real net worth between 1983 and 1997, as 80 percent of our wealth was shifted into the pockets of the top 10 percent. The 13,000 richest families in America have more assets than its poorest 20 million people. Another way to look at it is to see the top one percent of households holding nearly 40 percent of America's wealth, which is just about equal to what the bottom 95 percent of all households share.[184]

To fairly distribute wealth in its democratic society and to avoid concentrating its wealth in an economic elite or royalty,

---

* Bush fired his first Treasury Secretary, Paul O'Neill, after he publicly questioned the wisdom of Bush's proposed tax cuts in the face of increasing deficits.

America has relied upon: (1) a progressive income tax, whereby those who earn more pay a higher percentage of taxes on their income; (2) an alternative minimum tax on income for high earners who claim no real income (after adjustments); (3) a capital gains tax that considers investment capital to be "working," and imposes a tax on its income resulting from interest, dividends and appreciation; and (4) an estate tax that imposes a tax upon the estates of the very wealthy. Since the working poor don't earn much income, have little investment capital, and do not leave large estates, they rarely think about these matters. But rich folks do. They think about them all the time. They don't think the tax system is fair, and they pay massive political contributions, primarily to Republicans, to get rid of those taxes that keep them from getting all the marbles.

Almost one third of working poor families, over 12 million, doesn't think about income taxes because they don't pay them. However, they do pay substantial payroll taxes for Social Security and excise taxes.* For a two-earner family making $25,000 a year, this amounts to about $3,825, including employer contributions. The economic elites resent that working folks don't pay more. An editorial in the *Wall Street Journal* called those who only earn $12,000 a year and who pay less than four percent income taxes "lucky duckies."[185]

So what happened to the middle class? They paid their taxes instead of making political contributions, they were forgotten by the politicians, they are fast disappearing, and nearly all their marbles have been swiped by the upper class.

As Plato said in *The Republic* over 2,300 years ago, "When there is an income tax, the just man will pay more and the unjust less on the same amount of income."

A Tax Cut for the Wealthy

During the presidential campaign, when Vice President Gore predicted that Bush's tax cuts would wreak havoc in Texas, Bush cutely replied, "I hope I'm not here to deal with it."[186] Too bad

---

* Excise taxes are levied on a specific good or service, such as cigarettes, alcohol or fuel.

he wasn't. For when the projected budget surplus failed to materialize, the Texas legislature had to cut spending further. The Texas budget deficit is currently around $10 billion and rising. Bush bragged, "The national spotlight gives us a chance to show how well limited government works. And together, we can show Washington how to handle a budget surplus." Well, that much, at least, he did, alright.

Bush promised to reduce taxes just like he had in Texas, and once he was elected, he set out to do just that. Unfortunately, just like in Texas, his tax cuts (or "tax relief" as he likes to say) primarily benefited the rich and caused untold harm to the rest of us.

In his first month in the White House, Bush proposed his "tax relief" package. He asked Congress to cut income tax rates, cancel the estate tax (he likes to call it a "death tax"), eliminate the marriage penalty (which taxes couples at a higher rate than they would each pay individually), double the child tax credit from $500 to $1,000, and extend it to those earning between $110,000 to $200,000 a year.[187]

Bush promised that the cuts would help millions of the working poor to move up to the middle class, would prime the pump of a slowing economy, and avoid the breakup of family farms and the forced sale of small businesses upon the death of their owners. And, he said, just like he had in Texas, not to worry, there was an adequate surplus to cover the cost and to have enough money left over to pay for existing and new programs. These were all lies, but it sure sounded good.

Bush said that his plan would "reduce taxes for everyone who pays taxes" and that "the bottom end of the economic ladder receives the biggest percentage cuts" from his tax package. He promised that the poorest "six million families, one out of every five families with children, will no longer pay federal income taxes at all under our plan."[188] All lies and misrepresentations.

In fact, those earning over $147,000 annually (the top five percent) would receive almost 53 percent of the benefit, and the top one percent, with incomes over $373,000, would receive 45 percent of the tax relief once all cuts were made. At the same time, the bottom 20 percent, who earn less than $15,000, would receive less than a one percent cut, and the bottom 40 percent, earning less than $27,000, would be "relieved" by only 4.3 percent.[189]

Because of the increase in the child tax credit, Bush promised, "We will return $1,600 to the typical American family with two children." Since a "typical" American family didn't earn the $39,200 a year required to get the full $1,600, eighty-five percent of families didn't get the "relief." However, since the credit was to be extended to families earning between $100,000 and $220,000, nearly half of its benefit went to the top 20 percent of earners.[190]

Let's talk about Bush's "death tax." He said, "To keep family farms in the family, we're going to get rid of the death tax." A complete lie. A review of 1999 Internal Revenue Service returns found "almost no working farmers" owing estate taxes. The reason was that under existing tax laws, a married couple could already pass along a family farm worth up to $4.1 million to their children, as long as they agreed to work the property for 10 years. The average value of a farm in Iowa (a state with a lot of farms) was only $1.2 million.[191]

So why the big "whoop-de-do?" The estate tax only applied to the top 1.9 percent of estates, because to qualify they had to be valued in excess of $675,000, and the amount was already scheduled to increase to $1 million in 2006. Nor did the tax apply to estates left to spouses, and a married couple could leave an estate of $1.35 million (up to $2 million in 2006) to their children without taxes.[192]

The reason Bush pushed this "relief" is that the estate tax would have brought in an estimated $300 billion over the ten-year period of tax cuts.[193] Yep! It's not a typo, $300 billion, paid only by the super rich, the top 1.9 percent of Americans. That's why they laid out the big bucks to elect Bush; they demanded a return on their investment, and the rest of us will pick up the tab.

The outgoing Clinton administration estimated it was leaving a multi-trillion-dollar tax surplus over the next ten years, and it had actually reduced the national debt for the first time in modern history.[194] Bush's last big lie was that there was enough of a surplus over the next ten years to pay for his tax relief. He promised to not touch the Social Security surplus and said that, after the cuts, there would still be "almost a trillion dollars ... for additional needs." He joked, "My plan reduces the national debt ... so fast, in fact, that economists worry that we are going to run out of debt to retire." Just like in Texas, he overestimated the surplus at $3.1 trillion and low-balled the cost of the tax cuts at $1.6 to $1.8 trillion.[195]

In April 2001, President "What, me worry?" Bush promised, "We can proceed with tax relief without fear of budget deficits, even if the economy softens." He predicted a $125 billion surplus for the year. In May 2001, the Republican-controlled Congress passed and Bush signed the measure that reduced the government's income from taxes by a total of $1.65 trillion over the next 10 years.

In August 2001, the Congressional Budget Office (CBO) confirmed what many had feared. Because of the declining economy and Bush's tax cuts, the year's surplus had disappeared. The CBO estimated the year's deficit at $9 billion; to cover the difference, the government would have to dip into the Social Security surplus.[196] So much for Bush's promises, and, as he told the Texans, he sure showed us how to handle a surplus.

What did Bush do? He lied, naturally: "I've said that the only reason we should use Social Security funds is in case of an economic recession or war."[197] When did he say this? What he had said, over and over, was that his cuts would not contribute to deficits and that they would not threaten the Social Security surplus.

Did you get $1,600 from the tax cuts? What percentage of your salary goes to pay income and payroll taxes? You're not stupid! Get the truth.

Another Tax Break for the Rich and Richer

In 2003, President Bush took another run at getting rid of some ugly taxes that were troubling his constituency. This time he took aim at the capital gains tax. His father had tried to get rid of it when he was president, but he wasn't as slick as his son. Bush Jr. called for the elimination of the tax on "dividends," and said that it was to benefit the elderly.

The overall proposal called for cutting taxes by $726 billion over the next 10 years. It included the dividend tax cut (which accounted for half) and an acceleration of other cuts included in the previous year's legislation. These cuts had been scheduled for 2004 and 2006, and included early implementation of the expanded child tax credit and elimination of the marriage penalty.[198]

Bush claimed "These tax reductions will bring real and immediate benefits to middle-income Americans. Ninety-two million Americans will keep an average of $1,083 more of their own money." However, Bush was again playing word games with "average." Only about 20 percent of tax payers would get that much. Almost half would receive less than $100.[199]

Bush said he wanted the dividend tax eliminated for "the good of our senior citizens." However, what he didn't say was that, while it was true that 41 percent of the reduction would go to people over 65 years, three-quarters would go to those earning over $75,000, and 40 percent would go to the top 2.5 percent, those earning over $200,000. Another estimate gave 70 percent of the cut to those earning over $133,000.[200] In fact, the proposal would do little or nothing to aid most of the elderly in America, over half of whom would live in poverty if it was not for Social Security.[201] But again, it sounded good.

To those who questioned his proposal, Bush retorted, "Oh sure, you hear the typical class warfare rhetoric, trying to pit one group of people against another." He had earlier said that he expected critics to "turn this into class warfare."[202] What else would you call tax cuts for the richest of the rich, which shove more and more of the tax burden onto the working- and middle-class?

Bush blamed Congress for the need to accelerate reductions in tax rates that had been scheduled for the future in his first tax cut, saying that Congress had decided to phase them in over "three or five or seven years. If the tax relief is good five years from now, it makes a lot of sense to put the tax relief in today." However, the year before, he had said, "The tax relief package that I talked about in the campaign was phased in based upon projections so we wouldn't run a deficit."[203] Which was the truth, and which was the lie?

In April 2003, the Congressional Budget Office predicted a record $400 billion deficit for the year, and it predicted that Bush's tax cuts were "unlikely" to stimulate the economy.[204] No matter, on May 23, the Republican-controlled Congress passed a $320 billion tax cut plan that reduced the tax on most dividends and capital gains to 15 percent. This reduction composed almost half of the tax cut.

The program contained several accounting deceptions, and it has been estimated that the true cost of Bush's new round of tax cuts will fall between $800 billion and $1 trillion.[205] All for what? In the 2003 tax cut, half of the families in America got only $100 or less; however, those earning over $1 million each walked away with $93,500. Bush personally pockets an extra $11,000 this year; his top contributors Charles Cawley, CEO of the MBNA Bank, saves $276,000 and William MaGuire, CEO of United Health Group gets to keep $329,000.[206] How much did you get?

In an editorial, the *Washington Post* noted that "Whatever relief such measure will provide, it cannot offset the enormous damage that will be done to low-income families and low-income children over the next few years. ... The effective federal tax rate on households earning more than $416,000 will have fallen from 32.7 percent when Bush took office to 26.9 percent by 2010, while their share of federal taxation will have dropped from 24.3 percent to 22.8 percent. ... Conservatives and liberals alike agree that Bush's tax policies have shifted more of the tax burden to the middle class."[207] This was obviously what Bush wanted to do, but was it what you wanted him to do? Perhaps you can now see why more and more of the marbles are ending up in the bags of the upper class, and the rest of us are working harder for less.

On January 28, 2003, in his State of the Union address, Bush stated, "We will not deny, we will not ignore, we will not pass along our problems to other Congresses, to other presidents, and other generations."[208] Well, who the heck does he think is going to clean up the mess resulting from his tax cuts? Perhaps he really doesn't have a clue. Whenever he hit a dry hole in the oil patch, his father's wealthy friends or his Saudi and bin Laden connections always came along and bailed him out. Who's going to do it this time? Who else? You and me, our children, and our grandchildren.

Do you believe that Bush was truly concerned about the elderly, or do you think he cares only for the rich and mighty? You're not stupid! Get the truth.

177. Ivins, op. cit., p. 42.

178. Ibid., p. 283.

179. Kellner, op. cit., pp. 16, 18.

180. Conason, op. cit., pp. 27, 28.

181. Ivins, op. cit., p. 42.

182. Alterman and Green, op. cit., p. 55.

183. Conason, op. cit., p. 28.

184. Ivins, op. cit., p. 44.

185. Hightower, op. cit., p. 39.

186. Zagorin, Adam, "When tax cuts hit Texas: Beyond the beltway." www.cnn.com/ALLPOLITICS/time/2001/03/12/texas, March 5, 2001.

187. Corn, op. cit., p. 79.

188. Ibid., p. 80.

189. Ibid., pp. 80, 81.

190. Ibid., pp. 83, 84.

191. Ibid., pp. 84, 85.

192. Ibid., p. 86.

193. Ibid.

194. Ibid., p. 87.

195. Ibid., p. 88.

196. Ibid., pp. 90, 91.

197. Ibid., p. 91.

198. Ibid., p. 243.

199. Ibid., pp. 243-245.

200. Ibid., pp. 245, 246.

201. http://www.concordcoalition.org/entitlements/justgenintro.pdf.

202. Corn, op. cit., p. 248.

203. Ibid., p. 252.

204. Ibid., p. 256.

205. Ibid., pp. 258, 259.

206. "Polls: Americans Not Buying Bush Tax Cut Rhetoric,"
The Daily Mis-Lead, April 15, 2004,
daily.misleader.org/ctt.asp?u=1218302&l=29034.

207. Corn, op. cit., p. 262.

208. Ivins, op. cit. p. 38.

9/11: WHO KNEW WHAT AND WHEN, AND WHAT, IF ANYTHING, DID HE DO?

The terrorist attacks on September 11, 2001, shocked the nation. But what may be nearly as shocking is how much information the government had beforehand, and how stupendous were the incompetence and chicanery that attended its failure to prevent that catastrophe.

I was less than a year old on December 7, 1941, but as the youngest of eight children, I was later told the stories of where and how we all learned about the attack on Pearl Harbor as a part of our family's oral history. Similarly, the events of September 11, 2001 are imprinted in our consciousness.

We've had 60 years to figure out why the Japanese government decided to start a war with the United States, but we've yet to answer why the hijackers, primarily highly skilled, well educated, middle-class professionals, acting contrary to their own government's policies, would want to simultaneously commit suicide in violently attacking the most visible symbols of American culture.*

We will never know why each individual terrorist participated, since they all died in the plane crashes, but if we are to begin to comprehend their motivation, we must try

---

* Although President Bush's most common explanation is that the terrorists hate freedom, a more thoughtful analysis by political scientist Gilles Kepel reveals, "The terrorism of September 11 was above all a provocation – albeit a provocation of gigantic proportions. Its purpose was to provoke a similarly gigantic repression of the Afghan civilian population and to build universal solidarity among Muslims in reaction to the victimization and suffering of their Afghan brothers." (Miller, Mark Crispin, *The Bush Dyslexicon*, p. 331) The hijackers could not seriously have expected to defeat America and eliminate our freedoms, but as we will see, they were wildly successful in causing our own government to take away our freedoms *and* to violently repress the Afghan people.

looking at things from their point of view. If we are to make rational decisions leading to peace with our neighbors and security in our neighborhoods, we must be prepared to abandon some deep-seated prejudices and to draw some uncomfortable conclusions.

America is not blameless. We, regrettably, have a long history of having violently interfered with the societies, cultures and governments of other peoples, beginning with annihilation of the indigenous inhabitants of this country. We enslaved millions of Africans and we denied the rights of citizenship to Asian immigrants. It was not that long ago that we colonized Hawaii and the Philippines, killing hundreds of thousands of natives; that we routinely rotated the leadership of the republics of Central and South America at will; and, more recently, that we conspired in the removal of lawfully elected leaders of nations such as Chile and Iran.

We have allied ourselves with repressive regimes and supported their brutal policies. Commencing in 1965, the United States backed the Indonesian army as it took control of the country and organized the slaughter of hundreds of thousands of people, mostly landless peasants.[209]   Between 1984 and 1990, the United States provided 80 percent of the arms for Turkey's counterinsurgency campaign against its Kurdish minority. Tens of thousands were killed, and 2-3 million were driven from their homes, leaving 3,500 villages destroyed.[210]

President Reagan came into office in 1980 proclaiming that "international terrorism" sponsored by the USSR was the greatest threat faced by the United States. To combat Russian influence in Nicaragua, we mined its harbors and supported a "Contra" army that regularly and routinely engaged in terrorist activities.

After Nicaragua filed a lawsuit, the United States was condemned by the World Court of Justice for its unlawful acts and was ordered to desist and to pay reparations. We vetoed a United Nations Security Council resolution calling on all states (including the U.S.) to adhere to international law, and we and only two other nations, Israel and El Salvador, voted against the same resolution in the U.N. General Assembly.[211]

In 1985, the United States sponsored the setting of a truck bomb outside a mosque in Beirut, targeted at a Muslim cleric who had angered us. The bomb was timed to kill the maximum number of people as they left prayer services. It missed the cleric, but it killed 80 and wounded 250, mostly women and children. Wouldn't we define this as an act of terrorism had it occurred in the United States?[212]

There is more, much more, but this is enough. It is one thing to acknowledge our past policies of failure, which we are slowly doing, but it is another to understand that history and to adopt successful policies for the future based upon that understanding.

Sowing the Wind and Reaping the Whirlwind

President Carter's National Security Adviser, Zbigniew Brzezinski, claims that he instigated secret support for the Mujahideen, who were fighting against the communist government of Afghanistan in 1979, in an effort to draw the USSR into what he called an "Afghan trap."[213] After the USSR sent in its army to prop up the government, the United States and its allies organized, trained, and armed a mercenary army of more than 100,000 to resist the "invasion." Many of the Mujahideen were drawn from the most militant fighters available, the radical Islamists, who viewed the Russians as infidels and occupiers of Muslim lands. The United States encouraged these extremist views as "war values" that made the Mujahideen fierce fighters.

Osama bin Laden, a Saudi citizen, joined the fighters sometime in 1980. He was one of nearly two dozen sons born to Sheikh Muhammad bin Laden, who established a family construction company that built roads, airports and other infrastructure projects in the Middle East. The firm grew into a conglomerate of companies and had become the largest private construction contractor in the world by the time Sheikh Muhammad died in a plane crash in Texas in 1966. One of his older sons, Salem bin Laden took over control of the business. Both the family and the Saudi government supported a younger son, Osama bin Laden, in Afghanistan as he and the family company, under contract with the CIA, brought in engineers and heavy equipment to build roads and warehouses for the fighters.

Osama bin Laden obtained millions of dollars from his family and his own inheritance to fund the establishment of al Qaeda* in 1985. Osama bin Laden went on to supervise construction of an extensive tunnel complex near the Pakistan border used to store armaments and as a training and medical facility. He also established extensive funding networks, which remained in existence after the USSR retreated from Afghanistan in 1989. In all of this, bin Laden worked closely with his friend, Saudi Prince Turki Bin Faisal al-Saud, head of the Saudi intelligence service.[214]

Through al Qaeda, bin Laden continued to associate with other fundamentalist Islamists, who believe they are fighting a "Holy War" against the corrupt, repressive, and "un-Islamic" regimes of the region and their supporters.† They believe it is their duty to support Muslims everywhere who are defending themselves against the invasion of infidels. It was for this reason that Egyptian President Sadat was assassinated in 1981, and the Marine barracks were bombed in Beirut in 1983, driving the United States out of Lebanon. The Islamists consider the governments of Saudi Arabia and others in the region, including Iraq, to be corrupt, repressive, and not truly Islamic.

Following the Gulf War and the establishment of permanent U.S. military bases in Saudi Arabia (where Mecca, Islam's holy city is located), bin Laden and the organizations he was associated with zeroed in on America as an infidel invader.

Not only did the USSR abandon Afghanistan in 1989, but Bush Sr. did as well. Following the Russian withdrawal, the United States did nothing as Afghanistan suffered through a continuing civil war in which tens of thousands of civilians were killed. A collection of warlords known as the "Northern Alliance" brutally established limited control between 1992 and

---

* In Arabic, "al Qaeda" means a register (*not* "base"). It was a record book of visitors to the bin Laden guesthouse in Peshawar.

† Islamists comprise a number of factions in Islam that want to rely upon the Sharia (Islamic Law) to govern all aspects of their societies.

1995. The Alliance engaged in drug trafficking into Tajikistan, a major way station for drugs en route to Europe and the United States. The Alliance left a trail of burned out villages, and carried out such terror that the population generally welcomed the Taliban, a movement of fundamentalist Islamists with which bin Laden and his al Qaeda network became associated.[215]

The CIA was involved in the training and arming of Islamist fighters against the USSR, bringing many of them to the United States on visas issued in Saudi Arabia, and some of these relationships were maintained. In 1990, during the administration of President Bush Sr., a radical Islamist Egyptian cleric by the name of Sheikh Omar Abdel Rahman entered the United States with the full knowledge of CIA officials. Sheikh Rahman was a member of the Egyptian Islamic Jihad, which had affiliated itself with al Qaeda. Rahman, who was wanted by Egypt on charges of terrorism, quickly attracted a following of young radical Islamists.[216]

In 1993, the Pentagon commissioned a study that discussed how airplanes could be used as suicide bombs by terrorists to crash into national landmarks, such as the CIA headquarters, the White House or the Pentagon. The study was circulated through the Pentagon, the Justice Department and the Federal Emergency Management Service, but it was not publicly released because of fears it might give terrorists ideas.[217]

On February 26, 1993, the group of Islamists associated with Sheikh Omar Abdel Rahman parked a rented truck containing a huge fertilizer bomb and tanks of hydrogen in the underground parking basement of the World Trade Center, and set off an explosion intended to topple one tower into the other. The explosion killed six and injured a thousand.[218]

Within days, law enforcement authorities were able to trace the vehicle to the Islamists associated with Sheikh Rahman and to begin making arrests. One of the primary organizers, Ramzi Ahmed Yousef, escaped and became a fugitive. During subsequent criminal trials, ten of the conspirators, including Sheikh Rahman, were convicted of conspiring to wage a war of urban terrorism against the United States, including planned attacks against the United Nations building and the bridges and tunnels leading into New York City. All were sentenced to prison, with the Sheikh receiving a life term. Osama bin Laden was named in the case as an unindicted co-conspirator.[219]

In 1994, Clinton directed an extensive review of the administration's terrorism policy. Once agreement was reached between the various agencies and departments, Clinton signed Presidential Decision Directive 39 (PDD-39), "U.S. Policy on Counterterrorism." The Directive outlined actions to "reduce terrorist capabilities" in order to "reduce vulnerabilities at home and abroad." The Directive established there would be "no greater priority than preventing the acquisition of weapons of mass destruction" by terrorists. Failing that, there was no greater priority than "removing that capability."[220]

Although President Clinton was shrinking the overall federal budget, he increased the counterterrorism budget from $5.7 billion in 1995 to $11.1 billion in 2000. During the same period, he increased the FBI counterterrorism budget over 280 percent.[221]

Following the first World Trade Center bombing, Ramzi Yousef escaped from the U.S. and lived for a time in a boarding house in Pakistan operated by Osama bin Laden. In January 1995, Yousef was in the Philippines, where he and others were conspiring to blow up eleven U.S. commercial airplanes in one day, or as an alternative, to simultaneously crash the planes into symbols of American culture, such as the CIA headquarters, the Pentagon, the World Trade Center, the Sears Tower in Chicago, the TransAmerica Tower in San Francisco, and the White House. One of the conspirators had obtained a commercial pilot's license from a U.S. flight school. Fate interrupted these plans when Yousef accidentally started a fire while mixing explosives in a Manila apartment. He had to flee, but computer data found in the room led to his arrest a month later by Pakistani authorities.[222]

Yousef was extradited to the United States and as a helicopter transported him into New York City, an FBI agent pointed out the World Trade Center towers and said, "They're still standing." Yousef said, "Next time, if I have more money, I'll knock it down."[223] Yousef was tried and convicted of both the World Trade Center bombing and the conspiracy to destroy the eleven aircraft. He was convicted on *September 11, 1996* and was sentenced to 240 years in federal prison.[224] Exactly five years later, the World Trade Center towers were no longer standing!

In 1995, the United States began to back the Islamist Taliban organization in its civil war against the Northern Alliance for control of Afghanistan. While the Northern Alliance was supported by Russia and Iran and was recognized by the United Nations, the Taliban's march on Kabul was encouraged by the CIA and funded with Saudi petrodollars. The Taliban took power in 1996, with the support of the Pakistani secret service.[225]

In 1996, the FBI began to investigate why so many Arab students were attending flight schools in the United States to learn how to fly commercial airplanes.[226]

On June 25, 1996, Islamist terrorists associated with the radical Saudi Hezbollah group exploded a truck bomb loaded with 5,000 pounds of plastic explosives at the Khobar Towers in Dhahran, Saudi Arabia. The goal of the terrorists was to drive the United States military from Saudi Arabia. The Towers were used as dormitories for U.S. Air Force personnel, 19 of whom were killed and 372 injured. Following a comprehensive FBI investigation, 14 members of Hizballah were indicted.[227] During a trial of four defendants between February and July 2001, there was testimony that two of bin Laden's operatives had received pilot training in the United States.[228]

Another seemingly unrelated event that was to become critically significant in the future occurred on October 27, 1997, when following a feasibility study by Enron Corporation, six international oil companies (led by the Union Oil Company of California (Unocal) and the Delta Oil Company, Ltd., of Saudi Arabia) incorporated Central Asia Gas Pipeline, Ltd. (CentGas) along with the Government of Turkmenistan to build a 48-inch pipeline across Afghanistan to Pakistan. The Afghan Taliban had selected Unocal (which owned 46.5 percent of CentGas) over a Brazilian competitor.[229]

In February 1998, bin Laden issued a religious announcement known as a "fatwa," which stated, "The ruling to kill the Americans and their allies–civilians and military–is an individual duty for every Muslim who can do it in any country in which it is possible to."[230]

In May 1998, President Clinton appointed Richard A. Clarke as the first National Coordinator for Security, Infrastructure Protection, and Counterterrorism. Clarke was the Deputy Assistant Secretary of State for Intelligence in the Reagan administration and was the Assistant Secretary of State for Politico-Military Affairs in the Bush Sr. administration. He had been a member of Clinton's National Security Council staff with the primary responsibility for counterterrorism.

Clarke chaired meetings of the Counterterrorism Security Group and four committees made up of senior and midlevel managers from the departments. The four committees reported to the Cabinet-level Principals Committee, chaired by the national security advisor, with cabinet-level representatives from the departments and agencies. Clarke became a member of the Principals Committee[231]

On August 7, 1998, Islamists bombed the U.S. embassies in Nairobi, Kenya, and Dar es Salaam, Tanzania, killing 257 people and injuring thousands. A suspect, Mohammad Sadik Howaida, escaped from Nairobi but was arrested soon after his arrival in Karachi, Pakistan.[232] Howaida, an associate of bin Laden, was extradited to Kenya.

Two weeks later, the Clinton administration lashed out with a barrage of ship-based Tomahawk missiles launched at al Qaeda training bases in Afghanistan and at the al-Shifa Pharmaceutical Company in Khartoum, Sudan, believed to be linked to bin Laden, where the CIA thought a component of nerve gas was being produced. It is not known what damage was done at the training camps, but the pharmaceutical building was destroyed. The Sudan attack was a horrible mistake because the plant actually produced at least half of the nation's essential medicines for the Sudanese and their herds of cattle.[233]

On November 4, 1998, bin Laden was indicted in the Manhattan federal district court for the embassy bombings and for conspiring to kill Americans. The indictment alleged that bin

Laden and four others were members of al Qaeda, and that they conspired with a number of other terrorist organizations, including one led by Sheik Rahman.[234]

President Clinton issued a presidential order authorizing bin Laden's assassination. President Clinton ordered two Tomahawk cruise-missile submarines to remain on standby in waters near Afghanistan, and he exhausted intelligence sources attempting to pinpoint the time and location when bin Laden could be hit with a missile attack.[235]

On December 4, 1998, in another seemingly unrelated event, Unocal withdrew from the CentGas consortium for "business reasons" and denied that it had ever entered into a commercial agreement with the Taliban, although it had provided support.[236] However, as we will see, the pipeline deal was not dead.

The United Nations imposed economic sanctions on Afghanistan that further isolated the Taliban, whose "government" was only recognized by three countries, Saudi Arabia, Pakistan, and the United Arab Emirates.[237]

From at least 1998 forward, the Clinton administration was entirely hostile to the Taliban regime. It made repeated requests to the Taliban to arrest bin Laden and extradite him to the United States. In April 2000, the Taliban were informed that "If bin Laden or any of the organizations affiliated with him attacks the United States or United States interests, we will hold you, the leadership of the Taliban, personally accountable."[238]

In 1999, the National Intelligence Council prepared a report seeking to anticipate the al Qaeda response to Clinton's bombing of the bin Laden camps in Afghanistan. The report stated, "Suicide bomber(s) belonging to al-Qaida's Martyrdom Battalion could crash-land an aircraft packed with high explosives (C-4 and semtex) into the Pentagon, the headquarters of the Central Intelligence Agency (CIA), or the White House." The report referred to Ramiz Yousef's plans to engage in a suicide jetliner mission.[239]

In December 1999, the CIA learned that al Qaeda was planning an attack in the U.S. around the Millennium rollover. President Clinton instructed his national security advisor to hold daily meetings with the attorney general and the directors of the FBI and CIA to brief Clinton on what they had done and learned in the last day about the al Qaeda terrorism threat.[240]

When a U.S. Customs agent attempted to question Ahmed Ressam as he was crossing into the United States from British Columbia, he ran from the ferry. Ressam was arrested after a brief chase, and an intensive federal investigation ensued. Information was developed which led to an al Qaeda sleeper cell in Montreal. Other leads resulted in at least one additional arrest of an al Qaeda member in New York City.[241]

Security planning for the 2000 Olympic Games in Sydney, Australia included the danger of a fully loaded, fueled airliner crashing into the opening ceremony before a worldwide television audience, and bin Laden was the top suspect. Similar concerns had caused the prohibition of aircraft above event venues in Atlanta during the 1996 Olympic Games and the deployment of military helicopters to intercept aircraft that strayed into the restricted airspace.[242]

On October 12, 2000, al Qaeda operatives set off a bomb alongside the USS *Cole*, which was being refueled in the harbor at Aden, Yemen. Seventeen U.S. sailors were killed, and 39 were injured. President Clinton, who had increasingly concentrated on the terrorist threat during his administration by doubling counterterrorism funding and by identifying, arresting and convicting individual terrorists, turned to Richard Clarke, the White House Chief of Counterterrorism, and instructed him to develop a plan to destroy the al Qaeda terrorist network.[243]

Clarke immediately developed a comprehensive program to: (1) target al Qaeda cells and arrest their members; (2) track and attack al Qaeda financial networks; (3) freeze its assets and block its funding through charity fronts; (4) support other governments fighting against al Qaeda; (5) engage in covert actions in Afghanistan against al Qaeda training camps; and (6) go after bin Laden directly and forcefully.[244]

On December 20, 2000, Clarke presented the program to President Clinton's National Security Advisor, Sandy Berger, who immediately approved it. However, since the U.S. Supreme

Court had just decided on December 12, 2000, that George W. Bush could have the presidency as a gift, the Clinton administration decided to hold off launching any immediate attacks against bin Laden and al Qaeda to avoid spoiling Bush's Christmas and to allow him to implement the plan.

Two former counterterrorism officials of the Reagan administration evaluated the Clinton administration's fight against terrorism. Robert Oakley said, "Overall, I give them very high marks. ... The only major criticism I have is the obsession with Osama, which made him stronger." L. Paul Bremer (the current administrator of Iraq) believed that Clinton had "correctly focused on bin Laden." The *Washington Post* agreed, "By any measure available, Clinton left office having given greater priority to terrorism than any president before him. ... [It was] the first administration to undertake a systematic anti-terrorist effort."[245]

Neglect of Duty

On the day he left office, Bill Clinton took a few minutes to discuss with the new president what he considered to be the most urgent matters. "First," he said, "There is bin Laden. He is angry, and we have intelligence that indicates he is coming after us, somehow. We've put together a plan to deal with terrorist threats, and my people will brief you and your staff on its details. I consider this the top priority." Clinton went on to warn about the dangers of the Israelis and Palestinians, North Korea, and Pakistan and India. He concluded, "Lastly, I'd watch Saddam Hussein very closely. He's got oil money and anger against the U.S." Bush responded, "I think you've got your priorities wrong, I'm putting Saddam at the top of the list."[246]

At Clinton's instructions, Sandy Berger met with Bush's new National Security Advisor, Condoleezza Rice, during one of the ten briefing sessions he arranged for her that was dedicated to terrorism. He told her, "I believe that the Bush administration will spend more time on terrorism in general, and on al Qaeda specifically, than any other subject." Rice continued the meeting with Richard Clarke, who fully briefed her on the plan he had developed to combat bin Laden and al Qaeda, and Rice decided to keep Clarke on as the head of counterterrorism.[247] However, Rice downgraded Clarke's position and ordered that the Counterterrorism Security Group would no longer report to the Principals Committee.

In addition to Rice, Clarke also briefed her deputy, Steve Hadley, Vice President Cheney and Secretary of State Powell. Clarke provided the same warning to each: "al Qaeda is at war with us, it is a highly capable organization, probably with sleeper cells in the U.S., and it is clearly planning a major series of attacks against us; we must act decisively and quickly, deciding on the issues prepared after the attack on the *Cole*, going on the offensive."[248]

Immediately following the Inauguration, Clarke wrote to Rice and Hadley urgently requesting a meeting of the Principals Committee to discuss the imminent al Qaeda threat.   Rice decided that the Principals would not discuss terrorism policy until it has been "framed" by the Deputy Secretaries.[249]

In the meantime, the Bush administration had other more pressing priorities than terrorism. Bush's Secretary of Defense, Donald Rumsfeld, testified at his Senate confirmation hearing, "We must develop the capabilities to defend against missiles, terrorism and newer threats against our space assets and information systems." He said, "The American people ... must be protected against the threats with which modern technology and its proliferation confront us." Rumsfeld said that improving force readiness and strengthening intelligence and space capabilities should be top priorities.[250]

On February 9, 2000, Robert Walpole, the National Intelligence Officer for Strategic and Nuclear Programs, testified in Congress that while missile defense was an issue, an attack with weapons of mass destruction delivered by non-missile means was a significant concern, because these weapons are less expensive than ICBMs, they "can be covertly developed and employed; probably would be more reliable, accurate and effective" and they would "avoid missile defenses."[251]

Undeterred, the Bush administration continued to go forward with Rumsfeld's expensive missile defense system and did nothing immediate to defend against the most critical threat, the hijacking and use of civilian aircraft to crash into America's major cultural landmarks.

On February 7, 2001, CIA Director George Tenet testified before Congress and stated Osama bin Laden and his al Qaeda network were the single greatest threat to U.S. interests here and abroad. He said: "Terrorists are also becoming more operationally adept and more technically sophisticated in order to defeat counter-terrorism measures. For example, as we have increased security around government and military facilities, terrorists are seeking out "softer" targets that provide opportunities for mass casualties. Employing increasingly advanced devices and using strategies such as simultaneous attacks, the number of people killed...Usama bin Laden and his global network of lieutenants and associates remain the most immediate and serious threats."[252]

On February 15, 2001, former senators Gary Hart and Warren Rudman issued the final report of their commission that had studied national security over a period of years. The report warned that "mass-casualty terrorism directed against the U.S. homeland was of serious and growing concern," and that America was not prepared for a "catastrophic" terrorist attack. The report concluded, "This commission believes that the security of the American homeland from the threats of the new century should be *the* primary national security mission of the U.S. government." The report called for better information sharing between federal agencies, and called for the establishment of a National Homeland Security Agency to combine some of the government's national security agencies and departments. Bush opposed creation of such an agency, and ignored the report.[253]

On April 30, 2001, Clarke presented his al Qaeda plan to a meeting of second-tier deputies of the Vice President, the Defense Department, State Department, and CIA. The deputies agreed to a leisurely meeting schedule to individually consider the issues of al Qaeda, Pakistan, and the India-Pakistan relationship, and to then to meet a fourth time to integrate the issues.[254]

Rumsfeld's deputy secretary of defense, Paul Wolfowitz, said, "I just don't understand why we are beginning by talking about this one man bin Laden." Clark replied, "We are talking about a network of terrorist organizations called al Qaeda, that happens to be led by bin Laden, and we are talking about that network because it and it alone poses an immediate and serious threat to the United States."[255] As the spring wore on, Clarke e-mailed Rice and her deputies warning them that "al Qaeda was trying to kill Americans, to have hundreds of dead in the streets of America."[256]

On May 1, 2001, Bush gave a speech in which he argued the necessity of a missile defense system because "today's *most urgent threat* stems not from thousands of ballistic missiles in Soviet hands, but from a small number of missiles in the hands of ... states for whom terror and blackmail are a way of life. (emphasis added)"[257] Bush was determined to spend billions of dollars to fight a threat that did not exist, and to ignore, generally, the most dangerous threat, the use of civilian aircraft as fuel-loaded missiles.

To avoid congressional hearings on the Hart-Rudman report, Bush announced formation of an antiterrorism task force on May 8, 2001. The task force was to be chaired by Vice President Cheney to develop a plan to counter domestic terrorist attacks, and Bush said that he would "periodically chair a meeting of the National Security Council to review these efforts." Cheney's task force never met, and Bush never chaired a meeting to review the efforts. Instead, the national security agency deputies began to attend their schedule of meetings and to leisurely talk about the issues.[258]

In May 2001, the Bush administration made it easier for Saudi visitors to come to the United States by allowing them to arrange visas through 10 travel agencies, avoiding the necessity of being interviewed and identified at the U.S. Embassy or consulate offices.[259]

On June 7, 2001, National Security Advisor Condoleezza Rice addressed the Council on Foreign Relations on "Foreign Policy Priorities and Challenges of the [Bush] Administration. While she discussed the "values gap" and "strategic split" between the

U.S. and Europe, she did not mention terrorism as a priority or challenge of the Bush administration.[260]

On July 10, 2001, an FBI agent stationed in Phoenix, Arizona, became concerned about the number of Middle Eastern students attending a local flying school. He sent a report to Washington D.C. in which he suggested al Qaeda operatives might be trying to gain access to the United States civilian aviation system. He recommended that the FBI contact other intelligence agencies to determine if they had related information and to canvass other flying schools to identify other Arab students.[261] The report was laid aside because it was too "speculative."[262] Nothing was done.

In the meantime, Clarke and CIA Director George Tenet were becoming increasingly concerned about the likelihood of an imminent major domestic terrorist attack. America's allies were forwarding highly specific warnings that could not be ignored. In June, Germany warned that Middle Eastern terrorists were "planning to hijack commercial aircraft to use as weapons to attack important symbols of American and Israeli culture."

On June 13, Egypt warned that a plane stuffed with explosives could be used as a weapon against Bush, possibly at the Genoa summit of industrialized nations. Russia warned the CIA that 25 terrorist pilots had been specially trained to execute suicide missions against civilian buildings.[263] Tenet, "nearly frantic" with worry, informed Rice in mid-July that there was going to be a major attack.

On July 5, 2001, Clarke warned all of the domestic security agencies, including the Federal Aviation Administration (FAA) and the FBI, to increase their security because of the impending attack. The FAA, which had received specific warnings in the past about the vulnerability of cockpit doors, failed to take any steps to prevent hijackers from taking control of commercial aircraft.[264]

In July 2001, the CIA issued an intelligence briefing to "senior government officials" that predicted that Osama bin Laden was going to attack "in the coming weeks." The report stated "The attack will be spectacular and designed to inflict mass casualties against U.S. facilities or interests.   Attack preparations have been made. Attack will occur with little or no warning."[265] As you will see later, the names of the recipients of the briefing (including you-know-who) have been classified.

In July 2001, several FBI agents contacted an attorney, David Philip Schippers, the former head prosecutor of Clinton's impeachment trial, with their concerns about a massive attack being planned by terrorists targeted against the financial district of lower Manhattan (where the World Trade Center is located) and their frustration at being restrained by their superiors. Schippers attempted to personally contact Attorney General Ashcroft with their concerns; however, his attempts were rebuffed.

Prior to September 1, the FBI agents confirmed that such an attack by bin Laden was imminent; however, they were ordered by their superiors to shut down their investigation, and they were threatened with prosecution under the National Security Act if they went public with the information they had learned in their investigation.[266]

On July 12, 2001, Osama bin Laden was in the American Hospital in Dubai for treatment. He had received visits from many members of his extensive family and from Prince Turki al Faisal, the head of Saudi intelligence, but on this day his guest was CIA agent Larry Mitchell, an Arab specialist.[267] Although bin Laden was wanted on an American arrest warrant for murder, he was not arrested, nor did we hear about the visit.

On July 16, 2001, after three months of talking, the second-tier national security agency deputies held their fourth meeting and agreed to recommend Clarke's program to the Principals Committee, composed of Cheney, Rice, Tenet, Powell, and Rumsfeld. An attempt was made to schedule the meeting in August; however, too many of the participants were unavailable.[268]

So what did Bush do? He did what he did best. On August 3, he took his dogs, Barney and Spot, on an extended vacation to his Texas ranch. At this point in his term, when America's "most productive workers on earth" are lucky to get a two-week paid vacation, Bush had spent 42 percent of his first seven months on the job taking it easy at his ranch, at Camp David, or the Bush family retreat in Kennebunkport. He had earned another month off.[269]

On August 6, 2003, the CIA delivered an intelligence report entitled "Bin Laden Determined to Strike in U.S." to Bush at his ranch. Bush briefly interrupted his vacation to read the page-and-a-quarter-long document. The briefing reported that al Qaeda was active in the United States, that it was suspected of recent surveillance of federal buildings in New York and that it could be planning domestic hijackings. The report referred to "patterns of suspicious activity in this country consistent with preparations for hijackings or other types of attacks."[270]

Prior to 9/11, Tenet attempted to warn Bush in more than 40 briefings of threats involving al Qaeda. Among the titles of the briefings were: "Bin Laden planning multiple operations," "Bin Laden network's plans advancing," and "Bin Laden threats are real."[271]

If you recall, when President Clinton was presented with intelligence that warned of possible terrorist attacks during December 1999, he ordered the heads of the FBI and the CIA to report to the White House on a daily basis and account for what they were doing to counter the threats. As a result, a terrorist who was bringing explosives into the U.S. to attack the Los Angeles airport was arrested, an intensive federal investigation ensued, an al Qaeda sleeper cell was located in Montreal, and another al Qaeda member was arrested in New York City. What did President "What, me worry?" Bush do? He continued to relax, played a little golf, cleared a little brush, and watched his dogs chase the armadillos.[272] Nothing too brain taxing.

In August, the Israeli Mossad warned the CIA and the FBI that as many as 200 al Qaeda members were infiltrating the United States and were planning a "major assault" in the U.S. against "a large-scale target" where Americans would be "very vulnerable."[273]

Bush's attorney general, John Ashcroft, did not list counterterrorism as one of his seven goals in a draft of his "Strategic Plan" dated August 9, 2001. Fighting terrorism was a secondary subgoal under gun violence and drugs. In April 2000, Clinton's attorney general, Janet Reno, had called terrorism "the most challenging threat in the criminal justice area."[274] She ordered the preparation of an elaborate counterterrorism plan known as MAX CAP 05, or Maximum Capacity by 2005 that called for a huge build-up in the FBI's counterterrorism operations. Ashcroft declined to adopt the plan once he took office.[275]

On August 16, 2001, the Immigration and Naturalization Service arrested Zacharias Moussaoui, who had earlier flunked out of a flight school in Oklahoma, and who was taking flight simulator training for commercial airplanes at a flying school in Minnesota. He was turned in by an instructor, who became worried that Moussaoui had more interest in how much fuel a commercial jet carried and how much damage it could do if it hit anything and less interest in learning how to actually take off or land an airplane. The instructor told agents, "Do you realize that a 747 loaded with fuel can be used as a bomb?" The arresting agent wrote that Moussaoui was "the type of person who could fly something into the World Trade Center," and an FBI agent seeking permission to obtain a search warrant to review Moussaoui's computer files suggested that a 747 airliner loaded with fuel could be used as a missile.

FBI Headquarters refused to allow its agents to seek a search warrant, even after France disclosed that Moussaoui had connections with bin Laden and al Qaeda. Of the 12,000 applications for national security search warrants made since they were authorized in 1978, only one had ever been denied.[276] There was no plausible reason to not obtain a warrant to follow up on Moussaoui's arrest.

Another terrorist, who *was* subject to telephone surveillance (by the Egyptian secret service) and whose movements *were* being monitored by the FBI, Mohamed Atta, had been allowed to reenter the United States on January 10, 2001, on an expired tourist visa, even though he informed immigration officers that he was taking flying lessons in the United States, which violated his expired visa. Moreover, Israel had earlier notified the United States that Atta had been involved in a bombing there even before he was issued his original visa.[277]

During the week before September 11, 2001, Lt. General Mahmoud Ahmad, the Director-General of Pakistani military intelligence, came to the United States to consult with high-level officials of the CIA and the Pentagon. Before the trip, he had ordered the transfer of $100,000 to Mohamed Atta in the United States![278]

Meanwhile, down in East Texas, Bush continued to laze about with Barney and Spot.[279]

Back in Washington, Thomas J. Pickard, the acting Director of the FBI, read a top-secret review of the Bureau's counterterrorism programs calling for a dramatic increase in funding. Concerned, Pickard met with his boss, Attorney General John Ashcroft, and requested an additional $58 million to improve the Bureau's capacity to deal with terrorist threats.[280] Note what later happens to Pickard's request in evaluating the priority that the Bush administration placed on the counterterrorism effort.

On September 4, 2001, the national security principals, Cheney *et al.*, met and discussed Clarke's plan. They agreed to implement it in phases by first demanding cooperation from the Taliban and by establishing liaison with the Northern Alliance.[281] In preparation for the meeting, Clarke asked Rice "to put herself in her own shoes when in the very near future al Qaeda had killed hundreds of Americans." He asked her "What will you wish then that you had already done?"[282]

On September 7, 2001, the U.S. State Department issued a worldwide alert warning that "American citizens may be the target of a terrorist threat from extremist groups with links to the al Qaeda organization."[283] However, the FAA did not take any steps to put the domestic airline industry on high alert. Are you beginning to get the feeling that there was little concern for the safety of ordinary citizens? Read on.

On September 9, 2001, Congress was considering an increase of $600 million for antiterrorist programs, with the funds to be taken from Rumsfeld's missile defense program. Rumsfeld sent a letter to Senator Carl Levin, then chairman of the Armed Services Committee in response to Levin's attempt to transfer money to counterterrorism. Rumsfeld said he would urge Bush to veto the measure.[284]

On September 9, 2001, two North African suicide bombers posing as journalists from "Arabic News International" exploded a bomb concealed in a video camera as they interviewed Ahmed Shah Massoud, the popular leader of the Northern Alliance and primary opponent of the Taliban. Massoud died while being transported by helicopter to Tajikistan.[285]

The National Security Agency began to intercept multiple phone calls from Abu Zabaida, bin Laden's chief of operations, to the United States. The U.S. had broken the al Qaeda code; however, the contents of these communications have never been officially disclosed.[286] However, Sibel Edmonds, a former FBI translator has come forward with detailed information that specific intelligence documents pointing to the use of aircraft against skyscrapers in major U.S. cities were in existence in April and May 2001.[287]

It has been revealed that bin Laden telephoned his mother on September 9th and told her that "In two days you're going to hear big news, and you're not going to hear from me for a while." The call was monitored by a foreign intelligence service and was passed on to U.S. intelligence.[288]

On September 10, 2001, Ashcroft turned down Pickard's request for additional funding. The budget he did send to Congress included spending increases in 68 different programs. None had anything to do with terrorism.[289] (A month after the 9/11 attack, the FBI requested an additional $1.5 billion to create 2,024 positions to staff an enhanced counterterrorism effort. However, the White House Office of Management and Budget cut that request to $531 million. In response, Ashcroft cut the FBI's request for "items such as computer networking and foreign language intercepts by half, cut a cyber-security request by three quarters and eliminated entirely a request for 'collaborative capabilities.'")[290]

As for Ashcroft personally, he had stopped flying on commercial jets, choosing to use a luxurious $40 million FBI Gulfstream 5 intended for special investigations and the transportation of terrorists instead.[291] An interesting coincidence?

The Pentagon had been on high alert for several weeks; however, a particularly urgent warning was received on the evening of September 10, 2001, causing a number of top officials to cancel their air travel plans for the next morning.[292] Why wasn't the American public given the same warning?

Without a doubt, if the American public were provided the same information available to the top government officials, many may also have chosen to avoid commercial air travel. The airlines may have suffered a loss of revenue, but it is equally likely that an informed and alert public might have focused attention on some, if not all of the hijackers before they were able to board the planes.*

On September 11, 2001, the United States suffered the first major attack on its "homeland" since the War of 1812. The White House escaped being burned this time, but in a 2-hour, 11-minute attack, 19 Islamist terrorists simultaneously hijacked and converted four commercial airliners into low-tech weapons of mass destruction which they piloted into their targets, killing over 3,000 in New York City, almost 200 in Washington, D.C., and 40 in Pennsylvania. The attack resulted in losses of hundreds of billions of dollars to United States property and its economy, and inflicted a massive blow to our collective sense of security from which we may never recover. Certainly not, unless we learn what went wrong and make changes for the future.

---

* Eleanor Hill, the staff director of the Congressional Committee that subsequently investigated the 9/11 attacks, noted that "prior to September 11th, the U.S. intelligence and law enforcement communities were fighting a war against terrorism largely without the benefit of what some would call their most potent weapon in that effort: an alert and committed public. One need look no further for proof of the latter point than the heroics of the passengers on Flight 93."

Do you think that Bush and his administration considered the fight against terrorism to be a priority? Do you believe Bush took all appropriate steps to protect the American people? You're not stupid! Get the truth.

The Attack

On September 10, 2001, President Bush spent the night at the Colony Beach and Tennis Resort on Longboat Key, Florida, in preparation for a political visit to Booker Elementary School in Sarasota the next morning to push his education plan. His schedule for the day was a matter of public record.

On September 11, 2001, Bush was awake at 6:00 a.m. and preparing for his daily run when several Middle Eastern men approached the Colony's guard station. They told the guard they had an appointment to conduct a "pool side" interview with the president and asked for a particular Secret Service agent by name. The message was relayed to a Secret Service agent inside the Colony, who had never heard of the requested agent, nor was he aware of any scheduled interview. He instructed the guard to turn the van away and to tell the men to contact the White House public relations office in Washington, D.C. for an appointment.[293]

It is not known whether this was a suicide assassination attempt similar to the one that had killed Ahmed Massoud two days earlier in Afghanistan. However, once the men were turned away without further investigation, they were never identified or located. At the same time, a total of 19 hijackers were preparing for and boarding at least four scheduled flights. Nine of the hijackers were selected for special screening. Of these, six were further selected for extra attention by a computerized selection process to scan their checked baggage for bombs or weapons, three because of irregularities in identification documents. The names of two hijackers, who had not been selected for special screening, were on a terrorists watch list for international flights; however, the FAA had not given this information to the domestic airlines. All 19 were allowed to board their scheduled flights.[294]

A brief summary of each flight and the day's major events follows:*

American Airlines Flight 11:

7:59 a.m. Departs Boston.

8:13 a.m. Becomes unresponsive to ground control.

8:20 a.m. Veers dramatically off course; considered to be hijacked.

8:35 a.m. President Bush departs in motorcade for Booker Elementary School (there are media reports that Bush was informed of the hijacking of Flight 11 before he departed the hotel).[295]

8:40 a.m. North American Aerospace Defense Command (NORAD) notified.

8:46 a.m. Plane piloted into the World Trade Center North Tower; FAA establishes open line with Secret Service.

8:48 a.m. Presidential Spokesman Ari Fleischer notified of first crash while presidential motorcade still en route to school; CNN broadcasts first film.

8:55 a.m. President Bush arrives at school. Rice notifies him of the first crash; however, he apparently was not advised that it was the result of a hijacking nor that there was a second hijacking, or he was so advised and failed to comprehend. He engages in photo opportunities.

9:00 a.m. President Bush enters classroom and begins the planned event.

9:03 a.m. Vice President Cheney is forcibly removed from his office by Secret Service agents and moved to a secure bunker.

9:07 a.m. President Bush notified of second crash in the classroom. He continues with the reading program and photo opportunity.

---

* Following the attack on September 11, 2001, there have been numerous time lines published. For more detail, *see*: www.cnparm.home.texas.net/911/911/911.html and www.geocities.com/spdster2003/dtail3.html.

9:12 a.m. President Bush leaves the classroom, goes to vacant classroom, meets with staff, watches television, and prepares speech.

9:26 a.m. National ground stop issued by FAA, freezing all takeoffs.

9:30 a.m. President Bush gives a brief speech at the school to students, teachers and reporters. He announces that two airplanes have crashed into the World Trade Center in an apparent terrorist attack.

9:34 a.m. Presidential motorcade leaves school en route to airport.

9:56 a.m. President Bush departs Saratoga airport on Air Force One. He speaks to Vice President Cheney and approves shooting down hijacked commercial flights.

10:28 a.m. North Tower collapses.

United Airlines Flight 175:

8:14 a.m. Departs Boston.

8:42 a.m. Hijacked and veers from its course over New Jersey, makes U-turn.

8:43 a.m. NORAD notified.

9:03 a.m. Plane piloted into the World Trade Center South Tower.

9:59 a.m. South Tower collapses.

American Airlines Flight 77:

8:20 a.m. Departs Dulles International Airport outside of Washington, D.C.

8:46 a.m. Hijacked and changes course.

9:05 a.m. West Virginia flight control notes eastbound plane without transponder.

9:24 a.m. NORAD notified.

9:33 a.m. Plane passes over Pentagon at 7,000 feet, executes complete circle, spiraling down, passes near White House.

9:38 a.m. Piloted into the Pentagon.

United Airlines Flight 93:

8:41 a.m. Departs Newark en route to San Francisco.

9:00 a.m. United warns all aircraft of cockpit intrusions and to barricade cockpit doors; Flight 93 pilots acknowledge; however, hijacker in uniform pretending to be a pilot may have already been in cockpit with permission.

9:27 a.m. (Or before) Three hijackers put red bandanas around head, force way into cockpit.

9:30 a.m. Transponder turned off.

9:34 a.m. Hijacker pretending to be Captain tells passengers there's a bomb on board; passenger on cell phone learns about other highjackings, determines plane is on suicide mission.

9:36 a.m. Plane turns around near Cleveland, Ohio; heads toward Washington, D.C.

9:47 a.m. Passengers vote to overcome hijackers;

9:50 a.m. Filling pitchers with hot water to use against hijackers;

9:57 a.m. Use galley cart in attempt to force cockpit door.

10:06 a.m. Plane crashes near Shanksville, Pennsylvania.

The Cover-up

At 8:30 p.m., President Bush made a speech to the nation in which he stated that, "We will make no distinction between the terrorists who committed these acts and those who harbor them." He also stated, "Immediately following the first attack, I implemented our government's emergency response plans." This was the first of many lies about 9/11.

What actually happened was that Bush did nothing for over an hour between 8:46 a.m. (the time of the first crash and three minutes after NORAD was notified of the second hijacking) and 9:56 a.m., when he approved shooting down hijacked airplanes. He continued to read to the children and to posture for the cameras. One can only wonder what he was thinking. Was he in denial because he had blown off so many warnings of just such an occurrence? Or is he just not that bright and failed to comprehend what was taking place?

When Bush was later asked about the attack, he stated, "I was sitting outside the classroom waiting to go in, and I saw an airplane hit the tower–the TV was obviously on. And I used to fly myself, and I said, well there's one terrible pilot. I said, it must have been a horrible accident. But I was whisked off there. I didn't have much time to think about it."

later said, "first of all, when we walked into the classroom, I had seen this plane fly into the first building."296   None of this could be true.   He wasn't whisked off and he could not have seen the first crash, because it wasn't shown on television until videotape later turned up.   He said that his Chief of Staff, Andrew Card, had informed him of the crash, saying, "here's what you're going to be doing: You're going to meet so-and-so, such-and-such.'   Then Andy Card said, 'by the way, an aircraft flew into the World Trade Center.'"

What we do know is that during a substantial period of time, while time stood still for the rest of us and when the nation was entitled to aggressive leadership, Bush continued to dither and did nothing.   He did not order the nation's commercial air fleet grounded.   It fell to a third-tier FAA manager, Ben Sliney, to take that initiative.297

Fighter jets were dispatched in an attempt to intercept the remaining hijacked airliners; however, the only person who could have authorized the use of weapons was reading to the children.   President Bush finally left for the airport and took off in Air Force One.   He wandered around the country for much of the day, perhaps thinking about what to say to the American people. We don't know.   All we do know is that he lied about taking immediate action, and he began to lie about his prior knowledge concerning the likelihood of just such an attack.

In an attempt to cover for Bush's all-day absence from duty, Karl Rove leaked that U.S. intelligence had received information that Air Force One was under threat of attack. The information was a complete lie.298   The presidential communication codes were not compromised; there was never any intelligence that there was a risk to the airplane; Bush and Rove just needed time to create a cover story.

There were immediate calls for an independent investigation of the attack. Initially Congress was unwilling to go against White House suggestions that congressional hearings would detract from the efforts to prevent further attacks and interfere with the war in Afghanistan against the Taliban.

In the meantime, Bush began to take action that would ensure that the truth would not come out. First, while air traffic was still grounded, he allowed 11 members of Osama bin Laden's family to leave the United States for Saudi Arabia without questioning.[299]

Next, although the FBI was miraculously able to identify all of the hijackers, complete with backgrounds and photographs, within a couple of weeks (which is strong evidence that it knew exactly who and where they were before the attack), on October 10, 2001, less than a month after the attack, FBI agents were ordered to close their investigation. The case was considered closed: "The investigative staff has to be made to understand that we're not trying to solve a crime now."[300]

The United States pressured Pakistani General Ahmad to quietly announce his early retirement. He was never questioned about his transfer of money to Mohamed Atta, the lead hijacker.[301]

On November 1, 2001, President Bush signed Executive Order 13233, which ended 27 years of congressional and judicial efforts to make presidential papers and records available.* Executive Order 13233 shifts the burden of proof from the former president to the person requesting presidential materials, to show why he should be given them; it makes the sitting president, rather than the Archivist of the United States, the judge of whether invocation of executive privilege by a former president should be honored; it allows a former president to indefinitely block access to presidential papers; it commits the Department of Justice to defend the former president's assertion

---

* Eleven months earlier Bush had transferred all of his Texas gubernatorial papers to his father's presidential library in College Station, Texas, in an attempt to remove them from the jurisdiction of the Texas freedom of information statutes.

of privilege against legal attack; and it allows the sitting president to withhold the records of a former president, even if the former president wants the records released.[302] What this means is that we may never have access to any of the documents that can tell us what Bush may have known or what he did or did not do in regard to 9/11.

In December 2001, resolutions were introduced in the Senate to establish an independent bipartisan commission to investigate 9/11. The Bush administration opposed such a commission and decided that an investigation by the House and Senate intelligence committees would be more narrowly focused and more easily controlled than either an independent outside commission (as in the Warren Commission) or a special congressional committee (as in the Watergate Committee).

In January 2002, Cheney attempted to quash even a limited congressional inquiry. He telephoned Senate Majority Leader Tom Daschle to warn that the investigation would divert resources from the "war on terrorism." Later, on January 28, Bush made the same request in person.[303] Nonetheless, the congressional "Joint Inquiry Into Intelligence Community Activities Before and After the Terrorist Attacks of September 11, 2001" was convened on February 14, 2002.

The first bombshell exploded under Bush's cover-up on May 16, 2002, when Condoleezza Rice revealed that beginning in May 2001, Bush's daily briefings had included reports of increasing numbers of general terrorist threats against the United States. She said, "The most important and most likely thing was that they would take over an airliner, holding passengers (hostage), and demand the release of one of their operatives." Rice added, "I don't think that anybody could have predicted that these people would take an airplane and slam it into the World Trade Center, take another and slam it into the Pentagon."[304] Apparently, serving on the board of directors of Chevron and having a tanker named after you really do not qualify someone to be the President's National Security Advisor.

Presidential spokesman Ari Fleischer said "The president did not receive information about the use of airplanes as missiles by suicide bombers. This was a new type of attack that had not been foreseen." In case you're wondering about this newly-found candor after eight months of secrecy on the subject, be reassured it didn't occur because of an attack of conscience. Congressional staffers had learned of the presidential briefing documents, and members of the joint committee were seeking to review them. The cat was out of the bag.

Suddenly, there was a shift of emphasis. Only a few months before, Bush had personally stated, "Never did we realize that the enemy was so well organized."[305] Now it became known that specific evidence of a high level of organization had been available, and that Bush was so informed. Senator Daschle said he was "gravely concerned," and asked President Bush to hand over to Congress all the information he had received. Daschle asked, "Why did it take eight months for us to receive this information?" And secondly, "what specific actions were taken by the White House in response?"

Rather than produce the information, the White House unleashed an attack. Cheney warned Democrats "to be very cautious" in blaming 9/11 on the Bush administration, saying that it is "thoroughly irresponsible and totally unworthy of national leaders in a time of war" to criticize Bush.[306] He cautioned that the inquiry should be carefully handled because "a very real threat of another perhaps more devastating attack still exists."[307] Bush piled it on, saying, "Second guessing has become second nature to Washington Democrats." He said, "Had I known that the enemy was going to use airplanes to kill on that fateful morning, I would have done everything in my power to protect the American people."[308] Remember those words.

On May 21, 2002, a second bombshell exploded under the cover-up when a letter written by FBI Special Agent Coleen M. Rowley, a 21-year veteran and Minneapolis Chief Division Counsel, to FBI Director Robert Mueller was made public. Rowley wrote about her "deep concerns that a delicate and subtle shading/skewing of facts by you and others ... has occurred and is occurring." She continued, "I feel that certain facts ... have, up to now, been omitted, downplayed, glossed over and/or mis-characterized in an effort to avoid or minimize personal and/or institutional embarrassment on the part of the FBI and/or perhaps even for improper political reasons."

Rowley's 13-page letter detailed the abundant probable cause that had existed to justify a search warrant for Moussaoui's computer disc and the improbable opposition of the FBI headquarters' staff to even approve an application for a warrant. Specifically, she complained about news accounts attributed to headquarters saying she had concurred that there was inadequate probable cause, saying these accounts were "in error (or possibly the leak was deliberately skewed in this fashion?)." Rowley directly contradicted the public statement made by Mueller that "if the FBI had only had any advance warning of the attacks, we [the FBI] may have been able to take some action to prevent the tragedy."[309]

The joint congressional intelligence inquiry employed a special staff under the direction of Eleanor Hill, a former federal prosecutor and Pentagon inspector general. The staff reviewed hundreds of thousands of pages of classified documents and conducted scores of interviews; however, investigators were not allowed to interview Condoleezza Rice, Donald Rumsfeld or Colin Powell.

During a public hearing in September 2002, Hill exploded another bombshell under Bush's cover-up. An even earlier CIA briefing in July 2001 had specifically predicted that bin Laden was about to launch a terrorist attack "in the coming weeks" and that "The attack will be spectacular and designed to inflict mass casualties against U.S. facilities or interests. Attack preparations have been made. Attack will occur with little or no warning." As Hill was about to disclose who, exactly, had received the briefing, CIA Director Tenet quickly stepped in and said that the *names* of the recipients were classified.[310] Huh?!!!! Perhaps the briefing can be classified, but the briefee? Hill was only allowed to say it was given to "senior government officials."

Now, remember Bush's words, "Had I known that the enemy was going to use airplanes to kill on that fateful morning, I would have done everything in my power to protect the American people." Do you believe it?

The joint congressional committee completed its 800-page report in December 2002; however, it largely remained a secret from the American people, and only a brief list of "findings" was made public. The Bush administration reviewed the report and blocked its publication by refusing to declassify many of its major conclusions.

Moreover, Bush attempted to reclassify some material that had been discussed openly in public hearings, such as the Arizona FBI memo. Democratic Senator Bob Graham accused the administration of covering up information that could be a political embarrassment. Even Republican Representative Porter Goss said, "Senior intelligence officials said things in public hearings that they [administration officials] don't want us to put in the report. ... That's not something I can rationally accept."[311]

The report was finally published in July 2003 with glaring omissions, including the most obvious conclusions. Either Bush was, in fact, aware that terrorists were likely to fly hijacked airplanes into major public buildings, or the CIA was criminally negligent in not providing him the information it had that the risk was real, specifically defined, and immediate. The report reveals its formal request to Bush for copies of the relevant President's Daily Briefs and Bush's denial on the grounds of executive privilege. (Remember Nixon?)

In answering the question as to whether it was Bush or the CIA who was criminally negligent, the report points out that on May 16, 2002, Condoleezza Rice conceded that Bush's August 6, 2001, briefing included "information about bin Laden's methods of operation from a historical perspective dating back to 1997." Going on to define an "historical perspective," the report lays out 36 instances of such information dating back to 1997, including: (1) September 1998 – "Bin Laden's next operation might involve flying an explosive-laden aircraft into a U.S. airport and detonating it"; (2) Fall 1998 – "Bin Laden plot involving aircraft in New York and Washington, D.C. areas"; and (3) March 2000 – "types of targets that operatives of bin Laden's network might strike. The Statute of Liberty was specifically mentioned, as were skyscrapers, ports, airports, and nuclear power plants."[312]

Needless to say, few outside the White House were satisfied with the joint Congressional Committee on Intelligence report, specifically the relatives of those murdered on September 11, 2001. They continued to lobby for an independent investigation, and over Bush's objections, Congress enacted legislation creating and funding the "National Commission on Terrorist Attacks upon the United States" to prepare a full and complete account of the circumstances surrounding the September 11, 2001 attacks. The commission was funded through May 2004.

When President Bush signed the legislation creating the commission on November 27, 2002, he said its investigation should "carefully examine all the evidence and follow all the facts, wherever they lead."[313] Remember these words.

Under the legislation, Congress selected the members and Bush appointed the Chair. So whom did the President select? Henry Kissinger, as being synonymous with "cover-up" in your thesaurus? You've got to be kidding. Kissinger, the guy wanted for questioning by judges in war-crime cases in Chile, France, and Spain, who can't even travel to Brazil because of protests by human rights groups.[314] Poor choice. At least, the relatives of 9/11 victims had a few questions about it. During a meeting with them, Kissinger reassured them that he would privately disclose to the commission's members any "potential conflicts of interests." That was not enough, as all members had to comply with Senate ethics guidelines, including financial disclosure requirements. Kissinger declined to release the secret list of clients served by his consulting firm, Kissinger Associates (more about this later), and resigned from the commission.[315]

President Bush then appointed former New Jersey governor Thomas Kean to take Kissinger's place. Kean agreed to work only one day a week on the commission and continued as president of Drew University. Kean's appointment posed a significant conflict of interest as Kean also continued to serve on the board of directors and executive committee at Amerada Hess, an oil company extensively involved in Central Asia.

In 1998, Amerada Hess established a joint venture with the Saudi oil company Delta Oil, which if you recall is involved with Unocal in the Afghanistan pipeline venture. Delta is controlled by Khalid bin Mahfouz, who is Osama bin Laden's brother-in-law and the financial benefactor of both Bush and al Qaeda.[316]

In another conflict of interest, Kean appointed Philip Zelikow as the commission's staff director. Not only had Zelikow co-authored a book in the 1990's with Condoleezza Rice, he also worked on Bush's 2000 presidential transition team, specifically in the area of reducing and redefining the role of the National Security Council in the Bush administration. Following 9/11, Zelikow publicly praised Bush as having reached down and found "the best elements in his character. He is being authentic and plainspoken."[317]

Thus, is there any surprise that the commission operated in a "polite, friendly fashion"? Although Bush had promised cooperation, requests for documents from the Department of Defense, the Federal Aviation Administration, and the White House itself were met with delays and objections.

As time dragged on, and with the May 2004 cutoff date approaching for delivery of the final report, the commission had yet to use its subpoena power to obtain needed documents. Advocates for the families of victims complained about the lack of subpoenas, the lackluster hearings in which nobody testified under oath, and staff comments that negotiations with the White House over the production of documents were being carried on in a "very congenial atmosphere."* The families didn't want congenial, they wanted answers.[318] Don't you?

The commission was not given the power to issue subpoenas unless the chairman approved. Thus, subpoenas were not issued to the Federal Aviation Administration until October

---

* Ellen Mariani, the widow of Louis Neil Mariani, who died in the crash of United Airlines Flight 175, has filed a lawsuit in the United States District Court, Eastern District of Pennsylvania, against Bush, Cheney, Ashcroft, Rumsfeld, Tenet, Rice and other members of the Bush administration. The complaint, which was brought under the Racketeer Influenced and Corrupt Organizations Act (RICO), alleges that the defendants failed "to act and prevent" the murder of her husband "for financial and political reasons" and that the defendants have since "obstructed justice" (www.nancho.net/911/mariani.html).

2003, when it was learned that the FAA had withheld dozens of boxes of requested documents concerning the 9/11 attack.[319] On November 8, 2003, the commission issued subpoenas to the Department of Defense because it had experienced "serious delays" in obtaining records involving the performance of NORAD on the morning of the attack. The commission stated, "In several cases, we were assured that all requested records had been produced, but we then discovered, through investigation, that these assurances were mistaken."[320]

The White House continued to stonewall the commission, even under the threat of a subpoena, citing executive privilege. Commission member Max Cleland, the former senator from Georgia, stated, "It's obvious that the White House wants to run out the clock here. ... It's disgusting ... as each day goes by, we learn that this government knew a whole lot more about these terrorists before September 11th than it has ever admitted."[321]

Fearing that a court battle over a rejected subpoena would likely extend past the May 27, 2004 cutoff date, the commission reached a wholly unsatisfactory agreement with the White House by which four members of the commission will review some of the documents, but only two of the four will get to review others.* Moreover, the documents will be truncated before they are turned over, and the White House will vet any comments made by the members after reviewing the documents.[322] (Remember Nixon and the "expletives deleted" tape transcripts?)

Initially, the White House attempted to run out the clock by refusing to allow Condoleezza Rice to testify in public and under oath and by refusing to allow more that the chairman and vice chairman to privately question Bush and Cheney for only one

---

* The Commission has requested Congress to give it two additional months, until July 26th, to complete its report, and Bush has relaxed his previous opposition to an extension. Moreover, the Commission has reached an agreement to allow all commissioners to review the White House edited notes taken by three commissioners and Zelikow summarizing their review of pre-9/11 briefing documents. ("9/11 Panel Is Granted More Access to Data," *Los Angeles Times*, February 11, 2004, p. A32.)

hour each. However, two things happened in March 2003 that changed the situation. First, Richard Clarke testified under oath in a public hearing of the 9/11 commission; second, his book, *Against All Enemies: Inside America's War on Terror* was published and immediately became a best seller.

In the book and in his testimony, Clarke reported that Bush "failed to act prior to September 11 on the threat from al Qaeda despite repeated warnings and then harvested a political windfall for taking obvious yet insufficient steps after the attacks; and...launched an unnecessary and costly war in Iraq that strengthened the fundamentalist, radical Islamic terrorist movement worldwide.

Clarke said that "the administration had squandered the opportunity to eliminate al Qaeda and instead strengthened our enemies by going off on a completely unnecessary tangent, the invasion of Iraq. A new al Qaeda has emerged and is growing stronger, in part because of our own actions and inactions. It is in many ways a tougher opponent than the original threat we faced before September 11 and we are not doing what is necessary to make America safer from that threat."[323]

On March 30th after the commission demanded that Rice appear and testify under oath, Bush agreed on the condition that she cannot be recalled for further questions and that the Commission will not call any other White House aides as witnesses. She appeared on April 8, 2004 and continued to insist that the August 6, 2001 intelligence briefing was "historical information based on old reporting—there was no new threat information." Despite the reports explicit reference to attacks on America, she said, "all of the threat reporting that was actionable was about threats abroad, not about the United States."[324] Bush, who was on vacation in Texas, called Rice from his pickup truck and congratulated her on her performance before the Commission.

Although Bush agreed under pressure that he and Cheney can be questioned by the entire commission, he insisted that they appear together at the same time and that there be no transcript made of the proceedings.[325] One has to wonder if Bush can't be trusted to appear without his neocon handler, who, exactly, is in control of our government, and why are we not entitled to know what Bush said to the Commission investigating his failures?

Although former President Clinton testified (alone) before the Commission that he had ranked Osama bin Laden as the number one problem the new administration would face, Bush told the Commission that Clinton "probably mentioned" terrorism as a national security threat but "did not make it a point of emphasis." Bush said that Clinton was more concerned about North Korea's nuclear program and the Israeli-Palestinian conflict.[326] Since Bush was not under oath, he can't be charged with perjury; however, we don't have to believe him.

We're still waiting for answers. What do you think? Is there a cover-up going on? You're not stupid! Get the truth.

The Why

Why the dilly-dallying? Why did Bush completely ignore all of the explicit warnings that a major terrorist attack using hijacked commercial airplanes as flying bombs against United States landmarks was imminent? Why the cover-up? The answer is spelled "O-I-L." It's crudely spilled all over, Bush's stepped in it, and he can't scrape it off his boots, no matter how hard he tries.

The incoming Bush administration wanted to change the aggressive tone of the Clinton administration into one more accommodating toward Saudi Arabia. There was "a major policy shift," and investigators were told to "back off" investigations into Saudi financing of terrorism if they involved the Saudi royal family or their associates, including the bin Laden family. Two of Osama's brothers, who were associated with the World Assembly of Muslim Youth, a suspected terrorist organization, were able to slip out of the United States before the 9/11 attacks after agents were ordered to stay away from them.[327]

If you recall, Bush Jr. earlier received bailouts in his failed business endeavors through his bin Laden and Saudi connections, one of whom was Khalid bin Mahfouz. One of Saudi Arabia's five wealthiest businessmen, Mahfouz diverted over $3 million in pension funds to bank accounts linked to terrorism.[328] Moreover, Bush Sr. continues to do business with the bin Ladens through the Carlyle group, the massive but largely unknown U.S. defense contractor.[329] The bin Laden family was a major investor in the Carlyle group until shortly after 9/11. Since leaving office, Bush Sr. has been employed to give speeches for Carlyle, which pays him $80,000 to $100,000 per speech. Bush Sr., along with former Secretary of State James Baker and former Secretary of Defense Frank Carlucci (Carlyle's CEO), has visited the bin Laden family at their home in Jeddah, Saudi Arabia, and called on Crown Prince Abdullah to discuss Carlyle's business interests.[330]

The FBI's deputy director for counterterrorism, John O'Neill, who was closing in on Osama bin Laden, quit in protest over the Bush administration's obstruction of his investigation. He stated, "The main obstacles to investigating Islamic terrorism were U.S. oil corporate interests and the role played by Saudi Arabia." Tragically, O'Neill retired to become the World Trade Center's director of security and was killed in the 9/11 attack.[331]

More specifically, remember another clue–the gas pipeline that Unocal and the Saudis wanted to build across Afghanistan. It was terminated in 1998 because of the way the Taliban treated their women and for other "business reasons," back when Clinton was sending cruise missiles to bin Laden in care of the Taliban.[332] Well, beginning in January 2001, things had changed: an MBA was in charge of the White House, and he believed he could do business with the Taliban.

The Administration commenced a series of meetings with the Taliban. The objectives: to stabilize the country, establish a coalition government, complete the Unocal pipeline, and have the Taliban arrest and extradite bin Laden.[333] The point of the meetings was to convey to the Taliban that "if they did certain things, then, gradually, they could win the jackpot, get something in return from the international community." The meetings were intended to persuade the Taliban that once a broader-based government (a coalition with the Northern Alliance) was in place and the gas pipeline underway, there would be billions of dollars in commissions, and the Taliban would have its own resources.[334]   In other words, everything has a price and everyone can be bought with money.

In March 2001, several Taliban officials, including Mullah Omar's personal advisor, came to Washington, D.C., where they met with representatives of the CIA and the State Department. The agenda included both the arrest and extradition of bin Laden, as well as access to the Central Asian oil and gas reserves by American oil companies.   Subsequently, there were other meetings outside the United States.[335]

In May 2001, Bush held out a carrot with his additional $43 million gift to the Taliban; however, in July 2001, during a meeting in Berlin, the Bush administration arrogantly waved its big stick.   The Taliban were bluntly told, "Either you accept our offer of a carpet of gold, or we will bury you under a carpet of bombs."

More diplomatically, the former U.S. ambassador to Pakistan, Tom Simons, said, "either the Taliban behave as they ought to, or Pakistan convinces them to do so, or we will use another option."[336]   The other "option" was an open-ended military operation from bases in Uzbekistan and Tajikistan. This was no idle threat.   The Bush administration already had a war plan in place to attack from the North in concert with Russia, with Pakistan's agreement and with logistical support from India and Iran.   General Franks had already visited Dushanbe, Tajikistan on May 16, 2001; Army Rangers were training Special Forces inside Kyrgyzstan; and 17,000 Russian troops were on standby.   The plan was to launch the attack before snow started falling, no later than October 2001.[337]   The invasion was set: the ultimatum had been given; all that was required was provocation.

Although the Taliban walked out of the Berlin meeting after the war threats, there was one further meeting in Islamabad, Pakistan.   In August 2001, the U.S. Assistant Secretary of State for Central Asian Affairs, Christina Rocca, met with the Taliban ambassador to Pakistan, Abdul Salam Zaeef.[338]

Note that the emphasis had shifted from Clinton's targeting of bin Laden, and telling the Taliban to not assist him, to Bush's targeting of the Taliban, telling them not to resist the pipeline, and, by the way, to turn over bin Laden. This was essentially a threat of war, not over terrorism but over oil. Unbelievable? Perhaps a little more information will help you understand why Bush's Business Administration thought the payoff was worth the risk.

We have to start with Vice President Dick Cheney, the man who is just a beer and pretzel away from the presidency. After he left government service with the first Bush administration, Cheney was appointed as the CEO of the Halliburton Corporation, a service firm that has worked the oil patch since the dry hole was invented. With its subsidiaries, Halliburton does just about every job connected with the production and transportation of oil and gas, worldwide. Among its subsidiaries is Bredero-Shaw, a Texas-based company that provides anti-corrosion coatings for oil pipelines and which is a joint partner of the Saudi bin-Laden Group, a pipeline construction company owned by the bin Laden family.[339]

Other Halliburton foreign subsidiaries sold $23.8 million (maybe as much as $73 million[340]) in oil field equipment to Iraq in 1998 and 1999, even though U.S. oil companies were prohibited from investing in or buying Iraqi oil, which is probably why Cheney called for an end to the sanctions against Iraq while he was still Halliburton's CEO.[341] Cheney has denied any knowledge of these sales; however, Halliburton's current CEO stated that Cheney "unquestionably" knew.[342] Cheney received $162,392 in deferred salary from Halliburton in 2002, and he continues to own 433,333 stock options in the company.

In a speech on June 23, 1998, Cheney proclaimed, "the good Lord didn't see fit to put oil and gas only where there are democratically elected regimes friendly to the United States. Occasionally we have to operate in places where, all things considered, one would not normally choose to go. But we go where the business is." And the "business" that is at issue here derives from the oil and gas reserves in the Caspian Basin. In 1998, Cheney stated, "I can't think of a time when we've had a region emerge as suddenly to become as strategically significant as the Caspian."[343]

In 1999, Congress passed the Silk Road Strategy Act to assist and support the "economic and political independence of the countries of the South Caucasus and Central Asia." Congress noted that the region "could produce oil and gas in sufficient quantities to reduce the dependence of the United States on energy from the volatile Persian Gulf region" and that one of the principal objectives was "to support United States business interests and investments in the region."[344]

The breakup of the USSR left a string of newly independent nations arranged around and near the Caspian Sea and along the southern border of Russia. These nations, Azerbaijan, Kazakhstan, Uzbekistan, Kyrgyzstan and Turkmenistan, have vast oil and gas deposits. The problem is that these countries are landlocked, and all of the existing pipelines run north into Russia, which, while no longer a cold war enemy, is a competitor in the worldwide energy business.

A 1997 study written by Zbigniew Brzezinski for the Council on Foreign Relations noted that any nation becoming predominant in Central Asia would pose a direct threat to U.S. control of oil resources and that "it is imperative that no Eurasian challenger emerges, capable of dominating Eurasia and thus of also challenging America. ... For America, the chief geopolitical prize is Eurasia."[345]

Cheney's energy task force projected a doubling of the United States' consumption of fossil fuels over the next 25 years and found that "A significant disruption in world oil supplies could adversely affect our economy and our ability to promote key foreign and economic policy objectives, regardless of the level of U.S. dependence on oil imports." With a projected yearly drop in domestic crude oil production, the report predicts the U.S. will become increasingly dependent upon imported oil, with a corresponding doubling of imports over the same 25 years.[346]

Among the areas targeted by the plan was the Caspian region with proven reserves of about 20 billion barrels of oil. With the potential of 270 billion barrels, or almost one-fifth of the world's oil reserves, it also has natural gas potential of 665 trillion cubic feet, almost one-eighth of the world's gas reserves. In 1997, all of this was estimated to be worth some $4 trillion.[347]

Development of the Caspian Basin became a priority of the Bush administration and a foundation of Cheney's energy plan.[348] In the early days of September 2001, the U.S. Energy Information Administration confirmed Afghanistan's strategic "geographical position as a potential transit route for oil and natural gas exports from Central Asia to the Arabian Sea."[349]

We have seen that Unocal was vitally interested in building at least one pipeline across Afghanistan; however, it was not alone in wanting to do business in the Caspian oil patch. In 1996, Enron signed a contract to explore gas fields in Uzbekistan, to sell gas to Russia, and to link up with Unocal's proposed Afghanistan gas pipeline. In addition, Enron wanted to build a gas pipeline north from its Dabhol generating plant in India to connect with Unocal's gas pipeline coming out of Afghanistan. It badly needed the supply of cheap natural gas to prop up its failing Dabhol operation.[350]

In 1998, Turkmenistan selected Enron to conduct a feasibility study funded by the U.S. Trade and Development Agency for a trans-Caspian gas pipeline, and in 1999, the country signed a contract with Bechtel and GE Capital Services to build the pipeline.[351]

While he was Halliburton's CEO, Cheney also sat on Kazakhstan's oil advisory board and helped broker a deal between that country and Chevron, at a time when Condoleezza Rice was on its board of directors, for half ownership of the Tengiz oil field. (We'll later talk about a criminal bribery investigation in this area.) Chevron and ExxonMobil are also heavily invested in Azerbaijan's oil and gas fields, and in 2001, Halliburton signed a 12-year contract with Azerbaijan.

Because Azerbaijan has blockaded Armenia over the disputed Nagorno-Karabakh area, Section 907 of the Freedom Support Act adopted by Congress in 1992 prohibited the United States from providing most forms of assistance to Azerbaijan. However, after Bush met separately with the leaders of Armenia and Azerbaijan in April and July 2001,[352] and after Congress granted Bush's request post 9/11, he waived Section 907 and extended $4.4 million in military assistance to Azerbaijan.[353] Bush also met with Uzbekistan's ambassador to the United States.[354]

In November 2001, Bush proudly announced the opening of a new pipeline by the Caspian Pipeline Consortium: "The CPC project also advances my Administration's National Energy Policy by developing a network of multiple Caspian pipelines."[355]

Interestingly enough, John J. Maresca, a Unocal Vice President, testified before Congress on February 12, 1998, and asked for the repeal or removal of Section 907. In addition to the Afghanistan gas pipeline, he also discussed other proposed pipeline projects involving American oil companies. One would run west from the northern Caspian to the Black Sea and another (to be built by Unocal, Amoco, Exxon and Pennzoil) would either run to the Black Sea or to the Mediterranean port of Ceyhan, Turkey. To accommodate the growing Asian energy markets, Maresca proposed a pipeline through China and the Afghanistan gas pipeline. In addition, Maresca discussed another pipeline to gather oil from the existing pipeline infrastructure in Turkmenistan, Uzbekistan, Kazakhstan and Russia, which would also run through Afghanistan to an export terminal on the Pakistan coast. The 42-inch pipeline would have a capacity of one million barrels of oil per day.

Maresca concluded, "We urge the Administration and the Congress to give strong support to the U.N.-led peace process in Afghanistan. ... U.S. assistance in developing these new economies will be crucial to business success. ... Unocal and other American companies like it are fully prepared to undertake the job and to make Central Asia once again into the crossroads it has been in the past."[356]

When Unocal speaks, Bush listens. To more fully answer the "Why" questions, we must continue to track Unocal's demands and Bush's jumps. Immediately following the U.S. blitzkrieg in Afghanistan, Bush appointed Zalmay Khalilzad as his special envoy to the country. Khalilzad was well informed about Afghanistan's oil issues because he and Henry Kissinger were originally employed by Unocal to arrange the details of its Afghanistan pipeline. Yes, Henry "no conflict of interest" Kissinger and his Associates, including the present Deputy Secretary of State Richard Armitage. Back in 1995, Kissinger had helped put together the original pipeline deal between Unocal and Turkmenistan, and he was present at the signing ceremony in New York City.[357] However, at that time, Afghanistan was still in turmoil, and the Taliban needed a little help to capture Kabul. Enter the CIA, arrange a visit by Saudi intelligence chief Prince Turki to spread some Saudi petrodollars, and *voilá*![358]

Khalilzad had served in Bush Sr.'s administration as a special assistant to the president and as a senior Defense Department official for policy planning. He was later employed as an advisor to Unocal to draw up the risk analysis for its proposed gas pipeline across Afghanistan, and to facilitate the talks between Unocal and the Taliban in 1997. Prior to Khalilzad's appointment by Bush Jr. as his special envoy to Afghanistan, Khalilzad worked for Condoleezza Rice in the National Security Council and served as a counselor to Secretary of Defense Donald Rumsfeld.[359] (It's a small, small world after all.)

Back in 1996, just after the fall of Kabul to the Taliban, Unocal Vice President Chris Taggart described the takeover as a "very positive step" and called for the United States to recognize the Taliban. Shortly thereafter, Khalilzad wrote an article urging the United States to work with the Taliban to form a broad-based coalition government. He wrote "we should use as a positive incentive the benefits that will accrue to Afghanistan from the construction of oil and gas pipelines across its territory. ... These projects will only go forward if Afghanistan has a single authoritative government."[360] As Yogi Berra once said, "It's *déjà vu* all over again."

At about the same time that Bush was appointing Khalilzad as his special envoy to Afghanistan, he also appointed another former Unocal employee, Hamid Karzai, as Afghanistan's interim Prime Minister. Karzai had helped negotiate the pipeline deal with the Taliban in 1997 on behalf of Unocal and was closely associated with the CIA and its former director William Casey.[361]

Karzai immediately set out to finish the job on behalf of his former employers. On February 8, 2002, Karzai met with the president of Pakistan, Pervez Musharraf, who agreed to reinstate the pipeline deal. He then met with President Saparmurat Niyazov of Turkmenistan the next month to seal up the northern end of the agreement. Niyazov stated the pipeline would allow the export of his country's vast natural gas resources, and he hoped that peace in Afghanistan would allow the work to go forward.[362]

With this agreement, Unocal may finally get to complete its pipeline, but at what cost? Billions and billions of dollars and thousands of lives? With this background information, we can now begin to understand why Bush dilly-dallied around trying to do business with the Taliban rather than stopping bin Laden. We can better understand why he lied and denied, and perhaps we are beginning to understand why Cheney refuses to turn over documents relating to his energy task force.

Do you believe Bush acted in the best interests of the American public, or did he act to defend oil company interests in the Caspian Basin and the Afghanistan pipeline? You're not stupid! Get the truth.

209. Chomsky, Noam, *9-11* (New York: Seven Stories Press, 2001), p. 67.

210. Ibid., pp. 44, 45.

211. Ibid., pp. 23, 73.

212. Ibid., p. 44.

213. Ahmed, op. cit. p. 22.

214. Ibid., pp. 176, 177, 191.

215. Chomsky, op. cit., p. 43.

216. Marshall, Andrew, "Terror 'Blowback' Burns CIA," *The Independent*, November 1, 1998, www.cooperativeresearch.org/ timeline/1990s/ independent110198.html.

217. Warrick, Joby and Joe Stephens, "Before Attack, U.S. Expected Different Hit," October 2, 2001, www.washingtonpost.com/ac2/ wp-dyn/A55607-2001Oct1/language=printer.

218. Williams, Dave, "The Bombing of the World Trade Center in New York City," 1998, www.interpol.int/Public/Publications/ICPR/ICPR469_3.asp_38k_Jan2, 2004

219. Ibid.

220. Clarke, Richard A., *Against All Enemies: Inside America's War on Terror* (New York: Free Press, 2004), p. 92.

221. Ibid., p. 97.

222. "Who is Ramzi Yousef?" www.terrorismfiles.org/individuals/ramzi-yousef.html.

223. Waller, Douglas, "Inside The Hunt For Osama," *Time* December 21, 1998, www.time.com/time/magazine/story/0,9171,1101981221-140773,00.html.

224. "Ramzi Yousef Gets 240 Years," January 8, 1998, www.ict.org.il/spotlight/det.cfm?id=5.

225. "Afghanistan, Turkmenistan Oil and Gas, and the Projected Pipeline," October 21, 2001, http://ist-socrates.berkeley.edu/~pdscott/q7.html; see also Cohn, Marjorie, "The Deadly Pipeline War: US Afghan Policy Driven By Oil Interests," http://www.commondreams.org/views01/1208-04.html.

226. Martin, Patrick, "Was the US government alerted to September 11 attack?" www.wsws.org/articles/2002/jan2002/sept-j16.shtml.

227. "U.S. Indicts Fourteen in Khobar Towers Bombing," June 22, 2001, http://www.ict.org.il/spotlight/det.cfm?id=628.

228. Appleson, Gail, "US appeals court upholds cleric's conviction," http://www.metimes.com/issue99-34/eg/us_appeals_court.html.

229. "Consortium formed to build Central Asia gas pipeline," October 27, 1997, http://www.unocal.com/uclnews/97news/102797a.html.

230. "Family Affair: the Bushes and the Bin Ladens," www.thedubyareport.com/bushbin.html.

231. Clarke, op. cit., pp. 166-171.

232. "Pakistan hands over embassies bombing suspect to Kenya," August 16, 1998, www.cnn.com/WORLD/africa/9808/16/embassy.bombings.

233. Chomsky, op. cit., p. 49; see also Riemer, Matthew, "The Destruction Of The Al-Shifa Pharmaceutical Company," September 19, 2002, (http://www.yellowtimes.org/article.php?sid=692).

234. Aita, Judy, "Bin Laden, Atef Indicted In U.S. Federal Court For African Bombings," November 4, 1998, usinfo.state.gov/topical/pol/terror/98110402.html.

235. Gellman, Barton, "Broad Effort Launched After '98 Attacks," *Washington Post,* December 19, 2001, www.washingtonpost.com/ac2/wp-dyn/A62725-2001Dec18?language=printer.

236. "Unocal statement on withdrawal from the proposed Central Asia Gas (CentGas) pipeline project," December 10, 1998, http://www.unocal.com/uclnews/98news/centgas.html.

237. Al-Issawi, Tarek, "Saudi Arabia severs ties with Afghanistan's Taliban," September 25, 2001, www.timesargus.com/Archive/Articles/Article/34434.

238. Gellman, op. cit.

239. Solomon, John, "1999 Report Warned of Suicide Hijack," *Associated Press,* May 17, 2002, www.commondreams.org/cgi-bin/print.cgi?file=/headlines02/0517-06.htm.

240. "Interview: Richard Clarke," *Guardian,* March 23, 2004, www.guardian.co.uk/september11/story/0,11209,1175817,00.html.

241. Clarke, op. cit., pp. 205, 211-212.

242. Martin, op. cit.

243. "Attack on the USS Cole," The History Guy, http://www.historyguy.com/uss_cole.htm.

244. Bernton, Hal, Mike Carter, David Heath and James Neff, "The Past is Prologue," *The Seattle Times,* June 23 - July 7, 2002, http://seattletimes.nwsource.com/news/nation-world/terroristwithin/chapter1.html.

245. Franken, op. cit., pp. 107, 110.

246. Moore, *Bush's War for Reelection,* op. cit., pp. 16, 17.

247. "9-11 Commission, Attack Was Preventable," www.dailykos.com/comments/2003/12/18/03850/244/27.

248. Clarke, op. cit., p. 225.

249. Ibid., p. 231.

250. Ferullo, Mike, "Rumsfeld urges missile defense system during confirmation hearing," January 11, 2001, www.cnn.com/2001/ALLPOLITICS/stories/01/11/rumsfeld.hearing?

251. "Statement by Robert D. Walpole, National Intelligence Officer for Strategic and Nuclear Programs," February 9, 2000, http://www.clw.org/coalition/walpole020900.htm.

252. Leopold, Jason, "CIA Intelligence Reports Seven Months Before 9/11 Said Iraq Posed No Threat To U.S., Containment Was Working, June 27, 2003, www.scoop.co.nz/mason/storiesHL0306/S00211.htm.

253. Franken, op. cit., p. 117.

254. Ibid., p. 118.

255. Clarke, op. cit., p. 231.

256. Ibid., p. 236.

257. Corn, op. cit., p. 126.

258. Franken, op. cit., p. 118.

259. Ahmed, op. cit., p. 106.

260. "Foreign Policy Priorities and Challenges of the Administration, June 7, 2001, Council on Foreign Relations, www.cfr.org/pub5161/condoleezza_rice/foreign_policy_priorities_and_challenges_of_the_administration.php.

261. Frankel, op. cit., p. 118.

262. Flocco, Tom, "Bush May Invoke 9/11 Executive Privilege and Secrecy," www.tomflocco.com.

263. Ahmed, op. cit., p. 114.

264. Ibid., pp. 88, 90.

265. Corn, op. cit., p. 142.

266. Ahmed, op. cit., pp. 106-113; see also Davis, Walter E., "September 11th and The Bush Administration: Compelling Evidence for Complicity," 2003, (www.yuricareport.com/911/davis_compellingEvidenceForComplicity.ltme).

267. Ahmed, op. cit., pp. 207-209.

268. Franken, op. cit., p. 119.

269. Ibid., pp. 119, 120.

270. Jehl, Douglas and David E. Sanger, "Pre-9/11 Secret Briefing Said That Qaeda Was Active in U.S.," *The New York Times*, April 11, 2004, http://www.nytimes.com/2004/04/11/politics/11NTE.html.

271. "Bush Contradicts Self At His Own Press Conference," April 14, 2004, http://daily.misleader.org/ctt.asp?u=2323986&1=28723.

272. Franken, op. cit., p. 120.

273. Ahmed, op. cit., p. 114.

274. Milbank, Dana, "FBI Budget Squeezed After 9/11:Request for New Counterterror Funds Cut by Two-Thirds," *Washington Post*, March 22,

2004, http://www.washingtonpost.com/ac2/wp-dyn/A13541-
2004Mar21?language=printer.

275. Shenon, Philip and Lowell Bergman, "9/11 Panel Is Said to Offer
Harsh Review of Ashcroft," *The New York Times,* April 13, 2004,
http://www.nytimes.com/2004/04/13/politics/13PANE.html.

276. Franken, op. cit., p. 121; see also Ahmed, op. cit., pp. 93-95.

277. Ahmed, op. cit., pp. 95, 96.

278. Ibid., pp. 218, 219, 224.

279. Franken, op. cit., p. 121.

280. Ibid., p. 121.

281. Ibid., pp. 121, 122.

282. Clarke, op. cit., p. 237.

283. Ahmed, op. cit., p. 116.

284. Kellner, op. cit., p. 9; see also Johnson, David and Eric Schmitt,
"Uneven Response Seen on Terror in Summer of 2001," *The New York
Times,* April 4, 2004, www.nytimes.com/2004/04/04/politics/
04SUMM.html.

285. Wood, Allan and Paul Thompson, "It was an interesting day,"
www.talkleft.com/archives/003127.html.

286. Ahmed, op. cit., p. 89.

287. Harpter, Tim, "Ex-FBI worker challenges 9/11 'lie,'" *Toronto Star,*
April 5, 2004, www.thestar.com/NASApp/cs/ContentServer?
pagename=thestar/Layout/Article_PrintFriendly&c=Article&cid=1081
116611085&call_pageid=968332188854.

288. Ahmed, op. cit., p. 117.

289. Franken, op. cit., pp. 121, 122.

290. Milbank, Dana, op. cit.

291. Ahmed, op. cit., p. 125.

292. Ibid.

293. Wood, op. cit.

294. Ahmed, op. cit., p. 96.

295. IrvingShapiro.tripod.com/cgi.bin/flight_93/bush.html.

296. Alterman, Eric, "9/11/01: Where Was George?"
www.thenation.com/doc.mhtml%3Fi=20031006&s=alterman.

297. Ibid.

298. Kellner, op. cit., p. 77.

299. Ahmed, op. cit., p. 184.

300. Ibid., p. 99.

301. Ibid., p. 226.

302. Flocco, op. cit.

303. Cornwell, Susan, "Daschle: Bush, Cheney Urged No Sept. 11 Inquiry," May 26, 2002, www.newsfrombabylon.com/article.php?sid=1680.

304. "White House 'not warned of attacks,'" BBC News, May 17, 2002, news.bbc.co.uk/hi/english/world/americas/newsid_19910000/1991689.stm.

305. Eggen, Dan and Bill Miller, "Bush Was Told of Hijacking Dangers," *The Washington Post*, May 16, 2002, www.washingtonpost.com.

306. "White House 'not warned of attacks,'" BBC News, op. cit.

307. Kellner, op. cit., p. 238.

308. "Bush defends his actions before 9/11," *USA Today*, May 17, 2002, www.usatoday.com/news/washington/2002/05/17/bush-defense.html.

309. "Coleen Rowley's Memo to FBI Director Robert Mueller," May 21, 2002, www.zpub.com/notes/rowleymemo.html.

310. Corn, op. cit., p. 143.

311. Isikoff, Michael and Mark Hosenball, "The Secrets of September 11," *Newsweek*, April 30, 2003, www.truthout.org/docs_03/050203B.shtml.

312. Dean, John W., "The 9/11 Report Raises More Serious Questions," July 29, 2003, www.yuricareport.com.

313. "Commission in a hurry," *Milwaukee Journal Sentinel*, October 28, 2003, http://www.jsonline.com/news/editorials/oct03/180742.asp.

314. Corn, David, "Kissinger's Back ... As 9/11 Truth-Seeker," *The Nation*, November 27, 2002, www.thenation.com/capitalgames/index.mhtml?bid=3&pid=176.

315. Grigg, William Norman, "Kean Steps in for Kissinger," *The New American*, January 13, 2003, www.thenewamerican.com/tna/2003/01-13-2003/vo19no01_kean.html.

316. Alterman and Green, op. cit., p. 223.

317. Boehlert, Eric, "Is the 9/11 commission too soft?" October 10, 2003, www.voicesofsept11.org/news/101003.php.

318. Ibid.

319. Shenon, Phil, "White House Faces Subpoena Threat," *International Herald Tribune*, October 27, 2003, www.iht.com.

320. Shenon, Philip, "Panel Subpoenas Pentagon on 9/11," *New York Times*, November 8, 2003, www.twincities.com/mld/PioneerPress.

321. "The Daily Briefing: October 27," www.thedailyenron.com/documents/20031027122859-17777.asp.

322. Harper, Tim, "What Did Bush Know Before 9/11?" November 4, 2003, www.commondreams.org; see also Shenon, Philip, "9/11 Commission 'Deal' With White House," November 14, 2003, (www.vermontindymedia.org/newswire/display/1832/indexphp).

323. Clarke, op. cit., pp. ix, x.

324. Shenon, Philip, "Members of the 9/11 Commission Press Rice on Early Warnings," *The New York Times*, April 9, 2004, http://www.nytimes.com/2004/04/09/politics/09PANE.html.

325. Shenon, Philip and Elisabeth Bumiller, "Bush Allows Rice To Testify on 9/11 in a Public Session," *The New York Times*, March 31, 2004, http://www.nytimes.com/2004/03/31/politics/31PANE.html.

326. "Bush, Clinton differ on security issue before 9/11 panel," *The Hindu*, May 3, 2004, www.hinduonnet.com/thehindu/holnus/003200405031072.htm.

327. Palast, op. cit., pp. 96, 97.

328. "Family Affair: the Bushes and the Bin Ladens," www.thedubyareport.com/bushbin.html.

329. Palast, op. cit., p. 104.

330. Kellner, op. cit., pp. 36, 37, 119; see also Ahmed, op. cit., pp.180-183; see also Rampton, Sheldon and John C. Stauber, *Weapons of Mass Deception: The Uses of Propaganda in Bush's War on Iraq* (New York: J.P. Tarcher, 2003), pp. 106, 107.

331. Rosebraugh, Craig, "Don't Mess with Unocal: The war against terrorism may really be a battle over oil," *Toward Freedom*, January 2002.

332. "Unocal statement on withdrawal from the proposed Central Asia Gas (CentGas) pipeline project," December 10, 1998, http://www.unocal.com/uclnews/98news/centgas.html.

333. Godoy, Julio, "U.S. Policy Towards Taliban Influenced by Oil - Authors," November 15, 2001, www.truthout.org/docs_01/11.17A.oil.taliban.html.

334. "Al-Qaeda monitored U.S. negotiations with Taliban over oil pipeline," June 5, 2002, www.salon.com/news/feature/ 2002/06/05/memo/index_np.html.

335. Steele, Jonathan, et. al., "Special Report: Pakistan," September 22, 2001, www.guardian.co.uk/Archive/Artilce/0,4273,4262511,00.html.

336. Godoy, op. cit.

337. Ahmed, op. cit., pp. 58-61.

338. Godoy, op. cit.

339. Ahmed, op. cit., p. 187.

340. "Halliburton Iraq ties more than Cheney said," June 25, 2001, NewsMax.com.

341. Solomon, Norman and Reese Erlich, *Target Iraq: What the News Media Didn't Tell You* (New York: Context Books, 2003), p. 110.

342. Kellner, op. cit., p. 251.

343. Cohn, Marjorie, "The Deadly Pipeline War: US Afghan Policy Driven By Oil Interests," www.commondreams.org/views01/ 1208-04.html.

344. Ahmed, op. cit., p. 70.

345. Ibid., p. 73-77.

346. "U.S. Department of Energy Plans an Accelerated Dependence Upon Foreign Petroleum Sources," www.rainbow.net/ongwhehonwhe/energy/poli.html.

347. Kellner, op. cit., p. 37.

348. Aslam, Abid, "Bush-Cheney Energy Plan Bears Watching," July 2001, www.fpif.org/commentary/2001/0107energy_body.html.

349. Cohn, op. cit.

350. Neville, Harry, "Bush's Homeland Security Pipeline," March 29, 2002, www.buzzflash.com/contributors/ 2002/03/29_homeland_security_pipeline.html.

351. "How Much Were Bush and Cheney Involved?" www.alternet.org/letters_ed.html.

352. Aslam, op. cit.

353. "Section 907 of The Freedom Support act," April 12, 2002, www.aaainc.org/press/section907.pdf.

354. Neville, op. cit.

355. Ahmed, op. cit., p. 259.

356. "It's All About Oil!" www.whatreallyhappened.com/oil.html.

357. "Kissinger, Unocal, Enron and Cheney," December 3, 2002, www.btinternet.com/~nlpwessex/Documents/kissingerunocal.html.

358. "Afghanistan, Turkmenistan Oil and Gas, and the Projected Pipeline," October 21, 2001, (http://ist-socrates.berkeley.edu/~pdscott/q7.html); see also Cohn, op. cit.

359. www.nationmaster.com/encyclopedia/zalmay-khalilzad.

360. "Al-Qaeda monitored U.S. negotiations with Taliban over oil pipeline," June 5, 2002, (www.salon.com/news/feature/2002/06/05/memo/index_np.html); see also Martin, Patrick, "USA: Unocal Advisor Named Representative to Afghanistan," January 3, 2002, (http://www.corpwatch.org/news/PND.jsp?articleid=1149).

361. Madsen, Wayne, "Afghanistan, the Taliban and the Bush Oil Team," 2002, http://www.globalresearch.ca/article/MAD201.A.html.

362. "Agreement On US 3.2 Billion Gas Pipeline Project Signed," December 28, 2002, www.truthout.org/docs_02/12.30A.afgh.pipe.htm; see also Yant, Martin, "Enron played key role in events presaging war," *Columbus Free Press*, April 10, 2002, (www.freepress.org/journal.php?strFunc=display&strID=54&strJournal=10).

THE PREVARICATOR II:
THE MIDTERM CAMPAIGN

The saga of the midterm elections in 2002 is not a shining hour for American politics. Rather, it's a tale of new lows in dirty tricks and a corrupt politicization of the war on terrorism.

Not only was the presidential election in 2000 one of the closest in history, but the total of all votes cast in the congressional and senatorial elections was equally close. Only half of one percent separated Bush and Gore, and approximately the same percentage separated all the votes cast for Republican candidates for Congress and for their Democratic opponents.[363]

In 2001, Republican Senator James Jeffords of Vermont, fed up with the extreme conservatism of the Republican Party, announced that he would become an Independent. However, since he no longer voted with the Republicans, his decision gave the Democrats control of the Senate.

Going into the 2002 elections, the Republicans held a six-seat advantage in the House of Representatives and, with reapportionment reallocating 12 congressional seats from states in the East and Midwest to states in the South and West, Bush had hopes of increasing the Republican margin.[364] But what Bush desperately wanted was to regain control of the Senate, where his legislative agenda was stalled.

The Republicans raised a total of $400 million in hard money compared to $220 million for the Democrats. Operating with White House leadership, the Republican National Committee organized the "72-Hour Task Force," and the Republican House leadership organized the Strategic Taskforce to Organize and Mobilize People (STOMP). So much for subtlety. The plan included celebrity visits by Bush, Cheney, and their wives to pump up Republican campaign workers and to gain news coverage.[365]

Karl Rove's Political War

Karl Rove proposed to turn the war on terror into a political weapon against the Democrats. At a meeting of the Republican National Committee in Austin, Texas, Rove stated, "We can go to the country on this issue, because they trust the Republican Party to do a better job of protecting and strengthening America's military might and thereby protecting America."[366]

The fact that Rove was politicizing the war was confirmed when a computer disc containing a power-point presentation was found in Lafayette Park across the street from the White House. Slide number 20 was entitled "Republican Strategy" and listed six ways to win the election. The first was to "Focus on War and the Economy."[367] Even Pat Buchanan observed, "I think the way they rationalize ... Rove would rationalize it, is to explain to the President the consequences ... the political consequences of each of the choices he is considering, and that so long as policy is not disturbed by doing something that helps us politically, we should feel free to do something that helps us politically."[368]

Karl Rove's favorite propagandist, David Horowitz, wrote a campaign booklet entitled "How to Beat the Democrats." He emphasized that "mainstream Democrats [were] ... significant players in the debacle of 9/11. And no one is more singularly responsible for America's vulnerability on that fateful day than the Democratic president, Bill Clinton, and his White House staff." Clinton was accused of having "simply refused to do anything serious about the threat." Horowitz concluded, "This is a story the Republicans must tell the American people if they are to be warned about the dangers of putting their trust in the party of Bill Clinton by casting their votes for Democrats come November."[369]

In 1999, Bush had promised, "I've learned you cannot lead by dividing people. This country is hungry for a new style of campaign. Positive. Hopeful. Inclusive." Well, we saw how he conducted the 2000 campaign, and like a movie that becomes a box office success, he set out to make a sequel. During the 2002 campaign, Bush campaigned through 15 states. He stayed on message throughout and repeatedly accused Democrats of sacrificing America's safety by supporting workplace protection for the new employees of the Department of Homeland Security, and that Democrats were therefore uninterested in the security of the American people.

In the final days of the election, Karl Rove began to play his usual dirty tricks. In Florida and Texas, two states considered crucial to reelect Jeb Bush as governor and a Republican Senator, voters began to receive telephone calls purportedly from gay rights organizations encouraging them to vote for the Democratic candidates because they supported gay marriage.[370]

A Cowardly Attack on an American Patriot

Democrat Max Cleland was the senior Senator from Georgia. Between 1965 and 1968, he had volunteered to fight in the Vietnam War as a Captain in the Army's 1st Calvary Division. He lost both legs and his right arm in a grenade explosion, and he received numerous awards for his bravery, including the Silver Star for Gallantry in Action.* He went on to serve as the youngest administrator ever of the Veterans Administration for President Carter. As a senator, Cleland gained respect for his work in health care, bio-terrorism preparedness, and homeland security.[371] He was a liberal on economic issues and a moderate on cultural and foreign affairs. He was an ardent conservationist, receiving a perfect score of 100 percent on environmental issues from the League of Conservation Voters. The polls showed that Georgia voters had a generally favorable impression of Cleland.[372]

In the Senate, Cleland co-sponsored the legislation to establish the Department of Homeland Security, which was initially opposed by Bush; however, Cleland opposed Bush's

---

* Cleland was awarded the Silver Star because, "during heavy enemy rocket and mortar attack, Capt. Cleland disregarded his own safety, exposed himself to rocket barrage as he left his covered position to administer first aid to his wounded comrades. He then assisted them in moving the injured personnel to covered positions. Cleland's gallant action is in keeping with the highest traditions of military service."

plan to deny civil service protection to Department employees. This was enough to make him a target of the Republican juggernaut. Cleland's opponent in the 2002 Senate race was Republican Congressman Saxby Chambliss, a Chicken Hawk, who had avoided service in Vietnam because of a "football injury" and four student deferments.[373] Chambliss had a score of zero percent on environmental issues. Chambliss once said that to combat terrorism, a Georgia sheriff could be turned loose to "arrest every Muslim that comes across the state line."[374]

A true believer in going nasty, Chambliss began to run television attack ads that questioned Cleland's patriotism. The ads featured photographs of Osama bin Laden and Saddam Hussein and attacked Cleland as supposedly voting against homeland security and questioned his courage to lead. Chambliss labeled Cleland as "the most liberal senator Georgia has ever had."

Bush visited Georgia five times to campaign for Chambliss. In October 2002, Bush spoke at a fund-raiser for Chambliss, where he blamed Democrats for trying to "tie the hands of this president and future presidents to be able to carry out one of our most solemn duties, which is to protect the homeland." Since Cleland was a Democrat, it wasn't hard for Georgia voters to get the message.[375]

After Bush put the boots to Cleland, his buddy Chambliss, the crass bully, went on to defeat the brave and dignified warrior, who had given so much for his country and who deserved so much better. Who cares? Out of habit, Bush lied that the Republicans had prevailed because they ran clean campaigns, saying, "Their accent was on the positive."

The *Weekly Scalawag* reports that after his election, Chambliss telephoned Senate Majority Leader Bill Frist to ask a favor. What he didn't know was that he was on a speaker phone and that a reporter's tape recorder was running. Chambliss said that a friend who helped "raise a chunk of money" to get him elected wanted an "ambassadorship to an overseas economic development organization." When Chambliss was later confronted about the incident on Meet the Press, he said the friend "just happens to be a donor." Nonetheless, he said, "the guy's qualified." Yet, he had told Frist, "I don't even know what the hell he is, but he wants it." So much for integrity in politics.

The Republicans outspent the Democrats by $184 million and succeeded in holding their House seats and regaining control of the Senate. The new employees of the Department of Homeland Security lost out on workplace protection, and the Department was politicized when the Republican-controlled Congress passed the law and Bush signed it.

Do you think Bush acted in the best interests of Americans when he and Rove cynically used the 9/11 attacks as a political weapon? Do you think he cared about Homeland Security when he helped stomp on a true patriot, one who had really wanted to fight in Vietnam, who was not afraid to volunteer, and who really did give his right arm (and two legs) for his country? You're not stupid! Get the truth.

---

363. Zogby, James J., "The stakes are high in the 2002 congressional elections," January 15, 2002, www.jordanembassyus.org/01152002009.html.

364. Ibid.

365. "The Last Hurrah? Soft Money And Issue Advocacy In The 2002 Congressional Elections," Edited by David B. Magleby and J. Quin Monson, Center for the Study of Elections and Democracy, Brigham Young University, Provo, Utah, 2003, www.byu.edu/outsidemoney.

366. Conason, op. cit., p. 192.

367. Moore, op. cit., pp. 290, 291.

368. Ibid., p. 291.

369. Conason, op. cit., p. 196.

370. Moore, op. cit., p. 320.

371. "Stories of Courage: Senator Max Cleland," www.loc.gov/cocoon/vhp-stories/loc.natlib.afc2001001.03512.

372. "Race At A Glance: Georgia Senate," League of Conservation Voters, www.lcv.org/Campaigns/Campaigns.cfm?ID=1517&c=1.

373. Conason, op. cit., p. 68.

374. "Rep. Saxby Chambliss: Arrest every Muslim That Enters Georgia," November 21, 2001, www/refuseandresist/org/newrepression/120501chambliss.html.

375. Corn, op. cit., p. 156.

BUSH'S WAR

Blood for oil? A closer look at the history of Iraqi-American relations can tell what is really at stake. Just how much have the interests of U.S. oil corporations influenced the government's policies and actions, including the invasion of Iraq? To whose benefit are we risking our soldiers, our national treasury, and our traditional alliances with other nations?

Following the defeat of the Ottoman Turks, England and France artificially created the nation of Iraq at the end of World War I when they occupied the Middle East as League of Nations' Mandates. Arbitrarily drawing lines on maps back in Europe, they dismembered Kurdistan, leaving half in Turkey and half in "Iraq." Ignoring other tribal boundaries, they created the nation of Iraq composed of Kurds, Sunnis and Shiites, and which for a while included Kuwait. They installed Feisal, son of Hussein of Mecca, to reign over their creation, and they installed another son, Abdullah, to rule Trans Jordan. Hussein had been an ally in the war against the Turks; however, he lost out to Ibn Saud for control of Arabia.

In 1920, there was a national uprising against English rule in Iraq. Although the revolt involved both Shiites and Sunnis, the majority Shiite religious and tribal leaders played the leading role. The revolt was violently put down by the English, and thereafter they primarily relied upon the Sunnis to govern Iraq.

In 1932, after the mandate ended, Iraq became a sovereign country and joined the League of Nations; however, its oil fields and production facilities continued to be operated by foreign interests. In 1958, a popular revolution led by Abd al-Karim Qasim removed the king and ended foreign control.

Iraq, along with Britain, Turkey, Iran and Pakistan, was a member of the "Baghdad Pact" formed in the 1950s to defend the region against Soviet aggression.

When Qasim began to purchase arms from the Soviets and to install communists in his government, the CIA recruited Saddam

Hussein to assassinate him. Saddam botched the attempt and was slightly wounded in his calf by a fellow would-be assassin. He escaped through Syria into Beirut, where he was provided an apartment and was briefly trained by the CIA, who then moved him to Egypt and installed him in an apartment in the upper-class neighborhood of Dukki. He spent his time playing dominos in a local café and visiting his CIA contacts at the American Embassy. After Qasim was killed in a CIA sponsored coup by the Ba'ath Party, Saddam returned to Iraq where he became head of the al-Jihaz a-Khas, the Party's secret intelligence service.[376]

The Ba'athists did not consolidate their power until 1968, when General Ahmed Hassan Bakr became president and Saddam Hussein was appointed as his vice president. Saddam created a secret police force to identify and eliminate all political opponents.[377]

In 1972, General Bakr nationalized Iraq's oil resources and production facilities and quickly rose to the top of President Nixon's list of foreign enemies. The United States placed Iraq on its list of terrorist-sponsoring nations and began to arm the Iraqi Kurds. However, once Iraq ceded control over the Shatt-al-Arab waterway to America's ally the Shah of Iran, the flow of arms ceased.[378]

Coincident with the overthrow of the Shah of Iran in 1979, Saddam's personal fortunes improved. In one bloody day, he eliminated General Bakr and all of his Ba'athist rivals and seized total dictatorial powers. In 1980, encouraged by President Carter's National Security Advisor, Zbigniew Brzezinski, Saddam invaded Iran to regain control over the Shatt-al-Arab waterway. Although the Reagan campaign had made a secret deal with Iran to hold off on the release of the American Embassy hostages until after Reagan was sworn in, once he was in office, Reagan increasingly tilted toward Iraq and began to actively supply arms and intelligence to Saddam. In 1982, Iraq was removed from America's list of nations that support terrorism, and full diplomatic relations were restored in 1984.[379]

America became fully involved in Iraq's war against Iran after it appeared that Iran might defeat Saddam. The United

States supplied advanced weapons, satellite and AWACS intelligence, and helped plan and evaluate air strikes. Moreover, there is substantial evidence that the Reagan administration, which included Vice President Bush, was fully aware of and condoned the regular use of chemical weapons against Iran.[380] Directly, and through other countries such as Chile,[381] the United States authorized the sale to Iraq of poisonous chemicals and biological viruses, including anthrax and bubonic plague.[382] The United Nations inspection teams later found documents showing that Iraq dropped over 13,000 chemical bombs during the war.

In 1984, Reagan sent Donald Rumsfeld as his special envoy to shake Saddam's hand and to tell him that the United States government "recognizes Iraq's current disadvantage in a war of attrition since Iran has access to the gulf while Iraq does not (and that the United States) would regard any major reversal of Iraq's fortunes as a strategic defeat for the west." Rumsfeld wrote to Secretary of State George Shultz, "I added that the U.S. had no interest in an Iranian victory; to the contrary, we would not want Iran's influence expanded at the expense of Iraq."[383]

In 1986, Reagan sent a secret message to Saddam through Vice President Bush urging Iraq to increase its air attacks and bombings of Iran. However, Reagan was playing both sides, and he approved the covert sale of 1,000 TOW missiles to Iran and the secret transfer of the purchase money to the Nicaragua Contras.

Vice President Bush also took a secret message in 1986 to Saudi King Fahd and asked him to pressure OPEC to raise prices. The Saudis complied with the request and raised the price of oil to $18 a barrel, resulting in higher gas prices in the United States and greater profits for American oil companies.[384]

To facilitate Iraq's shipment of oil through the Persian Gulf where Iran was bombing neutral Kuwaiti tankers, the United States "reflagged" the tankers with American registration and deployed the U.S. Navy to protect them.[385]

In 1987, Vice President Bush met with Iraq's ambassador to the United States, Nizar Hamdoon, and informed him that Iraq would be allowed to purchase dual-use technology, which could be used for military purposes.[386]

With the assistance of the CIA, U.S. military intelligence, and Saudi AWACS surveillance aircraft, Saddam was able to avoid defeat and reach an agreement with Iran in 1988 to end the war, which had consumed a million lives.

The next year, in 1989, President Bush Sr. signed a top-secret directive ordering closer relations with Iraq and providing for the delivery of $1 billion in aid over the objections of several federal agencies.[387]

Iraq's economy was in shambles, world oil prices were falling, and Saddam blamed Kuwait for his inability to earn more oil revenues. On July 25, 1990, Saddam met with U.S. Ambassador April Glaspie regarding his dispute with Kuwait, which Iraq claimed was an historical part of Iraq. Glaspie told Saddam, "I have direct instructions from President Bush to improve our relations with Iraq. We have considerable sympathy for your quest for higher oil prices, the immediate cause of your confrontation with Kuwait." Saddam stated he would "give up all of the Shatt (waterway) to defend our claims on Kuwait to keep the whole of Iraq in the shape we wish it to be." In other words, he wished Kuwait to be a part of Iraq. When Saddam asked what the United States' opinion was regarding this, Glaspie answered, "We have no opinion on your Arab-Arab conflicts, such as your dispute with Kuwait. Secretary (of State James) Baker has directed me to emphasize the instruction, first given to Iraq in the 1960's, that the Kuwait issue is not associated with America."[388]

Why would Bush Sr. do this? The answer is simple. Higher oil prices would also prop up American oil companies and increase their profits.

On August 3, 1990, apparently trusting in Bush Sr.'s lack of concern, Saddam invaded and occupied Kuwait, threatening Saudi Arabia and America's Middle East oil supply. The United Nations condemned the invasion and imposed economic sanctions that cut off 70 percent of Iraq's food supply. Acting pursuant to a United Nations resolution, an international coalition of military forces led by the United States deployed 400,000 troops in the region. On January 14, 1991, following an ignored ultimatum, the coalition launched a bombing blitz against Iraq that lasted for 42 days. The air assault had five basic targets, one of which was "population will." The Iraqi civilian infrastructure, including electricity, water, and sanitation, was almost entirely wiped out to "degrade the will of the civilian population."[389]

When Saddam continued to refuse to leave Kuwait, a ground invasion commenced on February 23, 1991; three days later Saddam abandoned Kuwait, and Iraq agreed to a cease-fire on February 28, 1991.

During the three-day invasion, thousands of Iraqi soldiers, most of them conscripts and reserves armed with rifles, had been deployed in World War I style trenches along Iraq's border. Although some of them were able to surrender before the mechanized invasion swept around and over them, thousands were buried alive as Abrams battle tanks, equipped with huge front plows, swept along both flanks of approximately 70 miles of trenches, pouring avalanches of sand down upon the Iraqi soldiers. The tanks were followed by combat earthmovers that filled in and smoothed over the trenches creating unmarked mass graves.[390]

The Geneva Convention prohibits "denial of quarter," that is, refusing to accept an enemy's offer of surrender. Following the war, then Secretary of Defense Dick Cheney justified the live burials in his report to Congress as being "a gap in the law of war in defining precisely when surrender takes effect or how it may be accomplished. ... Because of these uncertainties and the need to minimize loss of U.S. lives, military necessity required that the assault ... be conducted with maximum speed and violence."

The United States refused to disclose the location of the burials and has never officially published the numbers of military and civilian deaths in Iraq resulting from the Gulf War.[391] When later asked, Colin Powell stated it was not something he was particularly interested in. During the Gulf War, as many as 100,000 military personnel and 15,000 civilians died.[392]   Do you feel our government acted honorably in its failure to comply with the rules of war? Does it bother you that our government may have committed war crimes?

During the air assault, President Bush Sr. had urged the Iraqi people to rise up against Saddam, and following the cease-fire, there were rebellions by the Kurds in the north and the Shiites in the south. These revolts were violently put down by Saddam after Bush Sr. allowed him to fly his helicopters across U.S. lines to attack the rebels. Tens of thousands were killed and were buried in mass graves. When elements of the Republican Guard rose up against Saddam, they were not allowed access to their surrendered weapons. Once Bush Sr. failed to act, Saddam violently crushed all resistance to his rule.[393]

The United States, England, and France imposed, without the authorization of the United Nations, a "no-fly" zone in the north and south of Iraq.   France later withdrew from enforcement of the zone; however, the United States and England continued to fly at will over the zones and to destroy any radar installations that sought to "lock on" their planes.[394]

In response to criticism of Bush Sr.'s failure to remove Saddam, then Secretary of Defense Dick Cheney explained on April 13, 1991, why they had not tried to impose a regime change on Iraq during the Gulf War: "If you're going to go in and try to topple Saddam Hussein, you have to go to Baghdad. Once you've got Baghdad, it's not clear what you will do with it. It's not clear what kind of government you would put in place of the one that's currently there now. Is it going to be a Shia regime, a Sunni regime or a Kurdish regime? Or one that tilts toward the Ba'athists, or one that tilts toward the Islamic fundamentalists?   How much credibility is that government going to have if it's set up by the United States military when it's there? How long does the United States military have to stay to protect the people that sign on for the government, and what happens to it once we leave?"[395] Remember these words.

To end the Gulf War, Saddam agreed to eliminate all weapons of mass destruction and to allow verification inspections by the United Nations. In the meantime, the United Nations economic sanctions were to continue.   Because of the sanctions, and certainly because of the priorities set by Saddam, there were significant delays in obtaining spare parts to repair Iraq's infrastructure, including its power grid, water treatment plants and sanitation systems, much of which was destroyed in the air attacks. Moreover, the population was denied access to adequate food supplies and essential medicines. UNICEF has estimated that as many as a million Iraqis died as a result of the sanctions, and that 500,000 of them were children.[396]

Between April 14 and April 16, 1993, Bush Sr. visited Kuwait, ostensibly to commemorate the Gulf War victory. He was accompanied by two of his sons and his former Secretary of State, James Baker, who was there to arrange contracts for Enron to rebuild Kuwait's damaged power plants. Neil Bush tagged along because he wanted a part of the fees to operate Enron's power plants, and Marvin Bush wanted to sell an electronic security system to Kuwait on behalf of a Washington firm.[397]

After Bush and his commercial entourage left, the Kuwait government arrested 17 persons and accused them of having plotted to kill Bush Sr. using a car bomb. The CIA concluded that Saddam likely directed a plot to kill Bush Sr., and President Clinton launched a cruise missile attack against the building in Baghdad that housed the Iraqi intelligence service. The attack killed eight persons, including one of Iraq's most gifted artists. In an extensive article published on November 1, 1993, reporter Seymour M. Hersh found that the "government's case against Iraq–as it has been outlined in public, anyway–is seriously flawed."[398]

Between the end of the war in 1992 and 1998, the United Nations conducted intensive and intrusive inspections throughout Iraq and was able to verify that Iraq had destroyed virtually all of its mass destruction capability, including all factories used to produce nuclear, chemical and biological weapons and all long-range missiles. What Iraq did not destroy, the inspection teams did. Given the fact that chemicals and biologicals used in weapons degrade with time and become harmless within five years, and without factories to replace the materials, it is relatively certain that Iraq ceased to have a weapons capability.

Initially, Saddam refused to allow Americans to be included on the inspection teams; however, he relented, and CIA agents were included on all inspection teams, as they had valuable information useful to the inspection mission. However, the CIA ultimately took over the signals intelligence program and used it to directly spy on Saddam and his government.

Matters came to a head in 1998 when Richard Butler, the UN's chief inspector was encouraged by the U.S. to "carry out very sensitive inspections that had nothing to do with disarmament but had everything to do with provoking the Iraqis." Iraq agreed to a set of "Modalities for Sensitive Site Inspections;" however, Butler insisted on unrestricted access to the Ba'ath Party headquarters in violation of the Modalities. When Saddam balked, Butler ordered the inspectors to leave the country to clear the way for a U.S. bombing attack. The Iraqis did not order the inspectors to leave.[399]

On December 16, 1998, on the eve of his impeachment trial, President Clinton announced "Operation Desert Fox" by U.S. and British forces to "attack Iraq's nuclear, chemical and biological weapons programs." Over the next four days, there were repeated air strikes in central Iraq. However, none ever targeted weapons of mass destruction, because no such weapons could be identified. Instead, Iraq's conventional military assets were targeted, along with its industrial infrastructure. The inspectors did not return to Iraq, and over the next three years, U.S. and British forces continued to fly at will in the no-fly zones and to bomb radar targets.[400]

Meanwhile, back in the United States, President Clinton was acquitted in his impeachment trial; Vice President Gore received the Democratic nomination; and the American people voted to elect him. The Supreme Court gave the presidency to the losing candidate, Bush Jr., who came to office determined to make up for his father's failures in Iraq and to extend and consolidate the United States' power over the Middle East and Central Asia.

An Ideological History of Bush's Never-Ending Preemptive War

In 1986, Irving Kristol, co-editor of *The Public Interest* magazine, proposed a doctrine of "global unilateralism" that urged the United States to adopt a less risk averse policy and become "far less inhibited in its use of military power." He believed the U.S. would be better off acting alone than in concert with allies "who were hampered by a failure of will, a loss of faith in their own values, and a barely submerged hostility toward Jews–which they manifested in an incurable hostility to Israel." Irving Kristol is considered to be the "godfather" of neoconservatism, and is the actual father of William Kristol, who served as Vice President Dan Quayle's chief of staff. William Kristol is editor of *The Weekly Standard* magazine, and is one of America's most ardent "neocons."[401]

In 1991, shortly after failing to remove Saddam overtly, President Bush Sr. signed a secret directive ordering the CIA to conduct a covert operation to overthrow him. The CIA employed a public relations firm and spent more than $23 million producing videos and comic books ridiculing Saddam and broadcasting radio programs over Iraqi airwaves mocking his government. None of these were effective; however, the firm helped organize the Iraqi National Congress (INC) to merge various groups who opposed Saddam. The CIA appointed Ahmed Chalabi as the head of the INC in 1992, although he had been criminally convicted in 1989 in Jordan and was wanted to serve a 22-year prison term for fraud and embezzlement of $70 million. The CIA channeled $12 million to the INC between 1992 and 1996, even though Chalabi failed to properly account for the funds.[402]

In 1992, Paul Wolfowitz was working on a policy paper for then Secretary of Defense Cheney and included arguments for an invasion of Iraq in a draft of the "Defense Policy Guidance." The invasion proposal was leaked to the media, and President Bush Sr. publicly rejected it.[403]

In 1996, Richard Perle was working for Benjamin Netanyahu, who was seeking election as Israel's prime minister. Perle co-authored a study, "A Clean Break," in which he argued for a "focus on removing Saddam Hussein from power in Iraq–an important Israeli strategic objective in its own right–as a means of foiling Syria."[404]

In 1996, William Kristol co-authored a document entitled, "Toward a Neo-Reaganite Foreign Policy,"[405] which became an inspiration for the neocon movement. The next year, Kristol helped establish The Project for the New American Century (PNAC) at the American Enterprise Institute, a conservative think tank. Other founders included Dick Cheney, Donald Rumsfeld, Paul Wolfowitz, Newt Gingrich, Jeb Bush, and Richard Perle (an associate of Chalabi).* PNAC advocated taking a harder line with Iraq and lobbied for higher military spending in a return to the "peace through strength" policies of the Reagan administration.[406]

In 1998, Congress was considering the Iraqi Liberation Act, which endorsed a "regime change" in Iraq as U.S. policy and authorized $97 million to help opposition groups make the change. PNAC lobbied for its passage, and Paul Wolfowitz testified that the act would get rid of Saddam without the necessity of U.S. troops, saying "Help the Iraqi people remove him from power. However–and I think this is very important–the estimate that it would take a major invasion with U.S. ground forces seriously overestimates Saddam Hussein."[407]

In 1998, some of the PNAC founders, including Rumsfeld, Wolfowitz, Kristol, Perle and others, wrote to President Clinton and urged him "to take the necessary steps, including military steps [in Iraq] to protect our vital interest in the Gulf." They argued that Clinton "should aim, above all, at the removal of Saddam Hussein's regime from power."[408]

---

* Many neocons have also been labeled as "Chicken Hawks," because they successfully managed to avoid actual military service, including George W. and Jeb Bush, Cheney, Perle, Wolfowitz, William Kristol, and Rush Limbaugh. (Lobe, Jim, "The Chicken Hawk Factor," AlterNet.org.)

In concert with the 2000 presidential campaign, PNAC published a report entitled "Rebuilding America's Defenses: Strategy, Forces and Resources for a New Century" as a military battle plan for world domination.* The report was built upon the Department of Defense's published policy in 1992 under Cheney for "maintaining U.S. preeminence, precluding the rise of a great power rival, and shaping the international security order in line with American principles and interests."[409] According to PNAC, as the "world's only superpower," which "faces no global rival, America's grand strategy should aim to preserve and extend this advantageous position as far into the future as possible." The report called for the development of "a new family of nuclear weapons ... safer and more effective nuclear weapons" required "in targeting the very deep, underground bunkers that are being built by many of our potential adversaries." Conventional nuclear weapons and ICBM's were to "provide a secure basis for U.S. power projection around the world."[410]

To accomplish America's mission, the report stated that the United States must "perform the 'constabulary' duties associated with shaping the security environment in critical regions." The report called for the deployment of U.S. troops throughout the world as the "first line of defense" of America's "security perimeter," to serve as "the cavalry on the new American frontier." The report recommended new permanent and "forward operating" military bases in the Middle East and Southeast Asia. In the Persian Gulf, from an "American perspective, the value of such bases would endure even should Saddam pass from the scene ... and retaining forward-based forces in the region would ... be an essential element in U.S. security strategy given the longstanding American interests in

---

* PNAC called for the U.S. to "Control the New 'International Commons' of Space and 'Cyberspace,' and pave the way for the creation of a new military service–U.S. Space Forces–with the mission of space control." The report envisioned a world-wide deployment of an "effective, robust, layered, global system of missile defenses" based on an array of "global reconnaissance and targeting satellites ... linked to a global network of space-based interceptors (or space-based lasers)." ("Rebuilding America's Defenses," pp. v, 54.)

the region." The report goes on, "The United States has for decades sought to play a more permanent role in Gulf regional security. While the unresolved conflict with Iraq provides the immediate justification, the need for a substantial American force presence in the Gulf transcends the issue of the regime of Saddam Hussein."[411] Read "American interests" as "O-I-L" and "immediate justification" as an excuse for invasion.

As soon as he took office, Bush established the removal of Saddam as an immediate priority. The subject was discussed at his very first National Security Council meeting and a memorandum was circulated that outlined a "Plan for post Saddam Iraq."[412]

Upon hearing about the 9/11 attack, Rumsfeld made the following notes that were later leaked to the news media: "Best info fast. Judge whether good enough hit S.H. [Saddam Hussein] at same time. Not only UBL [Osama bin Laden]. Go massive. Sweep it all up. Things related and not."[413] Crazy or not, it is clear that Iraq was a target from the beginning and had been for a long time.

The day after the 9/11 attack, Rumsfeld and Wolfowitz pressured Bush to target Iraq in the first battles against terrorism, and Wolfowitz argued in a National Security Council meeting that Iraq was an easier target than Afghanistan.[414] Rumsfeld complained there were insufficient targets in Afghanistan and that the U.S. should consider bombing Iraq where there were better targets. Bush replied that the U.S. should change Iraq's government, not just strike it with cruise missiles.[415]

On September 12, 2001, Bush instructed Clarke "to go back over everything, everything. See if Saddam did this. See if he's linked in any way." Clarke responded, 'But, Mr. President, al Qaeda did this.... We have looked several times for state sponsorship of al Qaeda and not found any real linkages to Iraq." Bush again directed, "Look into Iraq, Saddam."[416]

Clarke complied with Bush's direction and developed an official position on the relationship between Iraq and al Qaeda. "All agencies and departments agreed there was no cooperation between the two. A memorandum to that effect was sent up to the President,..."[417]

At a National Security Council meeting on September 15, 2001, Secretary of State Powell spoke against starting a war with Iraq. He argued that since we weren't going after Iraq before 9/11 and there was no evidence that it was responsible for the attack, the coalition he was building would "view it as a bait and switch — it's not what they signed up to do."[418] Richard Clarke thanked Powell for his support saying, "Having been attacked by al Qaeda, for us now to go bombing Iraq in response would be like our invading Mexico after the Japanese attacked us at Pearl Harbor."[419] Powell later tells General Hugh Shelton, "What the hell! What are these guys thinking about? Can't you get these guys back in the box?"[420]

On September 20, 2001, PNAC sent a letter to Bush encouraging him to extend the war to Iraq, as well as destroying the al Qaeda network.* He was also urged to take measures against Iran, Syria, Lebanon and the Palestinian Authority.[421]

On September 20, 2001, Bush hosted British Prime Minister Blair and England's Ambassador to the U.S., Sir Christopher Meyer, at a private White House dinner where the subject of discussion was the U.S. intention to remove Saddam Hussein from power. According to Meyer, Blair told Bush he should not get distracted from dealing with the Taliban and al Qaeda in Afghanistan. Bush agreed saying, "We must deal with this first. But when we have dealt with Afghanistan, we must come back to Iraq. Even though forewarned, Blair continued to insist that "no decisions had been taken" regarding Iraq until just before the subsequent invasion.[422]

On January 8, 2002, the Pentagon provided Congress with a secret report that detailed its contingency plans to use nuclear weapons as a tool for fighting wars, as well as for deterrence. The Pentagon had to be prepared to use nuclear weapons against hardened targets designed to withstand conventional attack or "in the event of surprising military developments."[423]

---

* The letter was signed by 20 PNAC members, all but one of whom are Chicken Hawks.

So we establish all these new military bases where we may not be entirely welcome and then we go nuclear if they try to throw us out and we get into trouble? Somewhere along the way, we forgot the principles of "how to win friends and influence people" — to put it mildly.

In early February 2002, in response to rumors that U.S. attacks on Iraq were inevitable, Richard Perle, who had become one of Rumsfeld's senior advisors, stated, "I don't think there's anything Saddam Hussein could do that would convince us there's no longer any danger coming from Iraq." He said that Bush was on "a very clear path" in the direction of war with Iraq.[424]

In March 2002, Cheney confidentially informed a group of U.S. senators that "The question was no longer if the U.S. would attack Iraq." The only question was when.[425]

On June 1, 2002, President Bush spoke at the West Point graduation ceremony, telling cadets that "The only path to safety is action, and this nation will act." He said that all Americans must be "ready for preemptive action when necessary to defend our liberty and to defend our lives." "If we wait for threats to fully materialize, we will have waited too long."[426]

On September 20, 2002, Bush released "The National Security Strategy of the United States," in which enemies are to be prevented from even threatening us with weapons of mass destruction. In the future, the United States will be defended "by identifying and destroying the threat before it reaches our borders. While the United States will constantly strive to enlist the support of the international community, we will not hesitate to act alone, if necessary, to exercise our right of self defense by acting preemptively against such terrorists."

While in the past, the legitimacy of preemption was predicated upon the existence of "an imminent threat–most often a visible mobilization of ... forces preparing to attack," Bush now declared: "We must adapt the concept of imminent threat to the capabilities and objectives of today's adversaries." And, "The greater the threat, the greater is the risk of inaction– and the more compelling the case for taking anticipatory action to defend ourselves, even if uncertainty remains as to the time and place of the enemy's attack."[427] What then is the standard, and who judges us if we are wrong?

In 1953, after he reviewed plans to launch a preventive war against the Soviet Union, President Eisenhower stated, "All of us have heard this term 'preventive war' since the earliest days of Hitler. I recall that is about the first time I heard it. In this day and time ... I don't believe there is such a thing; and, frankly, I wouldn't even listen to anyone seriously that came in and talked about such a thing."[428]

As justification for Bush's War, the White House relied upon misleading information provided by Chalabi and the INC over the more accurate intelligence provided by the CIA. The Pentagon brought pressure on the CIA to produce more supportive intelligence reports; however, the CIA viewed Chalabi as being ineffectual and the INC as corrupt. Vincent Cannistraro, a former senior CIA official, stated that the INC's intelligence wasn't "reliable at all. ... Much of it is propaganda ... telling the Defense Department what they want to hear ... they make no distinction between intelligence and propaganda, using alleged informants and defectors who say what Chalabi wants them to say, [creating] cooked information that goes right into presidential and vice-presidential speeches."[429]

Two days before Baghdad fell, the Pentagon flew members of the "Free Iraqi Forces," the military wing of the INC, into Iraq. Chalabi set up shop with his daughter in the Hunting Club, a former hangout of Saddam's son, Uday.[430] On May 5, 2003, the U.S. administrator, General Jay Garner, appointed Chalabi as one of five members of the interim government.

Why was all the attention paid to Iraq? Why were so many members of the Bush administration so determined to fight a war against Iraq, and why was it so important to get Chalabi into power? The answer should not even require a clue, but let's spell it out. Iraq has proven "O-I-L" reserves of 112 billion barrels, second only to Saudi Arabia in the world.[431] Chalabi and the INC believe that Iraq's oil resources should be explored and extracted by a private consortium of oil companies, including British Petroleum, ChevronTexaco, and ExxonMobil.[432]

In September 2002, Ariel Cohen of the Heritage Foundation, which has close links with the Bush administration, presented "The future of a Post-Saddam Iraq: A Blueprint for American Involvement," which lays out a plan for the privatization of Iraq's oil industry, and a warning that French, Russian, and Chinese oil contracts would not be honored by the new INC-led government. Cohen's proposal would split up the Iraqi National Oil Company into three large companies, generally in line with the ethnic and geographic divisions of Shia, Sunni, and Kurd.[433] So much for self-determination.

In October 2002, Chalabi met with the executives of three U.S. oil companies to negotiate the division of Iraq's oil reserves once Saddam was eliminated. Although Iraq has existing oil contracts with Russia, France, and China, Chalabi has stated that he would reward the United States with lucrative oil contracts for removing Saddam, and that "American companies will have a big shot at Iraqi oil."[434]

In addition to simple greed on the part of the oil companies, the neocons want to destroy OPEC, which they believe to be evil, i.e., incompatible with American business interests. Strategically, they want to reduce the United States' reliance upon Saudi oil and diminish Saudi Arabia's influence on world oil prices through its dominance of OPEC. In their view, once the oil starts flowing from an Iraq controlled by the United States, it will be much more difficult for OPEC to control prices.

On January 16, 2003, the *Wall Street Journal* reported that government officials had been meeting informally with executives from Halliburton, Schlumberger, ExxonMobil, ChevronTexaco and ConocoPhillips to plan the expansion of Iraq's oil production once Bush's War secured the fields.[435]

Any question about Bush's business intentions in Iraq seems to have been laid to rest on July 17, 2003, when Judicial Watch, a conservative public interest group that investigates and prosecutes government corruption and abuse, revealed the product of its Freedom of Information Act lawsuit against the

Department of Energy.* Surrendered documents from Cheney's energy task force included a map of Iraqi oilfields, pipelines, refineries and terminals, as well as two charts detailing Iraqi oil and gas projects, and "Foreign Suitors for Iraqi Oilfield Contracts."[436] Perhaps now we can better understand why Cheney continues to be so afraid to reveal the participants and proceedings of his task force. Moreover, is it any surprise that, following the invasion, the Pentagon was more interested in protecting Iraq's oil infrastructure than its archeological treasures?[437]

Deputy Defense Secretary Paul Wolfowitz eliminated any doubt as to Bush's intentions in Iraq when he candidly answered a reporter's question about why North Korea, a nuclear power, was being treated differently than Iraq, where no weapons of mass destruction were located. Wolfowitz stated, "Let's look at it simply. The most important difference between North Korea and Iraq is that economically, we just had no choice in Iraq. The country swims on a sea of oil."[438]

More than the oil, there is yet another reason why Bush and his gang of neocons were so eager to go to war with Iraq. According to Olivier Roy, a specialist on the Islamic world at the Centre National de la Récherche Scientifique, the "professional thinkers" at the American Enterprise Institute believed "the Israeli-Palestinian stalemate is America's most worrisome foreign entanglement, and can be broken only if the overall existing order in the Middle East is shaken up first." Roy goes on to observe:

---

* Cheney continued to refuse to reveal who met with his energy task force and appealed the District Court's order. After the U.S. Court of Appeals in Washington upheld the order, U.S. Solicitor General Theodore B. Olson filed an appeal at the U.S. Supreme Court. On December 15, 2003, the Supreme Court agreed to hear the appeal. Three weeks later, Cheney flew with Justice Antonin Scalia on Air Force Two to a duck hunting expedition in Louisiana. Should Scalia recuse himself from hearing the case? He says no. "I do not think my impartiality could reasonably be questioned?" (Savage, David G., "Senators Inquire of Justices' Recusal Rules," *Los Angeles Times*, January 23, 2004, p. A10.)

In this sense, the rationale for the military campaign in Iraq was not that Iraq was the biggest threat but, on the contrary, that it was the weakest and hence the easiest to take care of. The invasion was largely aimed at demonstrating America's political will and commitment to go to war. Reshaping the Middle East does not mean changing borders, but rather threatening existing regimes through military pressure and destabilizing them with calls for democratization.

After Baghdad's fall, Tehran, Damascus and Riyadh should understand that America is back. The Israelis, for their part, are now insisting that the Iranian nuclear program be dealt with immediately. Pentagon officials hint that Syria is the next target.[439]

In late 2003, Bush poured gasoline on the flames of endless war in the Middle East by giving Israel 100 Harpoon cruise missiles, which Israel immediately equipped with nuclear weapons and installed aboard three submarines purchased from Germany. These missiles provide Israel with the ability to strike any of its enemies in the Middle East, including all sites where Iran may be working on nuclear weapons.

According to a story in the *Los Angeles Times*, "Arab diplomats and U.N. officials said Israel's steady enhancement of its secret nuclear arsenal, and U.S. silence about it, has increased the desire of Arab states for similar weapons. 'The presence of a nuclear weapon program in the region that is not under international safeguards gives other countries the spur to develop weapons of mass destruction,' said Nabil Fahmy, Egypt's ambassador to the United States. 'Any future conflict becomes more dangerous.'"[440]

Relying upon Bush's doctrine of preemptive war, a spokesman for Israel's foreign ministry insisted, "Israel views every state that is harboring terrorist organizations and the leaders of those terrorist organizations who are attacking innocent citizens of the state of Israel as legitimate targets of self defense."[441]

In February 2003, Undersecretary of State John Bolton reassured Israeli officials that America would deal with Syria, Iran, and North Korea after it finished with Iraq. He later argued to Congress that Syria's possession of chemical and biological weapons posed a threat to the stability in the Middle East. One CIA official said that the neocons "want to go there next."[442]

William Kristol would seem to agree. He writes, "President Bush is committed, pretty far down the road. The logic of events says you can't go halfway. You can't liberate Iraq, then quit."[443]

Richard Perle goes even further, "This is total war, ... We are fighting a variety of enemies. There are lots of them out there. All this talk about first we are going to do Afghanistan, then we will do Iraq ... this is entirely the wrong way to go about it. If we just let our vision of the world go forth, and we embrace it entirely and we don't try to piece together clever diplomacy, but just wage a total war ... our children will sing great songs about us years from now."[444]

When Rumsfeld was asked what would constitute a victory in Bush's War, he stated, "Now, what is victory? I say that victory is persuading the American people and the rest of the world that this is not a quick matter that's going to be over in a month or a year or even five years. It is something that we need to do so that we can continue to live in a world with powerful weapons and with people who are willing to use those powerful weapons. And we can do that as a country. And that would be a victory, in my view."[445]

Thus, Bush's War may never end and victory becomes our approval. On another occasion Rumsfeld said the war could last as long as the cold war, perhaps for 50 years, and Cheney said it could go on for a "long, long time, perhaps indefinitely."[446]

Bush himself says, "Our war with terror begins with al Qaeda, but it does not end ... until every terrorist group of global reach has been found stopped and defeated." In doing so, Bush doesn't mind if we alienate the rest of the world, "At some point, we may be the only ones left. ... That's OK with me. We are America."[447]

Thus it was that Bush's endless war came to be invented. Is this the kind of world you want to live in? Have you ever read *1984*? If not, you should. You're not stupid! Get the truth.

The Propaganda and Politics of Bush's War

During his trial for war crimes at Nuremberg, Hermann Goering stated, "Of course the people don't want war. But after all, it's the leaders of the country who determine the policy, and it's always a simple matter to drag the people along whether it's a democracy, a fascist dictatorship, or a parliament, or a communist dictatorship. Voice or no voice, the people can always be brought to the bidding of the leaders. That is easy. All you have to do is tell them they are being attacked, and denounce the pacifists for lack of patriotism, and exposing the country to greater danger. It works the same way in every country."[448] And it has worked that way in America for the past three years.

Shortly after 9/11, Rumsfeld established the Office of Strategic Influence (OSI) in the Department of Defense to provide news items, including false information, to foreign media organizations and the Internet. OSI was provided with a multimillion-dollar budget to use disinformation and other covert activities, any of which could easily flow back to the United States and be republished and rebroadcast to domestic audiences as fact.

Following an outpouring of opposition on editorial pages and in Congress, Rumsfeld closed down the operation, saying he had never seen its charter. Bush promised, "We'll tell the American people the truth." Another pair of lies. In a later moment of candor, Rumsfeld said, "And then there was the Office of Strategic Influence. You may recall that. And 'Oh, my goodness gracious, isn't that terrible, Henny Penny, the sky is going to fall.' I went down that next day and said fine, if you want to savage this thing, fine, I'll give you the corpse. There's the name. You can have the name, but I'm going to keep doing every single thing that needs to be done, and I have."[449]

In the summer of 2002, Bush's chief of staff, Andrew Card, told the *New York Times*, "From a marketing point of view, you don't introduce new products in August." Card described a "meticulously planned strategy to persuade the public, the Congress, and the allies, of the need to confront the threat from Saddam Hussein."[450] Far better to launch the campaign on a symbolic date, like September 11th and in conjunction with the Congressional mid-term elections.

The White House created an Office of Global Communications and funded it with $200 million to use advertising techniques to persuade targeted groups that Saddam must be removed. There was a daily meeting to plan media strategy and to keep everyone on message. The White House instructed all civilian and military employees to refer to the invasion as a "war of liberation," and to refer to Iraqi paramilitary forces as "death squads."[451]

An observer of Rove's tricks over the years shared his thoughts about Rove's use of provocative language in politics: "it was starting to look like we couldn't win the war on terrorism. Rather than lose that war we redefine that war. Suddenly it wasn't the people who were terrorists who killed us. It was evil itself. They [Bush and Rove] can apply that to anyone they want. Tom Daschle or Hussein."[452] Another observer added, "Timing is everything in politics and it certainly is helping. ... I think it happened slowly through the Pentagon and [Paul] Wolfowitz leading and Cheney right there with him and Karl put his arms around it and said, 'Yeah, this is gonna help us.'"[453] A merging of interests, "Chicken Hawks" plus "Turd Blossom" equals war without end.

Propaganda, or media manipulation, is used to influence the thinking of others. We have come to rely upon public opinion polls to gauge the results, and there are two sets of data that seem relevant here. On the morning of September 11, 2001, Bush's standing in opinion polls hovered at 50 percent, but with the crisis, it jumped to 82 percent within two days.[454] If only we had known then what Bush had known when.

Shortly before Congress authorized Bush's War against Iraq in October 2002, a CBS news poll found that 51 percent of Americans believed that Saddam was involved in the 9/11 attacks. Later, the Pew Research Center found that two thirds of

Americans agreed that "Saddam Hussein helped the terrorists in the September 11 attacks."[455] (The percentage later rose to approximately 70 percent, but more about that later.)

Another poll in January 2003 found that 44 percent of Americans believed "most" or "some" of the 9/11 terrorists were Iraqi citizens. Only 17 percent were aware that none were. From this we can see that Bush's propaganda had produced results.[456] We came to believe something that even Bush had never said. Of course, Saddam had nothing at all to do with the 9/11 attacks.

However, by March 14, 2003, Bush's approval ratings had again fallen to 53 percent, essentially where it was before 9/11. Then, once he declared Bush's War on March 18, 2003, he got the crisis bounce back up to 68 percent.[457]

Common sense tells us that the greater knowledge we have, the better decisions we make. However, war propaganda is not used to inform people; rather, it is intended to mislead people into believing that war is in their best interest. In 1991, a study at the University of Massachusetts correlated public opinion and knowledge of basic facts about the Gulf War. It found "a strong correlation between knowledge and opposition to the war. The more people know, in other words, the less likely they were to support the war policy."[458]

Were you misled by Bush's propaganda? Did you come to believe that Saddam was somehow responsible for the 9/11 attacks? You're not stupid! Get the truth.

A Litany of Lies

Once Bush decided to go to war against Iraq, he and senior members of his administration constantly lied to and misled the American public about Iraq's possession of weapons of mass destruction and its relationship to al Qaeda.

In July 2002, Richard Perle said, "It is likely that chemical weapons, biological weapons in the possession of the Iraqis derived during the Cold War from the Soviet Union, are now being disseminated to terrorists."[459] In truth, if Saddam had hidden such weapons and had provided them to these terrorists, it is just as likely that they would have used them on him as on us, since they despised him and his corrupt secular regime.

In August 2002, Rumsfeld lied in saying it "is a fact that there are al Qaeda in a number of locations in Iraq." When asked in September 2002, Condoleezza Rice repeated the lie: "There is certainly evidence that al Qaeda people have been in Iraq. There is certainly evidence that Saddam Hussein cavorts with terrorists."[460] In fact, Greg Thielmann, a former official in the State Department's intelligence office, later said, "The al Qaeda connection and nuclear weapons issue were the only two ways that you could link Iraq to an imminent security threat to the U.S., and the administration was grossly distorting the intelligence on both things."[461]

It was not that the Bush administration was ignorant about the absence of Iraqi links with terrorism. Even his father's former National Security Advisor attempted to educate him. General Brent Scowcroft wrote in August 2002: "But there is scant evidence to tie Saddam to terrorist organizations, and even less to the September 11 attacks. Indeed Saddam's goals have little in common with the terrorists who threaten us, and there is little incentive for him to make common cause with them."[462]

In August 2002, Cheney said: "Many of us are convinced that Saddam Hussein will acquire nuclear weapons fairly soon."[463] He may have been convinced by his own self-delusion, but in truth, the CIA had absolutely no evidence that Iraq had or would soon have nuclear weapons. In fact, the *Washington Post* later reported that Cheney and his chief of staff repeatedly visited CIA headquarters and that some analysts "felt they were being pressured to make their assessments fit with the Bush administration's policy objectives."[464]

On August 26, 2002, Cheney lied: "Simply stated, there's no doubt that Saddam Hussein now has weapons of mass destruction. There is no doubt he is amassing them to use against our friends, against our allies, and against us."[465] The truth is that Saddam no longer possessed weapons of mass destruction. The fact is that Cheney knew his statements were untrue, because he had been pressuring intelligence analysts to alter their findings. Christian Westermann, a senior intelligence analyst at the State Department and an expert on biological and chemical weapons, later revealed that he had been pressured to alter his conclusions to conform to the administration's policy.[466]

In September 2002, Cheney lied, or was at best disingenuous, when he stated that "Mohamed Atta, who was the lead hijacker, did apparently travel to Prague on a number of occasions. And on at least one occasion, we have reporting that places him in Prague with a senior Iraqi intelligence official a few months before the attack on the World Trade Center." In truth, the CIA had concluded there was no evidence to support the "reporting," and U.S. intelligence and law enforcement officials actually believed that Atta wasn't even in Prague at the time. In fact, Czech President Vaclav Havel quietly told the White House in October there was no evidence to support the claim.[467]

On September 3, 2002, Rumsfeld lied, "It is the Iraqis that ended the inspections; that we know. We protested when the Iraqis threw the inspectors out. ... Would it be nice if they had not thrown the inspectors out? Yes, that would have been preferable."[468] In truth, the United Nations pulled the inspectors out for their own safety because the United States was preparing to bomb Iraq.

On September 7, 2002, Bush lied about a report issued by the International Atomic Energy Agency (IAEA): "I would remind you that when the inspectors first went to Iraq and were denied, finally denied access, a report came out of the Atomic–the IAEA–that they were six months away from developing a weapon. I don't know what more evidence we need."[469] The truth is that the IAEA never issued any such report. In fact, the IAEA issued a report in 1998 that said, "Based on all credible information to date, the IAEA has found no indication of Iraq having achieved its program goal of producing nuclear weapons or of Iraq having retained a physical capability for the production of weapon-useable nuclear material or having clandestinely obtained such material."[470]

To cover up for the first lie, the White House told another and said that Bush had really been referring to a 1991 IAEA report that said Iraq was within six months of building a nuclear weapon. However, the truth is that there was no such report.

Then, to cover up for the second lie, the White House told yet another and said that Bush was actually referring to an International Institute for Strategic Studies report that had concluded that Iraq could develop a nuclear bomb in as few as six months. However, the truth is that first, the report didn't actually say that, and second, it wasn't even issued until two days after Bush's speech.[471] (Is it time to say, "Liar, Liar, pants on fire?")

On September 8, 2002, Condoleezza Rice confirmed Iraq's attempt to purchase aluminum tubes that "are only suited for nuclear weapons programs, centrifuge programs. ... The problem here is that there will always be some uncertainty about how quickly he can acquire nuclear weapons, but we don't want the smoking gun to be a mushroom cloud."[472]

On September 8, 2002, Cheney said, "We don't have all the evidence [but evidence] tells us that he [Saddam] is in fact actively and aggressively seeking to acquire nuclear weapons."[473]

Regarding Iraq's nuclear weapons program, former U.N. weapons inspector Scott Ritter stated, "When I left Iraq in 1998, when the U.N. inspection program ended, the infrastructure and facilities had been 100 percent eliminated. There's no debate about that. All of their instruments and facilities had been destroyed. The weapons design facility had been destroyed. The production equipment had been hunted down and destroyed. ... We can say unequivocally that the industrial infrastructure needed by Iraq to produce nuclear weapons has been eliminated."[474]

On September 12, 2002, Bush addressed the delegates of the United Nations and said that what makes Saddam Hussein dangerous are his weapons. Bush then lied to them: "United Nations inspections [in the 1990s] ... revealed that Iraq likely maintains stockpiles of VX, mustard and other chemical agents and that the regime is rebuilding and expanding facilities capable of producing chemical weapons."[475]

The truth is that when U.N. inspectors were pulled out of Iraq in 1998, they may have had some lingering questions about the existence of hidden chemical weapons, but they did not know it as an established fact. In fact, Rolf Ekeus, the former executive chairman of the inspection program, stated in 2000, "UNSCOM was highly successful in identifying and eliminating Iraq's prohibited weapons–but to the degree that everything was destroyed. ... In my view, there are no large quantities of weapons."[476]

In the same speech, Bush lied to the delegates of the United Nations and to the world when he referred to Iraq's "continued appetite" for nuclear weapons. As evidence, he claimed that Saddam purchased thousands of high-strength aluminum tubes to be "used to enrich uranium for nuclear weapons." He stated, "Iraq has made several attempts to buy high-strength aluminum tubes used to enrich uranium for a nuclear weapon. Should Iraq acquire fissile material, it would be able to build a nuclear weapon within a year."

In fact, the unanimous opinion of Department of Energy experts was that the tubes in question were not intended for use in centrifuges, since aluminum had not been used is centrifuge construction since the 1950s, they were too long, the walls were excessively thick, and the diameters were too narrow. However, the experts were ordered by the White House to remain silent.[477]

In addition, the IAEA, in January 2003, stated that the size of the tubes was identical to those Iraq had used previously to make conventional artillery rockets. Powell later repeated the lie in his speech to the U.N. on February 5, 2003.[478]

On September 13, 2002, Rumsfeld said: "There's no debate in the world as to whether they have those weapons. ... We all know that. A trained ape knows that."[479]

On September 19, 2002, Rumsfeld told Congress that "There are a number of terrorist states pursuing weapons of mass destruction, but no terrorist state poses a greater or more immediate threat to the security of our people than the regime of Saddam Hussein and Iraq.[480]

On September 26, 2002, Rumsfeld lied when he said he had "bulletproof" evidence that Saddam and bin Laden were connected.[481] In fact, there was no such evidence, and Rumsfeld has yet to produce a smoking gun. In September 2003, Rumsfeld, in response to a question about a poll that showed up to 70 percent of Americans believing that Hussein was connected with 9/11, stated, "I've not seen any indication that would lead me to believe I could say that."[482]

On September 28, 2002, Bush said: "The Iraqi regime possesses biological and chemical weapons, is rebuilding the facilities to make more, and according to the British government, could launch a biological or chemical attack in as little as 45 minutes after the order is given."[483]

On October 7, 2002, Bush lied during a speech in Cincinnati regarding Saddam's nuclear weapons program, saying that Iraq was "rebuilding facilities at sites that have been part of its nuclear program in the past."[484] The truth is that when inspectors searched those sites a few weeks later, they found "At the majority of these sites, the equipment and laboratories have deteriorated to such a degree that the resumption of nuclear activities would require substantial renovation."[485]

Bush continued to lie during his Cincinnati speech when he stated that Saddam was a "significant danger to America," and that "Iraq could decide on any given day to provide a biological or chemical weapon to a terrorist group or individual terrorists. Alliance with terrorists could allow the Iraqi regime to attack America without leaving any fingerprints."[486]

In truth, CIA director George Tenet reported that "Baghdad for now appears to be drawing a line short of conducting terrorist attacks with conventional or CBW (chemical and biological weapons) against the United States. Tenet then went on to warn, "*Should Saddam conclude that a U.S.-led attack* [against Iraq] *could no longer be deterred, he probably would become much less constrained in adopting terrorist actions.*" Saddam might conclude "*that the extreme step of assisting Islamist terrorists in conducting a WMD attack against the United States would be his last chance to exact vengeance by taking a large number of victims with him.* (emphasis added)"[487]

On November 7, 2002, Bush was asked during a press conference about Tenet's warning. Bush stammered and lied:

"I'm sure that he said other sentences. ... I know George Tenet well. I meet with him every single day. He sees Saddam Hussein as a threat. I don't know what the context of that quote is. I'm telling you, the guy knows what I know, that he is a problem and we must deal with him. ... Well, if we don't do something he might attack us, and he might attack us with a more serious weapon. The man is a threat. ... He's a threat because he is dealing with al Qaeda."[488] In truth, the intelligence community had no such evidence, and Bush knew that Saddam was not involved in the 9/11 attacks.

According to a story in *USA Today*, Cheney and Rumsfeld had pressured the CIA to confirm reports that al Qaeda members were "hiding in Iraq with Saddam's blessings." The agency could not. Another story in the *Los Angeles Times* noted, "Senior Bush administration officials are pressuring CIA analysts to tailor their assessments of the Iraqi threat to help build a case against Saddam Hussein." Sources identified these officials as Rumsfeld and Wolfowitz.[489]

On November 20, 2002, Bush gave a speech in Prague in which he lied: "Our goal is to secure the peace through the comprehensive and verified disarmament of Iraq's weapons of mass destruction." Or, was Cheney lying when he said in early September, "The president made it clear that the goal of the United States is regime change."[490]

On December 2, 2002, Wolfowitz said that Bush's "determination to use force if necessary is because of the threat posed by Iraq's weapons of mass destruction."[491]

On December 5, 2002, Fleischer said: "The president of the United States and the secretary of defense would not assert as plainly and bluntly as they have that Iraq has weapons of mass destruction if it was not true, and if they did not have a solid basis for saying it."[492]

On December 12, 2002, Rumsfeld said: "It is clear that the Iraqis have weapons of mass destruction. The issue is not whether or not they have weapons of mass destruction."[493]

On January 7, 2003, Rumsfeld said: "There is no doubt in my mind but that they currently have chemical and biological weapons."[494]

On January 9, 2003, Fleischer said: "We know for a fact that there are weapons there."[495]

The truth of the matter is that back in September 2002, the Defense Intelligence Agency had reported, "There is no reliable information on whether Iraq is producing or stockpiling chemical weapons, or whether Iraq has–or will–establish its chemical warfare agent production facilities."[496]

On January 28, 2003, in his State of the Union speech, Bush stood before the American people, looked us in the eye, and once more lied to us about Saddam's possession of nuclear weapons. Even though he had earlier been caught in three different lies on the same subject, he again lied when he said that the IAEA "confirmed in the 1990's that Saddam Hussein had an advanced nuclear weapons development program."[497] In truth, the IAEA had maintained for years that it had destroyed Saddam's program.

Bush again lied about Iraq's purchase of the high-quality aluminum tubes "suitable for nuclear weapons production," even though the IAEA had already concluded that they were "not directly suitable" for the refining of uranium. Moreover, there was no secret about the acquisition, as Iraq had posted its purchase order on the Internet.[498]

Bush delivered his most deliberate lie when he said, "The British Government has learned that Saddam Hussein recently sought significant quantities of uranium from Africa." In truth, the CIA had informed the White House in March 2002 that it could not confirm the "Niger" allegations and had labeled the allegations as "highly dubious." In fact, the documents had been shown to be crude forgeries.[499]

In his speech to the United Nations on February 5, 2003, Secretary of State Colin Powell was untruthful when he described the "Khurmal" compound in northeastern Iraq allegedly operated by the Islamist terrorist group Ansar al-Islam as a "terrorist chemicals and poisons factory."[500] The truth is the "compound" consisted of a few dilapidated concrete outbuildings, with no evidence of chemicals whatsoever. Tragically, the nearby town of Khurmal was mistakenly bombed by cruise missiles in the first week of Bush's War, and 45 villagers were killed.[501]

The Ansar al-Islam group was formerly known as Jund al-Islam; it is a splinter of the Iranian-backed Islamic Unity Movement of Kurdistan. Moreover, the group was actually located in the Kurdish area outside of Saddam's control in the northern no-fly zone. In fact, the group was attacked and many were killed by the Kurds in early 2003 and the rest fled into Iran.[502] Since the commencement of Bush's War, it appears that Ansar and al Qaeda have begun to cooperate in their resistance to the invasion. Ansar may be providing its knowledge of the countryside and al Qaeda is providing explosives and volunteers to act as suicide bombers.[503]

Powell also repeated Bush's earlier lie to the delegates when he said that "Most U.S. experts think they [the aluminum tubes] are intended to serve as rotors in centrifuges used to enrich uranium. Other experts, and the Iraqis themselves, say the tubes were really for rockets."[504] As we have seen, most experts did not believe the tubes were intended to enrich uranium.

On February 26, 2003, Bush addressed a partisan gathering of the American Enterprise Institute at the Washington Hilton Hotel, where he opined that at the Institute, "some of the finest minds in our nation are at work on some of the greatest challenges to our nation. You do such good work that my administration has borrowed 20 such minds. ... We meet here during a crucial period in the history of our nation, and of the civilized world. Part of that history was written by others; the rest will be written by us."

Unfortunately, the history written by the Institute moles in Bush's administration, and by Bush himself, is replete with lies. That night, Bush laced his speech with lies: "In Iraq, a dictator is building and hiding weapons that could enable him to dominate the Middle East and intimidate the civilized world. ... This same tyrant has close ties to terrorist organizations, and could supply them with the terrible means to strike this country. ... The safety of the American people depends on ending this direct and growing threat. Acting against the danger will also contribute greatly to the long-term safety and stability of our world."[505]

None of this was true. In fact, Bush's War has gravely threatened the safety of the American people, and the stability of the world has become greatly unbalanced as a consequence.

Do you believe Bush and his cohorts told you the truth to justify his war? You're not stupid! Get the truth.

Milestones Along the Road to Bush's War

On November 21, 2001, Bush stated, "Afghanistan is just the beginning of the war against terror. ... The most difficult steps in this mission still lie ahead ... [because] there are other terrorists who threaten America and our friends, and there are other nations willing to sponsor them."[506]

In his State of the Union address to Congress on January 29, 2002, Bush said that terrorist camps exist in "at least a dozen countries." He said, "The United States of America will not permit the world's most dangerous regimes to threaten us with the world's most destructive weapons." First mentioning North Korea and Iran, Bush said that Iraq had "agreed to international inspection–then kicked out the inspectors. This is a regime that has something to hide from the civilized world. States like these, and their terrorist allies, *constitute an axis of evil*, aiming to threaten the peace of the world. By seeking weapons of mass destruction, these regimes pose a grave and growing danger (emphasis added)."[507]

Following an eight-month campaign of propaganda and deception, Bush made a speech in New York City on September 11, 2002, with the Statute of Liberty in the background; the next day he requested the United Nations Security Council to authorize his march to war, and a week later he asked Congress to back him in his invasion of Iraq.

On October 10, the House of Representatives voted 296 to 133 to grant Bush the authority to attack Iraq, and the Senate approved 77 to 23 the next day. Although a few members of both parties crossed over the aisles to vote, the resolution was largely supported by the Republicans and opposed by the Democrats. Senior Senator Robert Byrd of West Virginia attempted to mount a filibuster, but was cut off. He said, "This is the Tonkin Gulf resolution all over again. ... Let us stop, look and listen. Let us not give this president or any president unchecked power. Remember the Constitution."[508]

The resolution authorized Bush "to use the Armed Forces of the United States as he determines to be necessary and appropriate in order to: "(1) defend the national security of the United States against the continuing threat posed by Iraq; and (2) enforce all relevant United Nations Security Council resolutions regarding Iraq."[509]

On November 8, 2002, the members of the United Nations Security Council, responding to intense pressure by the United States, voted to adopt Resolution 1441 which afforded Iraq "a final opportunity to comply with its disarmament obligations," and it "set up an enhanced inspection regime." It required Iraq to provide, within 30 days, "a currently accurate, full, and complete declaration of all aspects of its programmes to develop chemical, biological, and nuclear weapons, ballistic missiles, and other delivery systems." It required Iraq to provide inspectors with "immediate, unimpeded, unconditional, and unrestricted access" to anything the inspectors wished to inspect.

The Security Council decided "to convene immediately upon receipt of a report ... to consider the situation and the need for full compliance with all of the relevant Council resolutions in order to secure international peace and security;" it recalled "in that context, that the Council has repeatedly warned Iraq that it will face serious consequences as a result of its continued violations of its obligations;" and finally, it decided "to remain seized of the matter."[510] In other words, the Security Council took all appropriate action to ensure that Iraq did not possess weapons of mass destruction, and it kept the matter on its agenda. It did not turn over enforcement of its resolution to the United States!

The Security Council's intention to retain control was confirmed by the United States' UN ambassador, John Negroponte, who stated, "There's no 'automaticity,' and this is a two-stage process. ... Whatever violation there is, or is judged to exist, will be dealt with in the council, and the council will have an opportunity to consider the matter before any other action is taken."[511]

Two days later, Bush's chief of staff, Andrew Card, stated: "The U.N. can meet and discuss, but we don't need their permission" before attacking Iraq. "The U.S. and our allies are prepared to act."[512]

Secretary of State Powell stated, "I can assure you that, if he [Saddam Hussein] doesn't comply this time, we'll ask the U.N. to give authorization for all necessary means, and if the U.N. is not willing to do that, the United States, with like-minded nations, will go and disarm him forcefully."[513]

Richard Perle admitted that the U.S. would attack Iraq even if the inspectors failed to find weapons, "All he [Dr. Hans Blix, the Executive Chairman of the U.N. inspection teams] can know is the results of his own investigations. And that does not prove Saddam does not have weapons of mass destruction."[514]

On November 14, 2002, Rumsfeld was asked what would happen if the inspectors did not find weapons of mass destruction, he answered, "What it would prove would be that the inspection process has been successfully defeated by the Iraqis."[515]

On January 11, 2003, Cheney showed Saudi Ambassador Prince Bandar the plans for the invasion of Iraq and asked if Saudi Arabia was in or out. The Prince declined to commit until he knew for sure the invasion was going to occur. Cheney told him "You can count on this. You can take it to the bank. This is going to happen." The next day, Bush asked Prince Bandar, "Any questions for me?" Bandar replied no, and Bush said, "The message you're taking is mine."[516]

On January 27, 2003, Dr. Blix reported to the United Nations that (1) Iraq submitted a 12,000 page declaration in compliance with Rule 1441 and, while most was a reprint of earlier documents, "in the fields of missiles and biotechnology, the declaration contains a good deal of new material and information covering the period from 1998 and onward. This is welcome." (2) While there had been some problems, "Iraq has on the whole cooperated rather well so far with UNMOVIC in this field. The most important point to make is that access has been provided to all sites we have wanted to inspect and with one exception it has been prompt. We have further had great help in building up the infrastructure of our office in Baghdad and the field office in Mosul. Arrangements and services for our planes and our helicopters have been good. The environment has been workable." (3) In the preceding two months, 300 inspections at more than 230 different sites were conducted, including 20 sites never before inspected; and (4) UNMOVIC had established "an inspection apparatus that permits us to send multiple inspection teams every day all over Iraq, by road or by air," all of which was at the disposal of the Security Council.[517]

On February 14, 2003, Dr. Mohamed ElBaradei, Director General of the IAEA, reported to the United Nations Security Council that "Iraq has continued to provide immediate access to all locations." The IAEA completed a detailed reviev of the 2,000 pages of documents found at the private residenɔe of an Iraqi scientist and found nothing that was not already known to the IAEA, nor anything to alter "the conclusions previously drawn by the IAEA concerning the extent of Iraq's laser enrichment programme." The report reiterated "by December 1998, that it had neutralized Iraq's past nuclear programme and that, therefore, there were no unresolved disarmament issues left at that time." It concluded: "We have to date found no evidence of ongoing prohibited nuclear or nuclear related activities in Iraq."[518]

Bush refused to accept the observations and conclusions of the United Nations and IAEA inspectors and continued to push for a new Security Council resolution mandating an end to inspections and immediate military action; however, on February 24, 2003, France, Germany and Russia joined together to issue a memorandum in which they concluded: "Full and effective disarmament in accordance with the relevant UNSC resolutions remains the imperative objective of the international community. Our priority should be to achieve this peacefully through the inspection regime. The military option should only be a last resort. So far, the conditions for using force against Iraq are not fulfilled. While suspicions remain, no evidence has been given that Iraq still possesses weapons of mass destruction or capabilities in this field; inspections have just reached their full pace; they are functioning without hindrance; they have already produced results."519

With the threat of a veto in the Security Council by either Russia or France, or both, Bush decided to ignore the United Nations. He created a new "Transatlantic Alliance," consisting of the United States, England and Spain to "face and overcome together the twin threats of the 21st century: terrorism and the spread of weapons of mass destruction."520

On March 16, 2003, the transatlantic triumvirate met in the Azores and made their final plans for Bush's War. They issued a "Statement of the Atlantic Summit," which warned, "The responsibility is his. If Saddam refuses even now to cooperate fully with the United Nations, he brings on himself the serious consequences foreseen in UNSCR 1441 and previous resolutions."521 How was Saddam not cooperating? Who appointed the triumvirate as the United Nation's police force, and who gave Bush a badge?

On March 16, 2003, Cheney appeared on *Meet the Press* and stated, "I think, if you look at the track record of the International Atomic Energy Agency and this kind of issue, especially where Iraq's concerned, they have consistently underestimated or missed what it was Saddam Hussein was doing. I don't have any reason to believe they're any more valid this time than they've been in the past. We believe [Saddam] has, in fact, reconstituted nuclear weapons."522

The following day, on March 17, 2003, Bush addressed the American people and laid down a 48-hour ultimatum for Saddam Hussein and his two sons to leave Iraq; otherwise, "Their refusal to do so will result in military conflict, commenced at a time of our choosing."

As justification for his demand, Bush continued his pattern of lying to the American people: (1) "It [Iraq] has uniformly defied Security Council resolutions demanding full disarmament. ... .Peaceful efforts to disarm the Iraqi regime have failed again and again." (2) "Intelligence gathered by this and other governments leaves no doubt that the Iraq regime continues to possess and conceal some of the most lethal weapons ever devised." (3) Iraq "has aided, trained and harbored terrorists, including operatives of al Qaeda."[523] Time will tell that these were three of the greatest lies of this new century.

Bush stated, "No nation can possibly claim that Iraq has disarmed. ... Yet, some permanent members of the Security Council have publicly announced they will veto any resolution that compels the disarmament of Iraq. ... The United Nations Security Council has not lived up to its responsibilities, so we will rise to ours." He said, "The American people can know that every measure has been taken to avoid war."[524]

Every measure had not been taken to avoid war, and it was not only the reasonableness of continued U.N. inspections that could have avoided it. It later came out that Saddam was desperately trying to make a last-minute deal with Bush to avoid an invasion. Using a Lebanese-American businessman as a go-between, Saddam was offering oil contracts for American companies and to allow U.S. agents to search for weapons of mass destruction. The offer eventually made it to the office of Deputy Defense Secretary Paul Wolfowitz, where it was presented to his aide, Jaymie Durnan.[525] The offer was never acted upon because Bush was more interested in the ouster of Saddam than in confirming that he did not have weapons of mass destruction.

On March 19, 2003, at approximately 10:16 p.m., Bush announced that, on his orders, military operations had commenced "to disarm Iraq, to free its people and to defend the world from grave danger." He did so because we "will not live at the mercy of an outlaw regime that threatens the peace with weapons of mass murder."[526]

Who was the outlaw threatening the peace? According to a *TIME EUROPE* poll, 86.9 percent of over 700,000 respondents in Europe consider the United States to pose the greatest danger to world peace. Only 6.3 percent thought that Iraq was the most serious threat.[527]

Where are Iraq's weapons of mass destruction? Do you still believe Iraq posed a grave danger to the United States? You're not stupid! Get the truth.

The Shifting Mission in Bush's War

The United States had two objectives in its invasion of Iraq. One, a regime change, took place rather quickly when Saddam disappeared and the Iraqi army collapsed, with its soldiers either surrendering or deserting. Under the Geneva Convention, the United States and its coalition partners undertook the obligation to govern the country. The second, the elimination of weapons of mass destruction, was even easier, for there were none. To make a long story short: nada, zip, none.

On March 25, 2003, Bush announced his war budget of $74.5 billion to protect the United States "from a brutal regime that is armed with weapons that could kill thousands of innocent people."[528] Rumsfeld repeatedly said that the immediate task was "to find the weapons of mass destruction" and "to eliminate the weapons of mass destruction, their delivery systems, production capabilities, and distribution networks." On March 30, 2003, he said, "We know where they are. They're in the area around Tikrit and Baghdad and east, west, south, and north somewhat."[529]

Less than two weeks later, on April 11, 2003, Rumsfeld seemed to have become less concerned about weapons of mass destruction (WMDs). He stated, "When there happens to be a weapon of mass destruction site in an area that we occupy and if people have time, they'll look at it."[530] When they have time? What were they there for?

On April 17, 2003, Rumsfeld seems to have gotten lost somewhere east, west, south and/or north of Baghdad and/or Tikrit in his search for WMDs, admitting, "I don't think we'll discover anything, myself. I think what will happen is we'll discover people who will tell us where to go find it. It is not like a treasure hunt where you just run around looking everywhere hoping you find something."[531] The problem was, all of the captured Iraqi officials were spilling their guts, but what they were saying was that Iraq really, really did not have any WMDs.

Nonetheless, Bush continued to be convinced that he had saved the world from Saddam's weapons of mass destruction: "We know he had them. And whether he destroyed them, moved them, or hid them, we're going to find out the truth."[532] Even so, it was time for Bush to duck and weave. The new line from the White House was that the Iraqi had employed the very latest in business school theory and relied upon a "just in time" delivery system which ensured that no spare chemical precursors were lying around on the shelf until just before they were needed to be combined and loaded into shells or missiles— now you see it, now you don't.[533]

By mid-May, the 75th Exploitation Task Force, whose job it had been to find WMDs, was winding up and preparing to go home. According to a story in the *Washington Post*, members complained that they "consistently found targets identified by Washington to be inaccurate, looted and burned, or both."[534]

But in case all this is confusing you, rest assured you're not alone. When asked about reports of the missing WMDs, Rumsfeld stated, "Reports that say something hasn't happened are always interesting to me, because as we know, there are known knowns; there are things we know we know. We also know there are known unknowns; that is to say, we know there are some things we do not know. But, there are also unknown unknowns–the ones we don't know we don't know." This brilliant bit of logic earned Rumsfeld the BBC's 2003 "Foot in Mouth" award.[535]

With his usual regard for the truth, in late May 2003, Bush responded to a Polish reporter's question about the absence of WMDs: "We found the weapons of mass destruction. We found biological laboratories. ... And we'll find more weapons as time goes on. But for those who say we haven't found the banned manufacturing devices or banned weapons, they're wrong. We found them."[536] Perhaps he feels more secure telling such whoppers when he's out of the country. Maybe, in a simple-minded way, he actually believes that we won't hear about it, or that we don't know that we know that we don't know.

By June 2003, it seems the administration was finally giving up on actually finding WMDs, no matter Bush's delusions, and the new mission settled on fighting terrorism. Wolfowitz said, "The issue of WMDs has never been in controversy, where there's been a lot of arguing back and forth about whether the Iraqis have been involved in terrorism."537

Someone changed Bush's cue card, and he too began to shift the mission: "Intelligence throughout the decade showed they had a weapons program. I am absolutely convinced, with time, we'll find out that they did have a weapons program."538 The congressional resolution did not authorize him to find and destroy *weapons programs*; it authorized him to wage war to find and destroy actual weapons of mass destruction.

August 2003 brought yet another shift of mission in Bush's War. L. Paul Bremer, the U.S. civilian administrator for Iraq, marketed the latest theory. Regarding the influx of Islamic militants into Iraq, he stated, "I suppose they could calculate that if we can succeed in Iraq, it will change the entire structure of this area of the world. And so it certainly is attracting a lot of them here, and it shows what the stakes are for all Americans. We've got to win this fight here." *The Washington Times* reported, "Mr. Bremer avoided answering whether the Bush administration set Iraq as a deliberate trap to capture terrorists, although he previously has stated that it is 'better to fight it here than to fight it somewhere else, like the United States.'"539

Bremer was following Bush's lead, who had told reporters on July 2, 2003, "There are some who feel that conditions are such that they can attack us there. My answer is bring 'em on."540 Such is the braggadocio of a coward. One wonders if Bush might feel differently about the cost of his war if he had ever had a real fight in his life, if he had actually patrolled the sky over North Viet Nam, rather than Houston, Texas, or if he was a reservist facing hostile crowds in Falluja or Najaf. In the real world, as of May 14, 2004, 571 of America's sons and daughters have died in Iraq since Bush taunted the Iraqi resistance to "bring 'em on."541

Lt. General Ricardo S. Sanchez, the top military commander in Iraq, said that Iraq was becoming a "terrorist magnet," which was okay with him. He confided, "But this is exactly where we want to fight them; we want to fight them here, we prepared for them, and this will prevent the American people from having to go through other attacks back in the United States."[542] Let's make sure we understand this. We sent our sons and daughters to fight in Iraq because we were told there were weapons of mass destruction there, and when we find that there aren't any, we are going to leave our children there as live bait for terrorists? I don't think so.

And now we come to the enduring mission in Bush's never-ending war. We are in Iraq to fight terrorism. However, in actuality, we are fighting to overcome a primarily grassroots resistance to our illegal invasion and occupation. We euphemistically refer to this resistance as an insurgency.

There can be no retreat. On August 26, 2003, Bush stated, "The civilized world will not be intimidated. Retreat in the face of terror would only invite further and bolder attacks. There will be no retreat. We are on the offensive."[543] Perhaps Bush was suffering a hangover the morning in class when the battle of Stalingrad was discussed and he failed to learn that lesson of history. According to *The Washington Times*, Bush counsels that "Americans must have patience as the nation begins a lengthy battle to purge terrorism from the world."

Bush is wrong and his own experts know better. In January 2004, the Army War College published a report by Jeffrey Record, a visiting research professor at the College's Strategic Studies Institute, which called for a reduction in the war on terrorism and a refocus on the al Qaeda threat. The report finds Bush's endless war on terrorism may have set us "on a course of open-ended and gratuitous conflict with states and non-state entities that pose no serious threat to the United States."

According to the report, "The global war on terrorism as presently defined and conducted is strategically unfocused, promises much more than it can deliver, and threatens to dissipate U.S. military and other resources in an endless and hopeless search for absolute security. The United States may be able to defeat, even destroy, al Qaeda, but it cannot rid the world of terrorism, much less evil." Record says that Bush's War was "an unnecessary preventative war" that has "diverted attention and resources away from securing the American homeland against further assault by an undeterrable al Qaeda."[544]

In September 2002, Prince Moulay Hicham Ben Abdallah of Morocco gave a speech at Princeton University. He said, "Perhaps some American strategists now think it will be easy to roll over these 'stirred-up' Muslims with military force alone. But without a sophisticated concurrent political, diplomatic and especially ideological strategy–one that distinguishes and isolates the new *jihad* movement from the Muslim world in general–any military offensive will only exacerbate the polarization between America and the Islamic world. It will lead to upheavals throughout the Muslim world, in which democratic constituencies will find it even more difficult to mobilize, and will increase the probability of prolonged bloody conflicts."[545]

More simply, as Egyptian president Hosni Mubarak warned us about going to war in Iraq, "there will be 100 bin Ladens afterward."[546] Just like Hercules cutting off the heads of the Hydra, for each one cut off, two grow back. How long will it take us to understand that there is a whole generation of young people growing up in the Muslim "street" who can't wait to be old enough to give their lives to rid their world of infidel crusaders? There will always be more of them *there* ready to lay down their lives to defend their homes and their society, than there will ever be of us *here* prepared to die to enrich Bush's oil patch buddies.

Why do you think we invaded Iraq? Do you believe we had adequate justification? You're not stupid! Get the truth.

The Inhumanity of Bush's War

In the statement of the "Atlantic Summit" on March 16, 2003, Bush undertook "a solemn obligation to help the Iraqi people build a new Iraq at peace with itself and its neighbors. The Iraqi people deserve to be lifted from insecurity and tyranny, and freed to determine for themselves the future of their country."[547] On March 19, 2003, Bush promised every "effort to spare innocent civilians from harm."[548] In his efforts to liberate the Iraqi people, he immediately caused the deaths of approximately

9,200 military personnel and 3,750 noncombatants.[549] Given the tribal nature of Iraqi society, it is highly likely that the grief associated with the loss of these lives has been visited upon every family in Iraq. Especially if one considers the untold number of serious injuries, one cannot help but wonder if there is anyone in Iraq who does not have some good reason to hate us.

Civilian suffering has always been associated with the violence of war; however, the high ratio of civilian deaths to military casualties in Iraq (about one civilian for every three Iraqi soldiers) raises questions about Bush's concern for Saddam's victims.

On May 1, 2003, Bush lied when he stated, "Today ... with new tactics and precision weapons, we can achieve military objectives without directing violence against civilians."[550] We know this was untrue because only one month before, the United States had finally admitted that it was using conventional cluster bombs and artillery shells which were banned by a 1999 Ottawa agreement signed by Britain, France and more than 140 other nations and which have been condemned by Human Rights Watch, Amnesty International, Oxfam International, Christian Aid, and Save the Children.[551] The United States has since admitted that it has used more than 10,782 cluster munitions in Iraq.

The United States has refused to sign the Ottawa agreement and continues to use the bombs, each of which contains about 200 bomblets the size of a tin can, which separate and saturate an area the size of two football fields with tiny shards of razor-sharp steel. These bombs kill indiscriminately, much like land mines, because approximately 5 to 15 percent of the bomblets fail to explode immediately and lay about on the ground waiting for a curious child to pick them up. It has been estimated that over 1,000 Iraqis have been killed by cluster bombs in Bush's War.[552]

On one hand, Rumsfeld says, "No nation in human history has done more to avoid civilian casualties than the United States has in this conflict." Then on the other, he says, "of course we are using cluster bombs, and of course the purpose is to try to kill them ... to be perfectly blunt."[553] Such a lie. Such arrogance!

In addition, the Pentagon repeatedly targeted approximately 50 "high value" individuals by tracking their satellite phone use. When these targets were located, an area within a 100-yard radius was saturated with bombs, irrespective of the risk to non-combatants.[554]

A discussion such as this is, in some respects, an intellectual exercise, for we are not there, nor have most of us ever experienced such horror; however, a couple of stories reported by the Project on Defense Alternatives paints a human face on the blank canvas of suffering innocent children: "In the emergency room in the complex of hospitals in Baghdad's Medical City ... eight-year-old Hamed Ali lies unconscious after surgery. Ali, his parents say, had been a curious boy and was playing with unexploded ordnance when he was injured. ... Surgeons give him a 50 percent change of survival–not because of his injuries ... but because of the risk of infection in a ward terribly short of antibiotics. Safah Ahmed, 12 ... was wounded when an American bomb landed near her home. ... Now doctors have amputated her leg. One of the U.S. Marine guards outside the Medical City Complex ... recalls a boy brought in with all of his face except his lower jaw shot away. The child had been traveling in a car with his parents that had approached a U.S. checkpoint too fast."[555]

Following its occupation by U.S. troops, violence escalated in Baghdad, which resulted in a tripling of violent deaths from around 10 per day to over 28 per day. Prior to Bush's War, gunshot wounds accounted for approximately ten percent of all bodies brought to Baghdad's city morgue; however following the fall of Baghdad, gunshot wounds account for over 60 percent of deaths. Between April 14 and August 31, 2003, there were at least 1,519 excess deaths over the pre-war rates. Similar statistics are not available for other areas, but anecdotal evidence indicates that the phenomenon is widespread throughout Iraq.[556]

As the resistance to military occupation has become more entrenched, it has also become more deadly for those Iraqis who cooperate with the Americans. There have been repeated bombings of police stations and a series of deadly attacks on politicians, professors, and translators. More than 400 Iraqi police and security personnel, including six police chiefs, have been killed since May 2003. Even four women who worked in a laundry at a U.S. military base were killed on their way to work. An associate of the slain women said, "No one from around here wants to work for the Americans. It is a worry for everybody. We are just trying to make a living." A military spokesman stated, "We believe that the purpose behind [the attack] is to send a message of terror to those people that if you work for the coalition ... we can reach out and touch you."[557]

Deadly suicide attacks on their headquarters have caused the United Nations and the Red Cross to withdraw their workers from Iraq. The week ending February 14, 2004 saw two suicide bombings that killed more than 100 Iraqi military recruits and police officers and an organized attack on a police station in Falluja that killed at least 15 police officers and freed dozens of prisoners. Documents on four slain attackers identified two as Lebanese and one as Iranian.[558]

As an occupying power, the United States is bound by the Fourth Geneva Convention to set up an effective military government in Iraq to (1) maintain law and order; (2) provide health and hospital services to the local population; and (3) operate the basic infrastructure, such as electricity, water and roads. Under these conventions, the United States does not have an option. It has a legal duty to control rampant looting and to safeguard civilian lives from violence, including that caused by the negligence of the occupying power.[559]

Finally, as long as we occupy Iraq and interfere with its sovereignty in exercising government authority, we are subject to the laws of occupation and international law. We are responsible for the deaths of children killed and maimed by playing with unexploded cluster bombs. We are responsible for the deaths of children who die from a lack of basic medical care, and we are responsible for the deaths of the elderly who die from exposure and insufficient nutrition. For this reason, we should withdraw, and we should withdraw as quickly as possible.

Shall we deny the truth and continue to commit war crimes? Or, should we acknowledge our error and encourage the United

Nations to undertake a humanitarian mission to stabilize Iraq, aid its people, and establish a government? Should we provide all possible support and play no further role in the occupation of Iraq, or shall we continue to sacrifice our own children on the altar of greed, attended by the oil-rich elite? You're not stupid! Get the truth.

The Shameful Treatment of American Soldiers

The United States also has a legal, moral, and ethical duty to protect the lives of the military personnel Bush has put in harm's way. In launching his war on March 19, 2003, Bush stated: "I know that the families of our military are praying that all those who serve will return safely and soon. Millions of Americans are praying with you for the safety of your loved ones and for the protection of the innocent. For your sacrifice, you have the gratitude and respect of the American people."[560] This at least was true, *we* are praying for the safety of our children, and *we* are grateful and respectful of their sacrifice. The problem is that Bush does not share our concern, and his treatment of those who have died and suffered grievous wounds in his war is shameful.

As of May 14, 2004, and the numbers mount every day, 777 U.S. service members have died in Iraq since March 20, 2003 and one has been captured.[561] The majority of these are attributed to hostile action; the remainder is due to accidents, suicide and illness. During the same period, 4,327 soldiers have been wounded in action in Iraq.

When Bush engaged in his phony "Mission Accomplished" carrier landing on May 1, 2003, the death toll stood at 138. It has now more than quintupled, and the attacks against our troops are increasing in accuracy and intensity. Following the invasion, the Iraqi army disintegrated, with most soldiers simply deserting and going home. Now they are regrouping and are engaging in a guerrilla resistance, injuring and killing more and more American soldiers with rocket-propelled grenades, remote-controlled mines, and "improvised explosive devices."

While the Pentagon cannot conceal the daily body count, it does go to extraordinary efforts to conceal the number of severely wounded soldiers. It does not announce such cases unless a death occurs, and it refers to the wounded as "injured," as in "on the job." In fact, since most soldiers wear body armor and many lives are saved by excellent trauma care in the field, the wounds they do suffer are horrible and disabling.[562]

Gene Bolles, the chief of neurosurgery at Landstuhl, Germany, has cared for many grievously wounded soldiers from Bush's War. He reports "a number of really horrific injuries now from the war. They have lost arms, legs, hands; they have been burned; they have had significant brain injuries and peripheral nerve damage. These are young kids that are going to be, in some regards, changed for life. I don't feel that people realize that."[563]

Other members of the coalition have also suffered loss of life: British, 59; Italy, 17; Spain, 11, including seven military intelligence agents killed in a single ambush; Bulgaria, 6; Thailand, 2; Denmark, 1; Estonia, 1; El Salvador, 1; Ukraine, 6; Poland, 4, and Netherlands, 1.[564] Some attacks have targeted civilian workers, including the deaths of two South Korean electricians, a Colombian working as a military contractor, and two Japanese diplomats killed when they stopped at a roadside stand to eat.[565]

A survey by *Stars and Stripes*, a military newspaper, found that half of those questioned described their unit's morale as low and their training insufficient for their assigned task. They had no intent to reenlist. About a third characterized Bush's War as of little or no value. Forty percent said their military assignments had little or nothing to do with their training. The article related that "Many soldiers, including several officers, allege that VIP visits from the Pentagon and Capitol Hill are only given handpicked troops to meet with during their tours of Iraq." And some soldiers who have complained of morale problems have been disciplined.[566]

Many of the troops deployed in Iraq are reserves, and they and their families have much to complain about. Their tours of duty have been extended to 12 or 15 months, and they are often made to feel like second-class soldiers. They are issued old and ineffective body armor, and they are assigned thankless tasks unrelated to their training. The military is offering bonuses of

$5,000 to $10,000 for soldiers who reenlist for three years. However, even if solders refuse to reenlist, they are not being allowed to come home. So far, thousands of soldiers have been prohibited from leaving the service when their enlistments expired.[567]

One of the differences between this and previous wars is that the soldiers have access to e-mail. One mother related what she had learned from her son: "I don't care what the administration says about flag-waving and children throwing flowers. It is just not true. The stories coming back are horrific. All he told me was that he had seen and done some horrible things, that they had all done and seen some terrible things."[568]

Reports are now coming to light about the torture of Iraqi prisoners in military prisons by reserve troops acting under the direction of active duty military intelligence personnel, CIA officers and private contractors. An Army report detailed "sadistic, blatant and wanton criminal abuses" at the Abu Ghraib prison near Baghdad, the very same prison where Saddam's regime tortured opponents. Detainees were beaten with a boom handle and one was sodomized with "a chemical light and perhaps a broom stick."

Photographs have been released showing a pyramid of naked Iraqi prisoners in the presence of smiling and clowning American soldiers, a naked Iraqi man kneeling in front of another naked Iraqi man, and another showing a female American soldier laughing and pointing to an Iraqi man with a bag over his head, who is masturbating. The purpose was to "set physical and mental conditions for favorable interrogation of witnesses." Much of the abuse was sexual, and such degradations "are particularly humiliating to Arabs because Islamic law and culture so strongly condemn nudity and homosexuality."[569]

This then is the emotional harm done to our children in uniform. By being used as live bait in a terrorist trap where they are unwelcome and do not speak the language, they become hardened and uncaring. According to a story in *The Guardian*, "Others said they detected anger and depression in their e-mails that would be difficult to fix when they returned. 'They're changing. They have dehumanized the Iraqis. They call them 'haji' now–that's like 'gook.'"570

How can it be different when our soldiers see or hear about swarms of Iraqis kicking and looting the bodies of those who are killed or injured? When they see crowds gather and cheer when helicopters filled with troops are shot out of the sky? They are human, after all. They are our children, and they deserve our support and comfort. They deserve to be told the truth, and they are entitled not to be used as pawns in an international chess game between competing business interests.

At least 24 service members are believed to have committed suicide, and as many as 4,500 returning troops have tried to obtain counseling from veteran centers, rather than seek help through military channels.571 In an effort to help soldiers cope with their depression, the military has commenced a furlough program to allow them to come home for 15 days. However, following the first flights home, about 30 soldiers declined to return to Iraq.572

The Pentagon announced in December 2003 that it plans to completely rotate all troops out of Iraq within the next five months, which will result in a dramatic rise in the number of reserves deployed in the country. Although reserves presently constitute approximately 20 percent of the deployment, after the rotation, they will comprise approximately 40 percent. It is likely that casualties will increase due to the inexperience of the replacement units. As Rumsfeld says, "You lose situational awareness, you lose relationships, you lose the experience."573 Remember the lines from the Vietnam War era song, "Well there ain't no time to wonder why, Whoopee! We're all gonna die."574

In addition to combat-related injuries and accidents, Bush's War has imposed other health costs as well. At least 100 soldiers have gotten severe cases of pneumonia; two have died and 13 had to be placed on respirators. *United Press International* reports the crusade of a father whose daughter died of pneumonia after she received anthrax and smallpox vaccinations in preparation for deployment to Iraq. The father, Moses Lacy, stated, "These young people have given their lives to the military and they are getting a raw deal. The Department of Defense is closing their eyes."575   A federal court ruled in December 2003 that the military could not force its members to be guinea pigs and to require them to undergo dangerous vaccinations for anthrax. Would you take an anthrax vaccination?

The most shameful aspect of Bush's War is the way the Department of Defense secretly brings home those who have given their lives and health because of Bush's lies. A military directive precludes any arrival ceremony or media coverage of "deceased personnel" returning to the Dover Air Force Base, the main reception area for those killed in action. Christopher Simpson, professor of communications at American University said, "In the beginning, the coverage was more personal. ... We saw photos, we were given names. But as the deaths kept coming it became more anonymous, more de-personalized."576

According to a story in the *Denver Post*, "There are no public ceremonies for the dead coming back through the military receiving center in Dover, Del. The flights of wounded to Walter Reed often arrive at night at Andrews Air Force Base in Maryland."

Senator Patrick Leahy said, "The wounded are brought back after midnight, making sure the press does not see the planes coming in. These are not a broken wrist, or scratched leg. These are terrible wounds: lost limbs, lost eyesight, lifetime disabilities. It is something the administration prefers not to talk about."

Pfc. Tristan Wyatt, who lost his leg in an ambush relates, "They say 'wounded' like they have a cast, or a splinter. There are people who lost both legs, in wheelchairs, here."577   If your son or daughter lost a limb or their eyesight in Bush's War, would you want them to feel ashamed to come home?

David Wood of the *Times Picayune* graphically described the injuries: "Explosions shatter and sever legs and arms. They char flesh and drive debris deep into the soft tissue that remains. Unattached muscles, nerves and tendons dangle.   Red-hot shrapnel sometimes punctures torsos below waist-length body armor, ripping bowels and bladders. Concussions bruise skulls and brains. Soldiers thrown into the air are injured again when they hit the ground." In an interview with French writer, Natasha Saulnier, a soldier who had lost one leg and the use of the other, says, "Thank God I'm single. I wouldn't want to have to go through what the other guys do. There's this one guy who lost his sight and had both of his arms blown off. His wife is pregnant but he's never gonna be able to hold his baby in his arms."[578]

Writing about "Our Wounded Warriors," Bob Herbert of *The New York Times* says, "Thousands of U.S. troops have been wounded and injured in Iraq. They have been paralyzed, lost limbs, suffered blindness, been horribly burned and so on. They are heroes, without question, but their stories have largely been untold."[579]

Retired Army Colonel David Hackworth, who has inside sources at the Pentagon, reports our military has suffered as many as 22,000 casualties since Bush's War started. Over 3,255 wounded-in-action soldiers and 18,717 non-battle casualties have been evacuated from Iraq.[580]

Although Bush has promised to give the troops whatever they need to defend themselves, the truth is that he has withheld funding and left major shortfalls in the military budget. Military commanders desperately need an additional $132 million shortfall for bolt-on vehicle armor and $40 million for body armor and combat helmets. However, the Bush budget that begins in October 2004 includes no money for Iraqi operations, and there will be no requests until after January 2005 (after the election). In the meantime, the Army has identified nearly $46 billion in funding needs that was not included in the 2005 budget.[581]

What does the future hold for these grievously injured and walking-wounded soldiers? On the same day it unanimously passed a resolution pledging "unequivocal support" for our soldiers in Iraq, the Republican-controlled House of Representatives voted 215 to 212, largely along party lines, to impose billions of dollars in cuts to veteran's programs over the next 10 years. As a result, veterans' pensions are threatened and almost half may lose their only source of medical care.[582] Why were our veterans stabbed in the back? Congress had to come up with the money to pay for Bush's $726 billion tax cut that primarily benefited his wealthy contributors.

Is it any surprise that support for Bush's reelection is waning among veterans, military personnel and their families? A bipartisan poll in September 2003 of military families found Bush's approval rating was only 36 percent. Jean Prewitt, the mother of a soldier killed in Iraq says she "just feels deceived. He just kept screaming, screaming, weapons of mass destruction, weapons of mass destruction; we've got to get in there. We got in there, and now there aren't any." A former Bush supporter, a Vietnam veteran, said he was basically "disappointed in his support of veterans... He's killing the active-duty military.... Look at the reserves call-ups for Iraq, the hardships. The National Guard—the state militia—is being used improperly. I took the president at this word on Iraq, and now you can't find a single report to back up or substantiate weapons of mass destruction."583

Military Families Speak Out has begun to organize demonstrations to protest the war. Fernando Suarez del Solar asks, "Bush lies and who dies? My son, Jesus Suarez del Solar Navarro, March 27." Del Solar says he is "very disillusioned with the American government. For it to get involved in an illegal war and to play with the emotions of the American people with 9/11 for politics is wrong."584

Military families and antiwar activists have united in asking Congress to censure Bush for his deception and manipulation of intelligence before the Iraq war. Sue Niederer, whose son was killed in Iraq, says "The best way that the United States Congress can honor those brave men and women in uniform who have served in Iraq, and who continue to serve in Iraq, is to honor the truth. They can do so by holding accountable those who deceived and manipulated the American people to justify the invasion and occupation of Iraq, starting with President Bush." The organization, Win Without War has gathered 460,340 signatures endorsing a censure resolution.585

Cheney has stated that the U.S. must expand its military in order to wage war quickly around the globe and with 49 percent of soldiers stationed in Iraq saying they will not reenlist, it is likely that Bush will reinstate the military draft next year if he is reelected. Legislation has been introduced in the House and Senate (S89 and HR163) to bring the draft back as early as spring 2005, just after the election.

The Selective Service System must report by March 31, 2005 that the system, which has lain dormant for years, is ready for activation. "The Pentagon has already had to double the deployment periods of some units, call up more reserves and extend tours of duty by a year..." Reflecting Rumsfeld's prediction that the permanent war on terrorism will be a "long, hard slog," the Pentagon has begun a public campaign to fill all 10,350 draft board positions and 11,070 appeals board slots. Under the new draft, there will be no college deferments, and both boys and girls will be drafted right out of high school.[586]

Are you prepared to allow your teenage sons and daughters, your nieces and nephews, to be drafted? Is the oil worth it? It was always for sale anyway. Is control of the whole wide world worth it? Is our President's ego worth it? What do you think? You're not stupid! Get the truth.

376. Sale, Richard, "Exclusive: Saddam key in early CIA plot," *United Press International*, April 10, 2003, http://www.upi.com/view.cfm?StoryID=20030410-070214-6557r.

377. Palast, op. cit., pp. 17, 18.

378. Ibid., pp. 18, 19.

379. Ibid., pp. 19, 20.

380. Ibid., p. 21.

381. Bowen, Russell S., *The Immaculate Deception: The Bush Crime Family Exposed* (Carson City, Nevada: American West Publications, 2001), p. 92.

382. Rampton, Sheldon and John C. Stauber, *Weapons of Mass Deception: The Uses of Propaganda in Bush's War on Iraq* (New York: J.P. Tarcher, 2003), pp. 19, 20.

383. Ibid., p. 20.

384. Bowen, op. cit., p. 150.

385. Clarke, op. cit. p. 42, 43.

386. Bowen, op. cit., p. 153.

387. Bowen, op. cit., pp. 150, 151; see also Rampton, op. cit., p. 22.

388. "Transcript of Meeting between Iraqi President, Saddam Hussein and U.S. Ambassador to Iraq, April Glaspie - July 25, 1990," www.ndtceda.com/archives/200311/0127.html.

389. Ahmed, op. cit., pp. 248, 249.

390. "Commentary & Opinion," *National Catholic Register*, December 8-14, 2002, (www.ncregister.com/register_news/120802war.html); see also Sloyan, Patrick J., "What Bodies?" *The Digital Journalist*, November 2002, (www.digitaljournalist.org/issue0211/sloyan.html).

391. "U.S. Defends Burying Iraqi Troops Alive: Pentagon Cites 'Gap' in International Law," *San Francisco Chronicle*, nucnews.net/nucnews/2002nn/0212nn/021204.nn.html.

392. Solomon, op. cit., p. 81.

393. Palast, op. cit., p. 24.

394. Solomon, op. cit., p. 145.

395. Landau, Saul, "The Iraq Ploy And Resemblances To The Start Of The Cold War," November 26, 2002, (zmag.org) www.organizepittsburg.org/theiraqploy.html.

396. Solomon, op. cit., pp. 87, 92-94.

397. Conason, op. cit., p.157.

398. Hersh, Seymour M., "A Case Not Closed," *The New Yorker*, November 11, 2001, www.tomfolio.com/books.sub.asp?catid=91subid=91.

399. Palast, op. cit., pp. 56-59.

400. Solomon, op. cit., pp. 145, 161.

401. Alterman and Green, op. cit., pp. 323, 324.

402. Rampton, op. cit., pp. 42-46.

403. Alterman and Green, op. cit., p. 275.

404. Ibid.

405. Ibid.

406. Rampton, op. cit., pp. 46-48.

407. Ibid., p. 48.

408. Ivins, op. cit., p. 265.

409. "Rebuilding America's Defenses: Strategy, Forces and Resources For a New Century," A Report of The Project for the New American Century, September 2000, p. ii, www.newamericancentury.org/.

410. Ibid., p. 8; see also Kellner, op. cit., p. 21; see also Rampton, op. cit., pp. 120, 121.

411. Ibid., pp. 14, 17, 19; see also Rampton, op. cit., pp. 121, 122.

412. Entous, Adam, "Bush Planned Iraqi Invasion Before 9/11, O'Neill Says," *Reuters*, January 11, 2004, iraqeconomy.com.

413. Kellner, op. cit., p. 258.

414. Alterman and Green, op. cit., p. 274.

415. Clarke, op. cit., p. 31.
416. Ibid., p. 32.
417. Ibid., p. 33.
418. Scheer, Christopher, et. al., *The Five Biggest Lies bush Told Us About Iraq*, (New York: Akashic Books and Seven Stories Press, 2003) pp. 40, 41.
419. Clarke, op. cit., pp. 30, 31.
420. Woodward, Bob, *Plan of Attack* (New York: Simon & Schuster, 2004), p. 25.
421. Rampton, op. cit., p. 49.

422. Rose, David, "Bush and Blair made secret pact for Iraq war," *Guardian*, April 4, 2004, http://www.guardian.co.uk/Iraq/Story/0,2763,1185438,00.html.
423. Ahmed, op. cit., p. 256.

424. "Attack on Iraq Unavoidable–North Iraq Bombed–4 Iraqis Killed," February 2, 2002, http://www.theexperiment.org/articles.php?news_id=1822.

425. Corn, op. cit., p. 206.

426. "U.S. President Says Preemptive Strike Necessary To Deter Terrorism," english.peopledaily.com.cn/200206/02/eng20020602_96946.shtml.

427. Kellner, op. cit., pp. 20, 21; see also www.whitehouse.gov/nsc/nssall.html.

428. Corti, Lillian, "Ultimatums and War," March 21, 2003, http://www.commondreams.org/views03/0321-01.html.

429. Rampton, op. cit., pp. 52, 53.

430. Steele, Jonathan, "Religion and Politics Resurface As the New Voices of Iraqi Freedom," http://www.buzzle.com/editorials/text4-21-2003-39381.asp.

431. Solomon, op. cit., p.107.

432. Rampton, op. cit., pp. 51, 52.

433. "Carve-up of oil riches begins," *The Observer*, November 3, 2002, www.guardian.co.uk/iraq/story/0,2763,825118,00.html.

434. Ibid.

435. "If ExxonMobil Is Not Indicted for Payments in Kazakhstan, What Has This To Do With Iraq?" ist.socrates.berkley.edu/~pdscott/qfmobil2.html.

436. "Cheney Energy Task Force Documents Feature Map of Iraqi Oilfields," judicialwatch.org.

437. Klare, Michael T., "It's The Oil, Stupid," *The Nation*, May 2, 2003, www.thenation.com/directory/view.mhtml?t=0B0602.

438. Moore, *Bush's War for Reelection*, op. cit., p. 20.

439. Roy, Olivier, "Europe Won't Be Fooled Again," May 13, 2003, http://titanus.roma1.infn.it/sito_pol/Global_emp/OL_Roy.htm.

440. Frantz, Douglas, "Israel's Arsenal Is Point of Contention," *Los Angeles Times*, October 12, 2003, http://www.latimes.com/la-fg-iznukes12oct12.story.

441. Beaumont, Peter and Conal Urquhart, "Israel deploys nuclear arms in submarines," *The Guardian*, October 12, 2003, http://www.guardian.co.uk/israel/Story/0,2763,1061399,00.html.

442. Ibid., pp. 322, 323.

443. Alterman and Green, op. cit., p. 322.

444. Ibid.

445. Rampton, op. cit., p.130.

446. Kellner, op. cit., p. 20.

447. Alterman and Green, op. cit., p. 231.

448. Rampton, op. cit., pp. 136, 137.

449. Ibid., pp. 67, 68.

450. Ibid., p. 37.

451. Ibid., pp. 38, 39, 127.

452. Moore, op. cit., p. 293.

453. Ibid., p. 310.

454. Rampton, op. cit., p. 143.

455. Solomon, op. cit., p. 43.

456. Alterman and Green, op. cit., p. 282.

457. Rampton, op. cit., p. 143.

458. Ibid., pp. 175, 176.

459. Corn, op. cit., p. 215.

460. Ibid.

461. Ibid., p. 281.

462. Scheer, op. cit., p. 49.
463. Corn, op. cit., p. 213.

464. Ibid., p. 218.

465. Ibid., p. 208.

466. Ibid., p. 283.

467. Ibid., p. 217.

468. Solomon, op. cit., p. 29.

469. Corn, op. cit., p. 213.

470. Ibid., p. 214.

471. Ibid.

472. Alterman and Green, op. cit., p. 264.

473. Ibid.

474. Pitt, William Rivers and Scott Ritter, *War on Iraq: What Team Bush Doesn't Want You to Know* (New York: Context Books, 2002), pp. 30, 31.

475. Corn, op. cit., p. 209.

476. Ibid., p. 210.

477. Moore, *Bush's War for Reelection*, op. cit., pp. 32-35.

478. Rampton, op. cit., p. 87.

479. Corn, op. cit., p. 211.

480. Daniszewski, John, "U.S. Combat fatalities in Iraq Surge Suddenly," *Los Angeles Times*, March 15, 2004, p. A5.

481. Corn, op. cit., pp. 214, 215.

482. "Rumsfeld: Saddam not linked to Sept. 11," September 17, 2003, *The Olympian*, http://www.theolympian.com.

483. Corn, op. cit., p. 211.

484. "Remarks by the President on Iraq," www.whitehouse.gov/news/releases/2002/10/20021007-8.html.

485. Corn, op. cit., pp. 214, 215.

486. "Remarks by the President on Iraq," op. cit.

487. Corn, op. cit., p. 220.

488. Ibid., pp. 221, 222.

489. Ibid., p. 223.

490. Ibid., p. 225.

491. Ibid.

492. Ibid.

493. Ibid.

494. Ibid.

495. Ibid.

496. Ibid.

497. Ibid., p. 228.

498. Ibid., p. 229.

499. Ibid., pp. 229, 230.

500. Ibid., pp. 232-235.

501. Rampton, op. cit., pp. 98, 99.

502. Corn, op. cit., p. 286; see also Palast, op. cit., pp. 50, 51; see also Solomon, op. cit., p. 136.

503. Sanders, Edmund, "Ansar, Al Qaeda Seen as Working More Closely," *Los Angeles Times,* February 26, 2004, p. A5.

504. Moore, *Bush's War for Reelection,* op. cit., pp. 32-35

505. Corn, op. cit., p. 236; see also "President Discusses the Future of Iraq," (www.whitehouse.gov).

506. Kellner, op. cit., p. 126.

507. "The President's State of The Union Address," January 29, 2001, http://www.whitehouse.gov/news/releases.

508. "Senate approves Iraq war resolution," www.cnn.com/2002/ALLPOLITICS/10/11/iraq.us.

509. "Authorization For Use of Military Force Against Iraq Resolution of 2002," Public Law 107-243-October 16, 2002, www.broadbandc-span.org/downloads/hjres114.pdf.

510. Solomon, op. cit., pp. 154-187.

511. Alterman and Green, op. cit., p. 285.

512. Solomon, op. cit., p. 70.

513. "White House: U.S. doesn't need U.N. permission on Iraq," November 10, 2002, www.cnn.com/2002/US/11/10/iraq.policy/.

514. Solomon, op. cit., p. 71.

515. Ibid., p. 97.

516. Woodward, op. cit., pp. 269-270.

517. "The Security Council, 27 January 2003: An Update On Inspection," www.aidanews.it/print.asp?IDarticle=529.

518. "The Status of Nuclear Inspections in Iraq: Statement to the United Nations Security Council," International Atomic Energy Agency, February 14, 2003, www.gwu.edu.

519. "Memorandum Submitted by France, Germany & Russia on Iraq Weapons Inspections - Feb. 24, 2003," c-span.org/resources/fyi/frenchresolution-asp.

520. "Statement of The Atlantic Summit: Commitment to Transatlantic Solidarity - March 16, 2003," www.whitehouse.gov/news/releases/2003/03/200316-2.html.

521. "Statement of The Atlantic Summit: A Vision For Iraq and the Iraqi People - March 16, 2003," c-span.org/resources.

522. Alterman and Green, op. cit., p. 271.

523. "President Says Saddam Hussein Must Leave Iraq Within 48 Hours," www.whitehouse.gov/news/releases.

524. Ibid.

525. Kamiya, Gary, "The case of the last-minute offer," November 7, 2003 www.salon.com/opinion/feature/2003/11/07/iraq/index1.html.

526. "President Bush Addresses the Nation," www.whitehouse.gov/news/releases.

527. "The Biggest Threat To Peace," *TIME EUROPE*, http://www.time.com/time/europe/gdml/peace2003.html

528. "Remarks by the President on the Wartime Supplemental Budget, March 25, 2003, www.whitehouse.gov/news/releases/2003/03/20030325-2.html.

529. Corn, op. cit., p. 267.

530. Ibid., p. 269.

531. Ibid., p. 270.

532. Ibid., p. 274.

533. "Vilified weapons inspectors may have got it right," May 1, 2003, http://www.smh.com.au/articles/2003/04/30/1051381997497.html.

534. Corn, op. cit., p. 276.

535. "Rum remark wins Rumsfeld an award," December 2, 2003, http://news/bbc.co.uk/2/hi/americas.

536. Corn, op. cit., p. 278.

537. Ibid., p. 280.

538. Ibid., p. 283.

539. Hudson, Audrey, "Foreign militants converging, making Iraq terror battlefield," *The Washington Times*, August 25, 2003, www.washingtontimes.com.

540. Alterman and Green, op. cit., p. 297.

541. "Iraq Coalition Casualty Count," http://lunaville.org/warcasualties/Summary.aspx.

542. Hudson, op. cit.

543. Curl, Joseph, "Bush pledges 'no retreat' from Iraq," *The Washington Times*, August 27, 2003, www.washingtontimes/national/20030827-120012-2591r.html.

544. Neubauer, Chuck and Ken Silverstein, "War College Study Calls Iraq a 'Detour,'" *Los Angeles Times*, January 12, 2004, p. A4.

545. Rampton, op. cit., p. 204.

546. Ibid.

547. "Statement of The Atlantic Summit: A Vision For Iraq and the Iraqi People - March 16, 2003," c-span.org/resources.

548. "President Bush Addresses the Nation," www.whitehouse.gov/news/releases.

549. Goldenberg, Suzanne, "Up to 15,000 people killed in invasion, claims thinktank," *The Guardian*, October 29, 2003, www.guardian.co.uk/Iraq/Story/0,2763,1073070,00.html.

550. Rampton, op. cit., p. 192.

551. Kellner, op. cit., p. 94.

552. Ibid., p. 24; see also Rampton, op. cit., pp. 194-198.

553. Kellner, op. cit., pp. 94, 205.

554. Farley, Maggie, "Report Notes Toll of Cluster Bombs, Strikes in Iraq," *Los Angeles Times*, December 12, 2003, p. A15.

555. Murphy, Melissa and Carl Conetta, "Civilian Casualties in the 2003 Iraq War: A Compendium of Accounts and Reports," Project on Defense Alternatives, May 21, 2003, http://www.comw.org/pda/.

556. "Over 1,500 violent civilian deaths in occupied Baghdad,"
http://www.iraqbodycount.net/ibc23sep03.htm.

557. Rubin, Alissa J., "4 Iraqi Women Slain on Way to Work at Base,"
Los Angeles Times, January 23, 2004, p. A5; see also Gettleman, Jeffrey,
"11 Iraqi Police Officers Are Killed by Gunmen," *The New York Times*,
March 24, 2004, www.nytimes.com/2004/03/24/international/
middleeast/24IRAQ.html.

558. Filkins, Dexter, "25 Slain and 40 Wounded in Iraq as Raid on
Police Frees Prisoners," *New York Times*, February 15, 2004,
www.nytimes.com/2004/02/15/interntional/
middleeast/15IRAQ.html?th.

559. Rudd, Kevin, "Australia Is One Of The 3 'Occupying Powers' In
Iraq–But As Hospitals Are Looted The Red Cross Says The Occupying
Powers Aren't Doing Their Job," (www.alp.org.au//media/0403/
20004160.html); see also "Over 1,500 violent civilian deaths in occupied
Baghdad," (http://www.iraqbodycount.net/ibc23sep03.htm).

560. "President Bush Addresses the Nation,"
www.whitehouse.gov/news/releases.

561. "Iraq Coalition Casualty Count,"
http://lunaville.org/warcasualties/Summary.aspx.

562. Loeb, Vernon, "Number of Wounded in Action on Rise: Iraq Toll
Reflects Medical Advances, Resistance Troops Face," *Washington Post*,
September 2, 2003, (washingtonpost.com); see also Goff, Stan, "The
Missing Wounded: Injury and Decorum in Iraq," *Counterpunch*,
August 1, 2003, (www.counterpunch.org/goff08012003.html).

563. Rampton, op. cit., p. 193.

564. Burns, Robert, "November Deadliest Month for U.S. Troops
in Iraq," *Associated Press*, November 9, 2003,
guestbooks.pathfinder.gr/read/HarryShannon?pass=&page=9.

565. Price, Niko, "U.S. Troops Kill Dozens of Iraqi Attackers,"
Associated Press, November 30, 2003,
www.siliconinvestor.com/stocktalk/mag.gsp?msquid=19548530.

566. "Poll: Many troops in Iraq dissatisfied," October 16, 2003,
www.msnbc.com/news/980954.asp?0c/=c3.

567. Hendren, John, "Big Bonus for Re-Upping With Uncle Sam,"
Los Angeles Times, January 6, 2004, p. A6.

568. Goldenberg, Suzanne, "Dissent on the home front: families of US soldiers in Iraq lead anti-war protests," *The Guardian,* October 25, 2003, www.guardian.co.uk/international/story/0,36041,00.html.

569. Shenon, Philip, "Officer Suggests Iraq Jail Abuse Was Encouraged," *The New York Times,* May 2, 2004, www.nytimes.com/2004/05/02/international/middleeast/02ABUS.html; see also Risen, James, "Report on Abuse Faults 2 Officers In Intelligence," *The New York Times,* May 3, 2004, www.nytimes.com/2004/05/03/international/middleeast/03ABUS.html

570. Goldenberg, op. cit.

571. Goldenberg, Suzanne, "Psychological Cost of Iraq War Evidenced by High Suicide Rate," *Guardian,* March 29, 2004, www.guardian.co.uk/international/story/0,3604,1179916,00.html.

572. Goldenberg, "Dissent on the home front," op. cit.

573. Schrader, Esther, "U.S. Plans Massive Rotation of Troops," *Los Angeles Times,* December 10, 2003.

574. "I Feel Like I'm Fixin' to Die Rag," © 1965 by Joe McDonald.

575. Benjamin, Mark, "Father of dead soldier claims Army cover-up," *United Press International,* August 7, 2003, www.avip2001.net/docs/cover-up.html.

576. Hewitt, Giles, "How US media cover military casualties in Iraq?" indiaink.net/forums/general/posts/3070.html.

577. Emery, Erin and John Aloysius Farrell, "Iraq has them wounded for life," *Denver Post,* November 23, 2003.

578. Saulnier, Natasha, "The Forgotten Soldiers of Operation 'Iraqi Freedom,'" March 7, 2004, www.gregpalast.com/detail.cfm?artid=317&row=0

579. Herbert, Bob, "Our Wounded Warriors," *The New York Times,* March 12, 2004, www.nytimes.com/2004/03/12/opinion/12HERB.html.

580. Hackworth, David, "14,000 and Counting," *Press-Telegram,* January 1, 2004, p. A19.

581. Weisman, Jonathan, "War May Require More Money Soon," *Washington Post,* April 21, 2004, www.washingtonpost.com/wp-dyn/articles/A31211-2004Apr21.html.

582. Decker, Ashley L., "Support the Warrior Not the War: Give Them Their Benefits!" *Common Dreams,* March 28, 2003, (www.commondreams.org); see also Smith, David, "Veterans' Benefits Cut," (www.futurenet.org/26courage/indicatorsmith.html); see also

Sweet, Phoebe, "Bush, GOP take aim at vets' benefits," April 11, 2003, (http://www.townonline.com/allston/news/local_regional/ab_covab vets04112003.html).

583. Douglas, William, "Bush Military Support Slipping," *Press-Telegram*, March 14, 2004, p. A10.

584. Douglas, William, "Democracy and Dissent," *Press-Telegram*, March 15, 2004, p. A7.

585. "Campaign Opens for Censure of Bush," *Los Angeles Times*, March 18, 2004, p. A22.

586. Stutz, Adam, "U.S. Preparing for Military Draft in Spring 2005," January 28, 2004, www.voiceoffreedom.com/draft/reinstatedraft.html; see also Lindorff, Dave, "Oiling Up The Draft Machine," *Salon*, November 3, 2003, www.informationclearinghouse.info/ article5146.htm; see also Cochran, Connor Freff, "The Coming Draft," *Alternet*, March 25, 2004, http://www.alternet.org/story.html?storyID=18255.

THE CRIMES OF GEORGE W. BUSH

International law establishes standards for national self defense and the treatment of POWs, who are accorded certain rights, but the Bush administration seems to be ignoring the law for political reasons. In the name of national security, is the United States becoming an outlaw state?

In the closing days of World War II, the nations of the world gathered together and established the United Nations to protect international peace and to avoid a repeat of the war that had just engaged practically every country on earth and cost millions of lives. In its Charter, the United Nations defined the duties of a nation to peacefully settle international disputes and provided only a very limited right for a country to wage war against another without drawing the condemnation of its peers. When the United States ratified the Charter of the United Nations, it became the supreme law of the land, binding on all those who thereafter occupied the Oval Office.

Illegal Use of Force

When the United States adopted "regime change" as an objective and when Bush threatened that he would use military force against Iraq unless Saddam and his two sons left the country, the United States violated sections three and four of Article 2 of the United Nations Charter which provides, "All members shall settle their international disputes by peaceful means in such a manner that international peace and security, and justice, are not endangered [and shall] refrain in their international relations from the threat or use of force against the territorial integrity or political independence of any state."[587]

Article 51 of the Charter provides that "Nothing in the present Charter shall impair the inherent right of individual or collective self-defence if an armed attack occurs against a Member of the United Nations, until the Security Council has taken measures necessary to maintain international peace and security." This legitimate right of self-defense has been defined as allowing anticipatory self-defense in response to an *imminent* attack; but it is justified only when the necessity for action is "instant, overwhelming, and leaving no choice of means, and no moment for deliberation." However, there is no legal basis in international law for Bush's new theory of preemptive war against the *potential* "threat" of danger.[588]

One reason that such preemptive wars are prohibited is demonstrated by what happened in Bush's War. He was determined to exact a "regime change" in Iraq, and although he tried to justify his aggression through a massive campaign of propaganda and deception, the invasion proved that there was no imminent threat in the first place. No weapons of mass destruction were found. Had the United States found ICBMs armed with atomic, biological or chemical weapons, targeted at America, the case might have been different. However, one should keep in mind that in America today there are thousands of ICBMs so armed and aimed at other countries. Does that give all of the targeted countries the right to conduct a preemptive strike against us?

We have to ask ourselves, assuming our invasion was something like the service of a search warrant, what if any evidence was found that might justify a prosecution of Saddam in a court in the United States for a crime against the United States, or its people? The answer is none. Without question, Saddam has committed monstrous crimes against his own people, and for that he should be prosecuted, convicted and sentenced, by the people of Iraq.

The terrorist attack on September 11, 2001, provides no justification for an invasion of Iraq. On January 31, 2003, before he launched his war, a reporter specifically asked Bush if there was any evidence of a direct link "between Saddam Hussein and the men who attacked on September the 11th?" Bush answered, "I can't make that claim."[589] Following the invasion, and after a poll found approximately 70 percent of Americans to believe that Saddam was connected, the White House denied ever linking Saddam to the 9/11 attacks.[*]   On September 17, 2003, Bush's spokesman Scott McClellan stated, "We said that we don't have any evidence to suggest a connection."[590]

Moreover, in July 2003, the joint congressional inquiry into the 9/11 attacks reported that it had found no evidence that Saddam was in any way connected with the al Qaeda terrorists.[591]

Therefore, what possible justification did we have to wage Bush's War?   One possibility might be Security Council Resolution 687, adopted at the end of the Gulf War, which authorized the continued use of force if Saddam was found to be in noncompliance. However, that doesn't work either, because it is the Security Council, and not member states operating unilaterally, that has the right to use force.

The Security Council, in Resolution 1442, which ordered the last minute inspections, remained "seized of the matter." Therefore, the matter remained on the agenda, and it was up to the *Security Council* to determine if Saddam was in compliance with its Resolution, *not* up to the United States. It was the *Security Council* which had the legitimate power to impose "serious consequences" in the case of violations, *not* the United States.

Bush lied when he declared, "The United Nations Security Council has not lived up to its responsibilities," and he placed himself in legal jeopardy when he continued, "so we will rise to ours."[592] When on his "orders" American troops invaded Iraq, he and those associated with him who shared his guilty knowledge and malicious intent became war criminals under international law.

---

[*] However, there is no stopping Cheney from lying about the connection and continuing to mislead the American people. On January 22, 2004, he stated, "There's overwhelming evidence there was a connection between al Qaeda and the Iraqi government. I am very confident that there was an established relationship there." (Miller, Greg, "Cheney Is Adamant on Iraq 'Evidence,'" *Los Angeles Times*, January 23, 2004, p. A1.)

It is becoming increasingly accepted that Bush and his administration lied to provide justification for his war, even by Bush's staunchest allies. Poland's President Aleksander Kwasniewski, recently remarked that Iraq "without Saddam Hussein is truly better than Iraq with Saddam Hussein," but went on to say, "naturally, I also feel uncomfortable, due to the fact that we were misled with the information on weapons of mass destruction."[593]

Upon his election following the train bombings that killed at least 200, Spain's new Prime Minister Jose Luis Rodriguez Zapatero said he would withdraw Spanish troops in Iraq by June 30 unless the United Nations issued a new mandate. Zapatero said that Bush and Blair needed "to engage in some self-criticism" over their war. "You can't bombard a people just in case they pose a perceived threat. You can't organize a war on the basis of lies." He said that such wars "only allow hatred, violence and terror to proliferate."[594]

Do you agree that the United States has the right to invade any country our president deems to be a threat, just because we have the military power to do so? You're not stupid! Get the truth.

Illegal Detention of Prisoners of War

On November 13, 2001, as the "Commander in Chief of the Armed Forces of the United States," Bush issued an executive order creating military tribunals for the detention and trial of non-American citizens taken into custody during the war against terrorism. Individuals subject to the order are defined as those who (1) are members of al Qaeda; (2) have engaged in, aided or abetted, or conspired to commit, acts of international terrorism, or acts in preparation therefor, that have caused, threaten to cause, or have as their aim to cause injury or adverse effects on the United States, its citizens, national security, foreign policy, or economy; or (3) have knowingly harbored one or more such individuals."[595] The order is so broadly written that it could be applied to anyone, anywhere in the world, who displays an intent to cause an adverse effect on citizens or the economy of the United States and to anyone who harbored them—which could be just about anyone.

The order empowers Secretary of Defense Rumsfeld to detain any subject individuals whenever and wherever he chooses and to appoint military commissions to try them "for any and all offenses triable by military commission that such individual is alleged to have committed, and may be punished in accordance with the penalties provided under applicable law, including life imprisonment or death." There is no right to access the civil courts of the United States, nor is there a right to appeal.[596]

Pursuant to the order, Rumsfeld established an outdoor camp at Guantanamo Bay in Cuba, where he has locked up approximately 650 "enemy combatants" in six-by-eight-foot chain-link cages open to the elements on three sides. Their only protection from the sun and rain is a low sheet metal roof and orange jumpsuits. They sleep on mats on the floor under floodlighted conditions. Rumsfeld stated that the detainees are not prisoners of war and have no rights under the Geneva Conventions. Bush later said that "official Taliban" troops would be considered as POWs; however, it is not clear if any of the detainees have been so designated.[597]

Many of the detainees have now been held in the cages for two years, without access to counsel, trials or visitors.* The military is considering constructing a death row and execution chambers where selected detainees can be tried, convicted and

---

* The United States is prepared to hold some of these prisoners for many years, perhaps indefinitely. Defense Department officials say that a military panel will review the long-term prisoners' cases annually to determine if they continue to be a threat to the United States. Even if an individual is convicted by a military tribunal and serves a long prison term, he would not be released if he were judged to remain a danger. The military is building a hard-walled traditional prison alongside the corrugated metal units which will house about 100 prisoners, although it denies that the prison will contain an execution chamber. (Lewis, Neil A. and Eric Schmitt, "Cuba Detentions May Last Years," *The New York Times*, February 13, 2004, http://www.nytimes.com/2004/02/13/politics/13GITM.html?th.)

executed by military tribunals without leaving the camp, all without a jury or right to appeal.

Although POWs are only required to provide their name, date of birth, rank and serial number, the prisoners are repeatedly subjected to intense interrogations and at least 18 have attempted suicide.[598] How would we feel if American citizens were being held under these conditions at any other location in the world? We would be outraged!

The United States has ratified the four Geneva Conventions of 1949, which establish the standards for protecting captured combatants and civilians during armed conflicts. The Third Geneva Convention defines prisoners of war (POWs) and lists the protection to be accorded them. "Unlawful combatants," who are not accorded POW status, are still entitled to the protections enumerated under the Fourth Convention, as they relate to the Protection of Civilian Persons in Time of War.

Under international humanitarian law, according to the Commentary of the Geneva Conventions of the International Committee of the Red Cross: "Every person in enemy hands must have some status under international law: he is either a prisoner of war and, as such, covered by the Third Convention, a civilian covered by the Fourth convention, [or] a member of the medical personnel of the armed forces who is covered by the First Convention. There is no intermediate status; nobody in enemy hands can fall outside the law."[599] Therefore, Bush and Rumsfeld violate international law each and every day they continue to deny basic rights to their prisoners.

The Third Geneva Convention establishes a presumption that any doubt as to whether a detainee belongs to the category of POW be resolved in favor of the individual. They are entitled to the protection of the Convention until a competent tribunal determines their status.

In 1997, the U.S. Military established detailed procedures for tribunals to resolve any doubts as to status. These regulations provide that detainees have the right to be advised of their rights, to attend all sessions, to call and question witnesses, to refuse to testify, and to address the tribunal. The standard of proof is a preponderance of the evidence, and the tribunal is required to issue a written decision in every case.[600]

POWs cannot be tried simply for having carried arms in combat, and if "unlawful combatants" are prosecuted for war crimes, they must be afforded the same rights provided to members of the trying military forces. The Pentagon has announced that the prisoners might not be released even if they were tried and acquitted.

One thing that has characterized Bush and Rumsfeld's detention of the prisoners is an information blackout. Visitors are not allowed, nor is any information provided regarding the prisoners. Although a few prisoners have been released, it does not appear that the vast majority has had any status tribunals, nor have there been any war crime trials.[601]

The information blackout has led to the arrest of at least four individuals who have attempted to get word out about the identity of prisoners and the conditions under which they are being caged. Colonel Jackie Farr was arrested as he attempted to leave Guantanamo Bay with "classified" material in his luggage, and Captain James (Yousef) Yee, a Muslim Chaplain, was arrested for espionage and treason after being found to have drawings of the camp and a list of prisoners in his luggage.

The charges against Yee were subsequently dropped in March 2004 after he was held in solitary confinement in a naval brig for nearly three months. Two Arabic translators, Senior Airman Ahmed Halabi and civilian linguist Ahmed Mehalba, were arrested for similar "offenses."[602] What are Bush and Rumsfeld trying to hide?

In a case filed by the brother of one of the individuals detained at Guantanamo Bay, the San Francisco-based 9th U.S. Circuit Court of Appeals ruled on December 19, 2003, that the prisoners of the war on terrorism should have access to legal counsel and the American court system. Judge Stephen Reinhardt wrote, "Even in times of national emergency–indeed, particularly in such times–it is the obligation of the Judicial Branch to ensure the preservation of our constitutional values and to prevent the Executive Branch from running roughshod over the rights of citizens and aliens alike. ... We simply cannot accept the government's position that the executive branch possesses the unchecked authority to imprison indefinitely any persons, foreign citizens included ... without permitting such prisoners recourse of any kind to any judicial forum."

The U.S. Supreme Court has already agreed to review another ruling by the Washington, D.C. Circuit Court of Appeals, which rendered an opposite opinion, holding that "enemy combatants" have no rights to the American legal system. Given the domination of the Supreme Court by the Federalist Society, it is unlikely that the opinion of the 9th Circuit will prevail.[603]

In one of his last official acts, President Clinton signed the "Rome" treaty establishing The International Criminal Court in the Netherlands, based on the principles of the World War II war crime trials, to judge individuals accused of mass murders, war crimes, and other gross human rights violations. Clinton said, "In taking this action, we join more than 130 other countries that have signed ... the treaty. We do so to reaffirm our strong support for international accountability and for bringing to justice perpetrators of genocide, war crimes and crimes against humanity." The Pentagon had opposed the court because it could try U.S. military personnel who commit crimes outside the United States.[604]

The Rome treaty became effective on July 1, 2002, and the Court assumed jurisdiction over war crimes; however, Bush had already "unsigned" the treaty on behalf of the United States in May 2002. He announced that the United States would provide neither information nor cooperation. Bush also threatened to veto any United Nations peacekeeping missions unless the Security Council provided immunity to all Americans engaged in the mission. He also announced that we were no longer bound by the Vienna Convention on the Law of Treaties, which establishes our obligations to conform to treaties that have been signed, but not yet ratified. Accordingly, we are no longer bound by the 1989 Convention on Children's Rights, because we want to continue sending 17-year-old boys and girls into battle.[605]

Among the prisoners held at Guantanamo Bay were five British citizens who had been held since their capture in 2001 and 2002. They were finally released in March 2004 with the United States insisting that they be "managed" with "appropriate and specific steps." However, the Blair government believes that "any evidence gathered under Guantanamo's vague legal standings probably would be ruled inadmissible in British courts."

Four British citizens remain in custody at Guantanamo, and the Blair government insists that "the right to a lawyer and the right to appeal were essential" in any U.S. trial. "Lord Justice Johan Steyn, a senior British judge, recently called the Guantanamo detentions 'a monstrous failure of justice,' and there is a sense in Britain that the Bush administration has abandoned some of the principles it claims to be fighting for in its campaign against terrorism."[606]

As "Commander in Chief," Bush is responsible for all acts committed under the authority of his orders, including the unlawful detention of prisoners under inhumane conditions at Guantanamo Bay in Cuba. Whether the International Criminal Court can or will assume jurisdiction is doubtful; however, Bush will be judged by the people of the world and by the voters of America when they go to the polls in November.

Are you proud of the fact that Bush and Rumsfeld are caging individuals who had nothing to do with the 9/11 attacks and who, by any reasonable measure, are entitled to protection under the Geneva Conventions? Under Bush's leadership, we are increasingly going it alone. Is he right? Are we right to blindly follow him? You're not stupid! Get the truth.

Impeachment

When Bush caused the United States to violate its duties under international law, he also subjected himself to impeachment. Article VI, Clause 2 of the United States Constitution makes international treaties such as the United Nations Charter, which was ratified by the Senate in 1945, the "supreme law of the land."[607]

Not only did Bush cause the United States to violate the Charter, but he also operated extralegally beyond the authority granted him by Congress in its resolution of October 10, 2002. He was not acting to enforce "all relevant United Nations Security Council resolutions regarding Iraq," nor was he acting to "defend the national security of the United States against the continuing threat posed by Iraq."[608]

Article II, Section 4 of the U.S. Constitution provides, "The President, Vice President and all civil officers of the United States, shall be removed from office on impeachment for, and conviction of, treason, bribery, or other high crimes and misdemeanors." By committing war crimes in violation of the supreme law of the land, Bush also committed a high crime or misdemeanor within the meaning of the Constitution.

Moreover, Bush is subject to impeachment for having lied to Congress, repeatedly, specifically during his State of the Union address on January 28, 2003, when he stated that the IAEA "confirmed in the 1990's that Saddam Hussein had an advanced nuclear weapons development program," and again when he stated, "The British Government has learned that Saddam Hussein recently sought significant quantities of uranium from Africa."

Title 18 of the United States Code, Section 1001 prohibits anyone from "knowingly and willfully" making "any materially false, fictitious, or fraudulent statement or representation" in "any matter within the jurisdiction of the ... legislative ... branch of the Government." The U.S. Supreme Court upheld felony prosecution under the statute in 1955, and a violation of the statute is a crime.[609]

Bush again violated Section 1001 when he wrote to Congress on March 18, 2003, as required by the Congressional resolution authorizing the use of military force against Iraq. In the letter, Bush stated he had determined that:

(1) reliance by the United States on further diplomatic and other peaceful means alone will neither (A) adequately protect the national security of the United States against the continuing threat posed by Iraq nor

(B) likely lead to enforcement of all relevant United Nations Security Council resolutions regarding Iraq; and

(2) acting pursuant to the Constitution and Public Law 107-243 is consistent with the United States and other countries continuing to take the necessary actions against international terrorists and terrorist organizations, including those nations, organizations, or persons who planned, authorized, committed, or aided the terrorist attacks that occurred on September 11, 2001.[610]

The letter is a complete lie and distortion. Iraq did not pose a threat to the United States, and further diplomatic and other peaceful means would have adequately protected our national security. The United States did not have to invade Iraq to enforce Security Council resolutions, as continued U.N. inspections would have likely succeeded. Most importantly, at the time Bush wrote the letter, he knew that there was no evidence that Iraq had "planned, authorized, committed, or aided" the 9/11 attack."

Increasingly, there is no doubt that Bush has, in fact, repeatedly lied to us. On January 8, 2004, the Carnegie Endowment for International Peace issued a comprehensive report, "WMD in Iraq: Evidence and Implications." The authors charge that the Bush administration "systematically misrepresented" the threat posed by Saddam's WMDs and called for the creation of an independent commission to fully investigate what the U.S. intelligence community knew about the true state of Iraq's WMD program. One of the authors, Joseph Cirincione said, "It is very likely that intelligence officials were pressured by senior administration officials to conform their threat assessments to pre-existing policies."

The report finds "no solid evidence" of cooperation between Saddam and al Qaeda. "The notion that any government would give its principal security assets to people it could not control in order to achieve its own political aims is highly dubious." Finally, the report concludes that the United Nations inspection process, which was terminated by Bush's War, "appears to have been much more successful than recognized before the war."[611]

Congressman Henry A. Waxman, the senior Democratic member of the House Government Reform Committee asked its Special Investigations Division to examine the public statements of Bush, Cheney, Rumsfeld, Powell, and Rice to identify the extent that the five made false and misleading statements regarding Bush's War.

On March 16, 2004, the committee staff submitted its report, "Iraq on the Record: The Bush Administration's Public Statements on Iraq," to the Committee. The investigators found that the five made misleading statements about the threat posed by Iraq in 125 public appearances and identified 237 specific misleading statements. The deceptive statements were divided into four categories. "There were 11 statements that claimed Iraq posed an urgent threat; 81 statements that exaggerated Iraq's nuclear activities; 84 statements that overstated Iraq's chemical and biological weapons capabilities; and 61 statements that misrepresented Iraq's ties to al Qaeda."[612]

The false statements commenced on March 17, 2002 when Cheney stated "We know they have biological and chemical weapons," and continued through January 22, 2004 when he claimed that "there's overwhelming evidence that there was a connection between al-Qaeda and the Iraqi government."[613]

The investigation found that most of the misleading statements—161—were made prior to the war, but 76 misleading statements were made after its commencement to justify the decision. During the 30-day period leading up to the congressional vote on the war resolution Bush and the other four engaged in a blistering pace of deception. They made a total of 64 misleading statements in 16 public appearances.[614]

The report found that Bush individually made 55 misleading statements about the threat posed by Iraq in 27 separate public statements or appearances. Of these, "4 claimed that Iraq posed an urgent threat; 14 exaggerated Iraq's efforts to develop nuclear weapons; 18 overstated Iraq's chemical or biological weapons capacity; and 19 misrepresented Iraq's links to al Qaeda."[615]

In just one speech, in Cincinnati, Ohio on October 7, 2002, Bush made a total of 11 misleading statements, "the highest number of misleading statements in any single appearance by any of the five officials."[616]

Some of the biggest whoppers told by Bush include:

• "On its present course, the Iraqi regime is a threat of unique urgency…. It has developed weapons of mass death."

• "The British government has learned that Saddam Hussein recently sought significant quantities of uranium from Africa."

• "The liberation of Iraq…removed an ally of al Qaeda."

• "We found the weapons of mass destruction…. [F]or those who say we haven't found the banned manufacturing devices of banned weapons, they're wrong, we found them."[617]

How many of his crimes will the American public tolerate before we insist that Bush be impeached? In fact, under the doctrine of preemptive strike, shouldn't the House of Representatives take action now before he brings down the fury of the rest of the world upon the United States? You're not stupid! Get the truth.

587. Mark, Peter, "The Case Against Preemption," *Asia Times Online*, October 9, 2002, www.atimes.com.

588. Lobel, Jules, "The United Nations Charter And The Use Of Force Against Iraq," October 2, 2002, www.lcnp.org/global/Iraqstatement.3.pdf.

589. "Bush Flatly Declares No Connection Between Saddam and al Qaeda," www.thememoryhole.org/war/no-saddam-qaeda.htm.

590. "White House denies tying Iraq to September 11 attacks," September 17, 2003, Agence France-Presse, http://quickstart.clari.net/qs_se/webnews.

591. Waterman, Shaun, "9/11 Report: No Iraq Link to al-Qaeda," July 23, 2003, *United Press International*, http://truthout.org/docs.

592. "President Says Saddam Hussein Must Leave Iraq Within 48 Hours," www.whitehouse.gov/news/releases.

593. Richter, Paul, "Poles 'Misled' on Iraq, President Says," *Los Angeles Times*, March 19, 2004.

594. Efron, Sonni and Bruce Wallace, "Spanish Victor Says Iraq War Based on 'Lies,'" *Los Angeles Times*, March 16, 2004, http://www.latimes.com/news/nationworld/world/la-fg-spain16mar16,1,7723246.story?coll=la-home-headlines.

595. "Military Order, Detention, Treatment, and Trial of Certain Non-Citizens in the War Against Terrorism," http://news.findlaw.com/cnn/docs/terrorism/bushtribunalord11301.

596. "President Bush Signs Executive Order Authorizing Military Tribunals," http://www.hrcv.org/hottopics/tribunal.

597. "Guantanamo Bay Prisoners," http://www.strange-loops.com.

598. Ibid.

599. Human Rights Watch, "Background Paper on Geneva Conventions and Persons Held by U.S. Forces," http://hrw.org/backgrounder/usa/pow-bck.html.

600. Ibid.

601. Ibid.; see also Seelye, Katharine Q., "War Captives Could Be Held If Acquitted," March 23, 2002, (why-war.com).

602. Tully, Andrew, "U.S.: Military Probes Security At Base In Cuba After Three Arrested," (www.rferl.org/nca/features); see also Rosenberg, Carol, "Officer Charged With Guantanamo Security Breach," (www.miami.com/mid/miamiherald); see also Lewis, Neil A., "Charges Dropped Against Chaplain," *The New York Times*, March 20, 2004, (www.nytimes.com/2004/03/20/national/20YEE.html).

603. Mintz, John, "Detainee to Get Hearing," *The Washington Post*, December 19, 2003, http://www.washingtonpost.com.

604. Charles, Deborah, "Clinton signs treaty to bring U.S. under jurisdiction of global criminal court," December 31, 2000, http://www.citizenreviewonline.org.

605. Ivins, op. cit., pp. 258, 259.

606. Wallace, Bruce, "5 Terror Suspects Return to Britain," *Los Angeles Times*, March 10, 2004, A3.

607. Lobel, Jules, "The United Nations Charter And The Use Of Force Against Iraq," October 2, 2002, www.lcnp.org/global/ Iraqstatement.3.pdf.

608. "Authorization For Use of Military Force Against Iraq Resolution of 2002," Public Law 107-243-October 16, 2002, www.broadbandc-span.org/downloads/hjres114.pdf.

609. Dean, John W., "Why a Special Prosecutor's Investigation Is Needed," July 18, 2003, writ.news.findlaw.com/dean/20030718.html.

610. "Text of a Letter from the President to the Speaker of the House of Representatives and the President Pro Tempore of the Senate," March 18, 2003, www.whitehouse.gov/news/releases/ 2003/03/print/20030319-1.html.

611. Cirincione, Joseph, et. al. *WMD in Iraq: Evidence and Implications*, Washington, D.C.: Carnegie Endowment for World Peace, January 2004, (www.ceip.org/files/Publications/IraqReport3.asp? p=8&from=pubdate); see also Lobe, Jim, "New WMD Report Slams Bush White House," Inter Press Service, January 9, 2004, (http://www.alternet.org/story.html?StoryID=17522).

612. "Iraq on the Record: The Bush Administration's Public Statements on Iraq," United States House of Representatives, Committee on Government Reform—Minority Staff, Special Investigations Division, March 16, 2004, www.reform.house.gov/min.

613. Ibid.

614. Ibid.

615. Ibid., p. 25.

616. Ibid., p. 26.

617. Ibid., p. 26

JUSTICE IN AMERICA

Superpatriots claiming that our nation is great because of personal freedom say in the next breath that national security demands less of it. America's top cop, while engaged in a wholesale attack on constitutional rights, has turned a blind eye to administration friends who break the law.

A self-employed Bavarian chicken farmer raised by a devout Catholic schoolmaster, Heinrich Himmler became convinced that Adolf Hitler was the messiah sent by God to lead Germany to greatness, and he marched beside Hitler in his failed 1923 Beer Hall *Putsch*.[618] Once the Nazis came to power and abolished the freedom of the press, the freedom of labor to strike, and the freedom of other political parties to participate in the government, Himmler quickly rose through Party ranks to become Germany's chief of police, second in absolute power only to Hitler himself. Himmler established the concentration camps, trained the guards, selected the inmates, scheduled the transports, and created the gas chambers and cremation ovens.[619]

Among those selected for transport was Pastor Martin Niemöller, who opposed Hitler's efforts to bring German churches under Nazi control. Pastor Niemöller was arrested in 1937 and was confined in concentration camps until 1945. He later wrote,

> "First they came for the Communists, but I was not a Communist, so I said nothing. Then they came for the Social Democrats, but I was not a Social Democrat, so I did nothing. Then came the trade unionists, but I was not a trade unionist. And then they came for the Jews, but I was not a Jew, so I did little. Then when they came for me, there was no one left to stand up for me."[620]

Discretionary Justice

The Attorney General is not a constitutional officer, and the Department of Justice was not created until 1870. Since then, the Justice Department has grown into the largest law firm in the country. Its primary task is to represent the citizens of America in enforcing the law in the public interest. In addition to supervising the U.S. Attorneys in the prosecution of the federal criminal code, it also enforces the drug, immigration and naturalization laws.[621]

The Department of Justice does much more than prosecute. It is also the nation's police force, fielding both the Federal Bureau of Investigation and the Drug Enforcement Agency. Moreover, through its Civil Rights Division, established in 1957, the Justice Department enforces the Civil Rights Acts, the Voting Rights Act, the Equal Credit Opportunity Act, the Americans with Disabilities Act, the National Voter Registration Act, the Uniformed and Overseas Citizens Absentee Voting Act; the Voting Accessibility for the Elderly and Handicapped Act, the Civil Rights of Institutionalized Persons Act, the Freedom of Access to Clinic Entrances Act, the Police Misconduct Provision of the Violent Crime Control and Law Enforcement Act of 1994, as well as Section 102 of the Immigration Reform and Control Act of 1986, which prohibits discrimination on the basis of national origin and citizenship status. It coordinates the civil rights enforcement efforts of other federal agencies and assists them in identifying and removing discriminatory provisions in their policies and programs.[622]

Thus, in one way or another, the activities of the Justice Department impact the lives of virtually every person in America. If we are to maintain our free society, the awesome power vested in the Justice Department must be exercised in a fair and even-handed manner, in accordance with the laws *and* the Constitution.

Perhaps more so than anything else, the manner in which our laws are enforced defines the very soul of our society. Are the officers of the law and the judges rigid and uncaring, or do they act with compassion and understanding? Are we treated equally? Does *our* government recognize that it is *our* government, that they are *our* laws that are being enforced by *our* justice system, and that they are *our* rights that are protected by *our* Constitution?

Law enforcement in a free society requires that there be a high degree of discretion exercised at every level. Do we really want robots making arrests for every single infraction, unthinking automatons prosecuting every chargeable offense, and heartless judges giving the maximum possible sentence in every case? Of course not. Individual justice must be administered in every individual case. Justice requires that all facts and circumstances, including aggravating and mitigating factors, be weighed and that discretion be exercised according to thoughtful written policies that take into consideration the wide range of human frailties and motivations, and the expectations of our free society.

Moreover, given the fact that a limited budget requires the establishment of priorities and the careful allocation of scarce resources, the decisions made by the Attorney General must be free of personal bias and political taint. Thus, there is the potential for great good to be performed on behalf of the people of the United States, and there is the risk of grave harm being caused to us and to our institutions. Therein lies the rub.

The Would-Be President and the Anointing of Ashcroft

John Ashcroft wanted to be president of the United States. He had the ambition, he had lived right, and he thought he had the nod from God, but he just didn't have the political horsepower.

Ashcroft grew up in a household dominated by his father, a second generation Assemblies of God minister, who taught his son that every child should grow up to be a preacher, learn to speak in tongues, engage in faith healing, and spread the word. Raised as a Pentecostal, Ashcroft doesn't believe in drinking, smoking, gambling, or even dancing. He doesn't believe in abortions, even in cases of rape or incest; nor the equal rights of women, even for those with great talent; he doesn't believe in equal rights of religion, especially for those "Oriental" ones; he doesn't believe in equal rights for minorities, especially affirmative action; he doesn't believe in the separation of church and state, except to "protect the church;" but he does believe in

Internet censorship, school vouchers, and everyone's right to pack a gun.[623]

In 1975, Ashcroft was appointed as an assistant attorney general in Missouri; the next year he got the top job in a close race. After serving eight years as attorney general, he was elected governor and served two terms. In 1993, he tried and failed to be elected chairman of the Republican Party, but he was elected to the U.S. Senate in 1994.[624]

On May 8, 1999, Senator Ashcroft gave a speech in which he stated, "Unique among the nations, America recognized the source of our character as being godly and eternal, not being civic and temporal. And because we have understood that our source is eternal, America has been different. We have no king but Jesus."[625] He has also said, "I think all we should legislate is morality."[626]

In 1999, Ashcroft thought he was positioned to become president. He gained the unofficial support of Dr. James Dobson, Pat Robertson and the Christian Coalition, as well as some of Pat Buchanan's former supporters. He thought he could beat Bush in the primaries, but he couldn't.[627] He thought he could be reelected Senator, but he wasn't. A dead man defeated him. That's right, for the first time in the history of the country. His opponent was former Governor Mel Carnahan, who was killed in a plane crash just weeks before the election. Ashcroft was defeated, and Carnahan's wife, Jean, was appointed to serve the term.[628]

Bush, a born-again Christian, was elected with the support of the religious right wing of the Republican Party, and to placate them, he nominated Ashcroft to be his Attorney General. It was as Ashcroft wrote in his memoir, "for every crucifixion there's a resurrection."[629] The only problem was to get him confirmed by the Senate. Ordinarily, the Senate would pay great deference to a former member of their exclusive club; however, those who knew Ashcroft best, knew him well. After a brutal hearing in which he swore he would not allow his religious beliefs to influence his administration of the law, Ashcroft was confirmed, barely, with 42 senators voting against him, including the new Senator Carnahan.[630]

Has he kept his promise? He immediately called upon Supreme Court Justice Clarence Thomas to anoint him with "holy oil" upon taking the office. (Like the messiahs of ancient Israel, Ashcroft has always been anointed with oil upon taking office, once with Crisco when nothing else was available.)[631] He has continued to preach that "The source of freedom and human dignity is the Creator. The guarding of freedom that God grants is the noble charge of the Department of Justice."

Ashcroft leads morning prayer meetings in his office, in which his staff has to join him in singing an inspirational song he wrote, "Let the Eagle Soar." The song includes these lines, "Let the mighty eagle soar. Soar with healing in her wings, as the land beneath her sings: 'Only God, no other kings.'... Built by toils and struggles God has led us through."[632] At a cost of $8,000, he ordered curtains to be hung in front of the bare-breasted Spirit of Justice statue in the Justice Department press room to avoid having its bronze nipple appear over his shoulder during photo opportunities.[633]

Referring to the morning Bible study classes, one of Ashcroft's lawyers said, "It strikes me and a lot of others as offensive, disrespectful and unconstitutional." The Government's guidelines on worship in the workplace seem to agree, "Because supervisors have the power to hire, fire or promote, employees may reasonably perceive their supervisors' religious expression as coercive, even if it was not intended as such."[634]

As we saw earlier, Ashcroft entirely failed in his management of the Department of Justice to avoid the terrorist attacks of September 11, 2001. Perhaps if he had spent more time listening to his FBI agents, who were worried about terrorists flying airplanes loaded with fuel into the World Trade Center, instead of preaching to them, he really could have led the "noble charge" and arrested all of the hijackers before their attack, or at least scared them off, instead of writing silly songs and violating the civil rights of his staff.

Do you believe Ashcroft represents your personal values? Do you believe he should be able to impose his personal values on you? You're not stupid! Get the truth.

Censoring the Freedom of Information Act

James Madison, one of our founding fathers, once observed, "A popular government, without popular information, or the means of acquiring it, is but a Prologue to a Farce or a Tragedy–or perhaps both. Knowledge will forever govern ignorance, and a people who mean to be their own Governors must arm themselves with the power which knowledge gives." Congress passed the Freedom of Information Act (FOIA), in 1966 to give meaning to Madison's words, and following the Watergate scandal, it amended the Act to essentially open up all public records to public view, with a few limited exceptions.[635]

The Act provides that "Each agency *shall* make" public information available, and empowered the federal courts to prevent agencies from withholding agency records, to assess reasonable attorney fees, and to punish irresponsible employees for contempt of court. In addition, the employee who is primarily responsible for improper withholding can be disciplined. Finally, the Act requires the Department of Justice to undertake efforts "to encourage agency compliance."[636]

The FOIA is truly one of the greatest acts of federal legislation ever enacted to facilitate the effectiveness of our free democracy. It allows ordinary citizens, journalists, historians, and any interested person or organization to request and to quickly receive public documents. It has provided transparency and avoided secrecy in the operation of our government.[637]

The Act was amended in 1996 to facilitate on-line and computer access to public records. When he signed the new legislation, President Clinton stated that the FOIA "was the first law to establish an effective legal right of access to government information, underscoring the crucial need in a democracy for open access to government information by citizens."[638] In accordance with her duties, Attorney General Janet Reno wrote, "We must ensure the principle of open government is applied in each and every disclosure." She required that "In determining whether or not to defend a nondisclosure decision, we will apply a presumption of disclosure."[639]

On October 12, 2001, Ashcroft pulled a fast one. One month after 9/11 and without a press release, he sent out a memo urging federal agencies to deny most FOIA requests.[640] In doing so, he listed the fundamental values held by our society, which included protecting "sensitive business information." He went on to "encourage your agency to carefully consider the protection of all such values and interests when making disclosure determinations under the FOIA. Any discretionary decision by your agency to disclose information protected under the FOIA should be made only after full and deliberate consideration of the institutional, *commercial*, and personal privacy interests that could be implicated by disclosure of the information. (emphasis added)"

Ashcroft promised, "When you carefully consider FOIA requests and decide to withhold records, in whole or in part, you can be assured that the Department of Justice will defend your decisions unless they lack a sound legal basis or present an unwarranted risk of adverse impact on the ability of other agencies to protect other important records."[641]

Federal agencies have never liked FOIA requests, and Ashcroft's memo gave them the green light to deny, deny, deny. Ashcroft is charged by the law to *encourage* compliance; however, he has taken steps to *discourage* compliance. What would Madison have to say about it? Probably that it was indeed the "Prologue to a Farce or a Tragedy–or perhaps both."

Do you believe that Ashcroft's censoring of the Freedom of Information Act protects your rights and freedom? You're not stupid! Get the truth.

Patriot Games

Following 9/11, Ashcroft fired another salvo in his war against freedom. He sent the Uniting and Strengthening America by Providing Appropriate Tools Required to Intercept and Obstruct Terrorism Act (USA Patriot Act) to Congress. With little consideration, Congress passed the Act on October 26, 2001, with but one dissenting vote in the Senate.* The title was more than a cute acronym; implicit in its selection is an assertion that if you oppose the act, you aren't patriotic.

Although Ashcroft had all the "appropriate tools" needed before 9/11 to "intercept and obstruct" that act of terrorism, and instead of falling on his sword in shame, he used the results of his own malfeasance to gather unprecedented powers. If you recall, his FBI agents in Minneapolis were pleading with headquarters to obtain a search warrant to review Moussaoui's computer files. They were telling headquarters that a 747 airliner loaded with fuel could be used as a missile, and that Moussaoui was connected with bin Laden and al Qaeda. Ashcroft had all the authority he needed to stop the 9/11 attacks, but he had been ordered to "back off" and didn't exercise his authority.

The official reason for the failure to prevent the 9/11 attack was information overload and a failure to coordinate reports, such as one from agents in Minneapolis screaming that they had a terrorist who wanted to fly a 747 into the World Trade Center, and another in Phoenix pleading with headquarters to check other flying schools. Mohamad Atta came and went as he pleased, even after Israel informed us that he was a terrorist, and two others hijackers on the international terrorist list were allowed to board domestic flights at will. Let's make sure we get this right: what Ashcroft wants is to dramatically increase the amount of information flowing in, and that, somehow, is going to make the bureaucrats at the top smarter and better at catching

---

* Congressmen got no chance to read the bill before it was pushed through during the frenzy of the anthrax scare. When attempts to implicate Iraq failed and the anthrax trail led instead to a U.S. military source, the investigation was pushed under the carpet–although U.S. troops in Iraq still had to take the dangerous anthrax vaccine. Russ Feingold, the only senator to vote against the bill, stated, "I believe we must, we must, redouble our vigilance. We must redouble our vigilance to ensure our security and to prevent further acts of terror. But we must also redouble our vigilance to preserve our values and the basic rights that make us who we are." (Alterman and Green, *The Book on Bush*, p. 91.)

terrorists? Wouldn't it be better for Bush to simply order Ashcroft to stop "backing off," or better yet, to hit the highway?

Clearly the Patriot Act had been planned for a long time, and 9/11 was just an excuse for Ashcroft to grab powers that had been denied by Congress or that had been found to be unconstitutional by the courts in the past.[642] One reason that the Act sailed through Congress so quickly was that nobody could understand what it said without referring to numerous other laws. For example, one section merely substituted the words, "a significant purpose" for "the purpose" in another law. However, that simple change allowed the government to obtain Foreign Intelligence Surveillance Act (FISA) warrants in primarily domestic "criminal" investigations, if the Attorney General says the investigation also has a significant foreign intelligence purpose.

The difference between criminal and intelligence investigations is that, in domestic criminal matters, the Bill of Rights prohibits unreasonable searches and seizures not based upon probable cause. Ashcroft already had ample probable cause to get a warrant to look at Moussaoui's computer disk; he just didn't do it.

Fortunately, the FISA court has refused to go along with Ashcroft's power grab. In August 2002, the secret court released an opinion for the first time in its history saying, "this Court (not Ashcroft) is the arbiter of the FISA's terms and requirements."[643]

In a six-part article, Professor Jennifer Van Bergen reviewed the history of the Alien and Sedition Laws passed in 1798 by the Federalist-controlled Congress, which "allowed the President to arrest, imprison, and deport 'dangerous' immigrants on mere suspicion of 'treasonable or secret machinations against the government.' If a deported alien returned, the President could imprison him for as long as he thought 'the public safety may require.'" For over two hundred years we have been taught that these were terrible laws used for a corrupt purpose to arrest and detain political opponents. Now, they are back in vogue.[644]

Since enactment of the Patriot Act, thousands of suspects have been rounded up and held for months. Without having to give any reason or explanation, all Ashcroft has to do is pronounce the magic words, "terrorist," or "threat to national security," and the suspect is locked up. For the first seven days, no charges are required and the suspect is not even allowed contact with legal counsel; thereafter, the Attorney General can detain suspects indefinitely for nothing more than a violation of their visa. Hearings, even the fact that they are held, and the names of the detainees are kept secret.[645]

Aliens can be deported because of what they "knew or should have reasonably known" about organizations with which they had contact. Even if they have only overstayed their visas and want to return home, they can be held indefinitely; they are being held as "material witnesses," and, administratively, under "emergency" conditions, they are being held for indefinite "reasonable" periods of time.[646]

The Act's "sneak and peek" provisions allow the government to obtain a warrant, sneak into your home, peek at your computer files (and dirty laundry), copy your computer hard drive (and digital photos of your girlfriend), and, if they say the magic words, that "[notice would] seriously jeopardize an investigation or unduly delay a trial," they don't even have to tell you they've been there.[647]

The Act allows the government to obtain blank search warrants for electronic surveillance, *without probable cause*, as long as the magic words, "relevant to an ongoing criminal investigation" are spoken. Agents can then trap and trace the telephone numbers you call *and* trace your e-mails and Internet usage.[648]

Under the Act, Ashcroft's agents can review "business records," including those of libraries, bookstores and Internet service providers, without establishing probable cause sufficient to show a connection to terrorism, espionage or another crime, *and* they can forbid any notification to the patron, buyer or user; they can issue "National Security Letters" to force production of records and information, without having to obtain a court order; and they can demand, without a court order, the production of confidential education records, based only on their declaration that the records are needed for a terrorism-related investigation.[649] For example, they can check on what library books you have been reading, and your librarian can go to jail for telling you about it. How far from here to the next Gulag?

Also hidden among the Act's stealth provisions is an amendment of the Bank Secrecy Act of 1970 that expands the definition of "financial institution" to include a variety of businesses including insurance companies, car dealers, real estate brokers and the U.S. Postal Service. Designed to prevent money laundering, Section 326 requires all such institutions to develop a Customer Identification Program for all new accounts that includes screening their customers through a database provided by the government. Section 314(a) requires these institutions to respond within 14 days to search requests by federal law enforcement agencies, and rules have been proposed that would compel them to file suspicious activity reports when they detect unusual activities by their customers. The effect of this law is to impose law enforcement responsibilities on small businesses, which are woefully ill equipped to keep track of their customers for the government.[650]

Most simply and most often, the Act changed the requirement that the government have "probable cause" to a requirement that it only has to show a "simple relevance" to an investigation. Although Ashcroft keeps saying that the Act "isn't something new ... this isn't some vast incursion into the freedoms of the American people,"[651] in fact, it is. Ashcroft himself argued several years ago against Clinton's attempts to expand the government's ability to monitor the Internet in fighting terrorism: "The protections of the Fourth Amendment are clear. The right to protection from unlawful searches is an indivisible American value. Two hundred years of court decisions have stood in defense of this fundamental right. The state's interest in effective crime-fighting should never vitiate the citizen's Bill of Rights."[652]

If you oppose Ashcroft and what he's doing, you risk being called (and investigated as) a traitor. He warns, "To those who scare peace-loving people with phantoms of lost liberty, my message to you is this: Your tactics only aid terrorists, for they erode our national unity and resolve. They give ammunition to

America's enemies, and pause to America's friends."*
Remember what Goering said: "All you have to do is tell them
they are being attacked, and denounce the pacifists for lack of
patriotism, and exposing the country to greater danger."653

If all this was not enough, Ashcroft had yet another card up
his sleeve as he played the Patriot Game. In February 2003, a
secret copy of the Domestic Security Enhancement Act of 2003
(Patriot Act II) was leaked from the Justice Department even
though, for months, the Justice Department had been denying to
Congress that amendments to the Patriot Act were being
prepared, and only a week previously, Ashcroft had personally
denied the existence of a proposed amendment. However, the
smuggled copy of Patriot Act II was quickly posted on the
Internet and alarm bells began to ring across America.654

Among other things, these "enhancements" would allow
Americans to be stripped of their citizenship without their
having to renounce it as is presently required. Patriot II says,
"the intent to relinquish nationality need not be manifested in
words, but can be inferred from conduct." So, if you provide
"material support" (whatever that means) to an organization
that has been designated a "terrorist organization" (whatever
that is), even if you were unaware of its activities, you could lose
your citizenship and be detained, indefinitely, as an alien.655

Patriot II also allows the government, among other things, to
secretly detain citizens; access credit reports without a subpoena;
encourage police surveillance of non-criminal organizations and
public events; extend the authorization periods for secret
wiretaps and Internet surveillance; and make it easier to use
secret evidence. It prevents someone subpoenaed to a grand
jury from even disclosing that they have been subpoenaed.656

To justify his new game, Ashcroft twisted the words of
Thomas Jefferson, who wrote in the Declaration of Independence
that governments are instituted to secure the "unalienable
rights" of the people. According to Ashcroft, "This then, is the
first responsibility of our government: to preserve the lives and

---

* Along with most of the other warmongers of the Bush administration,
Ashcroft is a Chicken Hawk.

liberty of Americans." He forgot two things: we also have an unalienable right to pursue happiness, and "whenever any Form of Government becomes destructive to these Ends, it is the Right of the People to alter or to abolish it."[657]

Idaho *Republican* Representative Butch Otter introduced legislation to de-fund the Patriot Act's "Sneak and Peek" provisions, which has passed in the House of Representatives by a vote of 309-118. He more accurately quoted Jefferson, "In questions of political power, speak to me not of confidence in men, but bind them down from mischief with the chains of a Constitution." Otter said, "That mischief is what we're seeing today and could see tomorrow."[658]

For now, it doesn't appear that Patriot II is going anywhere soon; however, that hasn't stopped Ashcroft from playing other games with our freedoms. The Justice Department has admitted that it is using Patriot Act provisions to pursue common criminals, such as suspected drug traffickers, white-collar criminals, blackmailers, child pornographers, and money launderers. Although Ashcroft has portrayed his new powers almost exclusively as a tool to fight terrorism, his use of the powers in traditional criminal investigations has caused critics to assert that Bush has "sold the American public a false bill of goods, using terrorism as a guise to pursue a broader law enforcement agenda."[659]

One of the primary characteristics of a totalitarian society is the widespread practice of citizens spying upon each other, with all of them reporting their observations to "big brother," who decides who goes away and who stays. Last year, Big Brother Ashcroft introduced Operation TIPS, another cute acronym for Terrorism Information & Prevention System. He envisioned millions of Americans, letter carriers, truckers, utility workers, etc., reporting their suspicions to a central FBI database. He didn't get away with it; even *Republican* Dick Armey opposed it.[660]

The government "has admitted that its failure to heed the warnings [about 9/11] was not because of a lack of law enforcement powers. Rather the failure was the result of an information overload."[661] Aside from its unconstitutionality, can you imagine the information overload if TIPS was put into place?

Meanwhile, under the supervision of John Poindexter, Reagan's disgraced National Security Advisor,* the Pentagon is creating a "prototype" database called "Total Information Awareness" (TIA). Working under the motto, "Knowledge is Power," the TIA system is being designed to predict future acts of terrorism through the correlation of hundreds of billions of bits of disparate information gathered about each of us.[662]

Conservative writer William Safire observed, "Every purchase you make with a credit card, every magazine subscription you buy and medical prescription you fill, every web site you visit and e-mail you send or receive, every academic grade you receive, every bank deposit you make, every trip you book and every event you attend–all these transactions and communications will go into what the Defense Department describes as 'a virtual, centralized grand database.'"[663] All of this would be done automatically, without a search warrant.

Viet Dinh, who formerly worked for Ashcroft as the head of the Office of Legal Policy and was one of the Patriot Act's authors, has come to have concerns about its application. Dinh has questioned Ashcroft's continued detention of Jose Padilla, the so-called "dirty bomber." Padilla, a Chicago street thug, has been called a "small fish" by the FBI, which has cleared him of any connection with al Qaeda.[664] Nonetheless, Ashcroft has held Padilla, an American citizen, as an enemy combatant for two years in a military prison without access to a lawyer. Dinh, who now teaches law at Georgetown University, has come to the conclusion that Ashcroft's detention of Padilla is not legally

---

* Poindexter was convicted in connection with the Iran-Contra scandal in 1990 of conspiracy, making false statements to Congress, and obstructing congressional inquiries. His conviction was subsequently reversed on a technicality associated with his receipt of Congressional immunity. (Nash, Timothy, "John Poindexter, 'Outstanding American,'" Slate, February 25, 2002, slate.msn.com/?id=2062542.)

"sustainable" and that it is unlikely to survive court review. It appears he may have been right.[665]

On December 19, 2003, the New York-based 2nd U.S. Circuit Court of Appeals ordered the government to release Padilla from custody within 30 days, and, if the government chooses, to try him in civilian court.[666] The U.S. Supreme Court has agreed to hear the case, along with another involving the secret detention of an American-born Saudi captured in Afghanistan.[667]

In 2002, Ashcroft relaxed FBI surveillance rules dating from the Vietnam era and gave agents authority to attend political rallies, mosques and any event "open to the public." The FBI has collected extensive information on the antiwar movement, and in November 2003, it circulated a memorandum urging local law enforcement to report any suspicious activity at protests to its counterterrorism squads. The memo reviewed "innovative strategies" used by demonstrators, such as videotaping arrests as a means of "intimidation" against the police. It revealed that protestors "often use the Internet to recruit, raise funds and coordinate their activities prior to demonstrations."[668]

If you protest too much, your name may show up on the government's "no fly" list designed to keep suspected terrorists from boarding commercial flights. The Transportation Security Administration confirms that it has a list of about 1,000 people who are deemed "threats to aviation" and who are not allowed on airplanes. However, others who have been repeatedly delayed and searched have been informed that their names are also on a "list." These include John Dear, a Jesuit priest and member of the Catholic peace group Pax Christi, Virgine Lawinger, a 74-year-old nun and member of Peace Action, Barbara Olshansky and Nancy Chang of the Center for Constitutional Rights, and Green Party activists Nancy Oden and Doug Stuber. Lawinger, with the help of the ACLU, filed a Freedom of Information request with the TSA to learn why she has been barred from flying.[669] Another group of antiwar protestors has sued the government to learn how members' names ended up on the list.[670]

Does the Patriot Act make you feel more secure? Do you think it is necessary for the government to collect information about your bank account, your library checkouts, and your real estate transactions? You're not stupid! Get the truth.

The Non-Investigation of Corporate Corruption

Ashcroft's Department of Justice lists "ensuring healthy competition of business in our free enterprise system" as one of its tasks in defining its "key role." In that connection, if you recall, we earlier saw that Vice President Cheney, when he was Halliburton's CEO, also sat on Kazakhstan's oil advisory board and helped broker a deal between that country and Chevron for half ownership of the Tengiz oil field.[671] ExxonMobil was also in on the deal for a quarter share of the same field, and it turns out that some palms also got greased in the deal. That's a crime, especially if the palm is in another country. In our free enterprise system, it's unfair competition to bribe some foreign despot to make a deal with you.[672]

Back in 1996, ExxonMobil (then Mobil), acting through a senior manager, J. Bryan Williams III, allegedly paid James Giffen, a broker acting on behalf of Kazakhstan, a $51 million "success fee" on top of Mobil's $1 billion purchase price. Giffen, in turn, paid over $20 million into the Kazakhs' Swiss bank accounts. Allegedly, ExxonMobil later tried to make an illegal oil swap with Iran to get the Kazakhstan oil to market more quickly.* In addition, in 1997, one of BP-Amoco's subsidiaries, Amoco Kazakhstan Petroleum, allegedly transferred $61 million into Swiss bank accounts, where it quickly flowed into private accounts benefiting several Kazakh leaders.[673]

All of these alleged shenanigans came to the attention of the Clinton administration, which initiated a major investigation to determine if there were violations of the Foreign Corrupt Practices Act and the 1996 Iran Trade Sanctions Act. The

---

* Executives of ExxonMobil (the second largest oil company contributor to the Republican Party) and BP- Amoco met several times in secret with Vice President Cheney and his Energy Task Force, after federal grand juries had been impaneled in their criminal cases. Any wonder why the Task Force report encouraged government agencies to "deepen their commercial dialogue" with Kazakhstan? Any wonder why Cheney continues to conceal the Task Force's working papers?

investigation was commenced in three locations, the Department of Justice, the U.S. Attorney's Office in Washington D.C., and in New York, where the U.S. Attorney, Mary Jo White, began to present evidence to the grand jury.[674]

Following the 9/11 attacks, the Department of Justice took over all prosecutions of terrorists, including 15 who were already under indictment in New York, even though the New York U.S. Attorney's Office had successfully investigated terrorists for almost ten years and had secured more than two dozen convictions. Mary Jo White resigned in December 2001.[675]

Immediately, there were reports from senior prosecutors in both New York and Washington D.C. that Ashcroft was taking control of the New York grand jury investigation of ExxonMobil and BP-Amoco and was exercising "unusual" influence over the Washington investigation.

One might wonder why, in the midst of the 9/11 investigations, Ashcroft would become personally concerned about an investigation into corruption that took place in Central Asia? Well, it turns out that ExxonMobil was the largest contributor from the oil and gas industry to Ashcroft's Senate race, followed by Chevron, Enron, The Independent Petroleum Association of America, BP-Amoco, and Halliburton.[676] Although sleeping with a close relative is called incest, covering for a major contributor is just good politics.

Ashcroft quickly recused himself from the Enron investigation (at least once his receipt of a total of $57,000 in campaign contributions from Enron and its employees was publicly questioned by Representative Henry Waxman).[677] However, he has not, apparently, done so in the Kazakh oil company corruption investigations.

Interestingly enough, when the indictments finally came down in April 2003, ExxonMobil itself was not indicted, but only its manager, J. Bryan Williams III, and the broker, James Giffen. However, the U.S. Attorney's Office has announced that ExxonMobil continues to be the subject of the government's ongoing investigation into the Kazakhstan contracts.[678]

Even FBI Director Robert Mueller got into the act. It seems that, back before he was appointed to direct the FBI, he was hired by Enron in 1993 to investigate a suspicious $600,000 payment by a subsidiary for a property worth only $41,000. He concluded that the deal was just fine, and his investigator quit in disgust. So, when Enron imploded and the FBI had to investigate its financial machinations, did Mueller conclude that he might have a conflict of interest? Of course not, and Deputy Attorney General Larry Thompson agreed. This is the same Larry Thompson who had earlier worked for the law firm that represented Enron.[679] It *is* a small, small world, isn't it?

Ashcroft is democratic when it comes to the prosecution of corporate crime. He doesn't just give energy companies a free ride. During the first six months of the 2002 fiscal year, the number of white-collar crimes referred to U.S. Attorneys was the lowest it had been since the late 1980s. And of these, Ashcroft's prosecutors only filed on 50 percent.[680]

Do you believe Ashcroft has a conflict of interest in the ExxonMobil and BP-Amoco investigations? Do you think he should be allowed to interfere in the investigations? Should Mueller recuse himself from the investigation of Enron? You're not stupid! Get the truth.

---

618. "Heinrich Himmler," en.wikipedia.org/wiki/Heinrich_Himmler.

619. "Heinrich Himmler (1900-1945) Reichsfuehrer SS," http://www.joric.com/conspiHeinrich_Himmler.

620. "Pastor Niemöller," http://www.liv_coll.ac.uk/pa09/europetrip/brussels/niemoller.htm.

621. Longley, Robert, "About the U.S. Department of Justice (DOJ)," http://wwwusgovinfo.about.com.

622. "Civil Rights Division Activities and Programs," August 2002 Edition, http://usdoj.gov/crt/activity.html.

623. Doherty, Brian, "John Ashcroft's Power Grab," reason.com/0206/fe.bd.john.shtml; see also Cogswell, Kelly, "Beware Minorities, Women, Queers: Ashcroft is Coming!" www.thegully.com/essays/america/001226ashcroft.html.

624. Doherty, Brian, "John Ashcroft's Power Grab," reason.com/0206/fe.bd.john.shtml.

625. Miller, op. cit., p. 335.

626. Doherty, op cit.

627. "The Two Faces of John Ashcroft," www.tylwytheg.com/enemies/Ashcroft/ashcroft.html.

628. Doherty, op. cit.

629. Ibid.

630. Espo, David, "Ashcroft confirmed in 58-42 Senate vote," *Portsmouth Herald*, February 2, 2001, www.seacoastonline.com/2001/news/2_2_w2.htm.

631. Doherty, op. cit.

632. "John Ashcroft," www.zpub.com/un/ashcroft.html.

633. Franken, op. cit., p. 161.

634. Borger, Julian, "Dismay at US attorney general's Bible classes," *The Guardian*, May 15, 2001, www.guardian.co.uk/international/story/0,3604,491125,000.html.

635. "Free Information For Our Free Country," www.aclu.org/library/foia.html.

636. The Freedom of Information Act, 5 U.S. Code, Section 552, As Amended By Public Law No. 104-231, 110 Statutes 3048.

637. Rosen, Ruth, "The Day Ashcroft Censored Freedom of Information," *San Francisco Chronicle*, January 7, 2002, www.commondreams.org/views02/0108-04.htm.

638. www.usdoj.gov/oip/foia_updates/Vol_XVII_4/page2.htm.

639. "Janet Reno Memorandum," www.usdoj.gov/oip/foia_updates/Vol_XIV_3/page3.htm.

640. Rosen, op. cit.

641. "New Attorney General FOIA Memorandum Issued," www.usdoj.gov/oip/foiapost/2001/foiapost/9.htm.

642. Van Bergen, Jennifer, "The USA PATRIOT Act Was Planned Before 9/11." *Truthout*, May 20, 2002, http://www.truthout.org/docs_02/05.21B.jvb.usapa.911.htm.

643. Van Bergen, Jennifer, "Secret Court Decision Silently Overrules Provision of PATRIOT Act," 2002, http://truthout.com/docs.

644. Van Bergen, Jennifer, "Repeal the USA Patriot Act," 2002, http://truthout.com/docs.

645. Ibid.; see also Cole, David, "The Ashcroft Raids," *Amnesty Now*, (www.amnestyusa.org/usacrisis/ashcroftraids.html); see also Taylor, Stuart Jr., "Congress Should Investigate Ashcroft's Detentions," *National Journal*, May 28, 2002, (www.theatlantic.com/politics/nj/taylor2002-05-28); see also Riley, Michael, "Lawsuits decry 'indefinite' detentions," *Denver Post*, March 20, 2002, (www.refuseandresist.org/detentions/art.php?aid=659).

646. Ibid.

647. Van Bergen, Jennifer, "Repeal the USA Patriot Act," 2002, http://truthout.com/docs.

648. Ibid.

649. Ibid.

650. Brom, Thomas, "Full Disclosure," *California Lawyer*, p. 31.

651. Hart, Peter and Rachel Coen, "John Ashcroft Needs Help," August 2003, http://www.fair.org/extra/0308/ashcroft.html.

652. Conason, op. cit., p. 108.

653. Ibid., p. 102.

654. Lumpkin, Beverley, "Patriot Act Redux," February 21, 2003, civilliberty.about.com/cs/patriotact/; see also Alterman and Green, op. cit., p. 95.

655. Hentoff, Nat, "Ashcroft Out of Control," *The Village Voice*, February 28, 2003, www.villagevoice.com/issues/0310/hentoff.php.

656. Welch, Matt, "Get Ready for PATRIOT II," April 2, 2003, Alternet.org.

657. Johnson, Jeff, "Congressional Opponents Lash out at PATRIOT Act, Ashcroft," 2003, http://www.crosswalk.com/news/1221745.html.

658. Ibid.; see also Lithwick, Dahlia and Julia Turner, "A Guide to the Patriot Act, Part 1," September 8, 2003, slate.msn.com/id/2087984/.

659. Lichtblau, Eric, "Feds widen use of Patriot Act beyond terror," *New York Times*, September 28, 2003, www.independent-media.tv/item.cfm?media_id=2773&fcategory-desc=under%20reported.

660. Conason, op. cit., p. 106.

661. Van Bergen, Jennifer, "Free Speech & G.W. Bush," *Truthout*, October 15, 2002, www.truthout.com/docs_02/11.16Ejvb.speech.html.

662. Hightower, op. cit., p. 88.

663. Conason, op. cit., pp. 106, 107.

664. Hightower, op. cit., p. 94.

665. Schmitt, Richard B., "Patriot Act Author Has Concerns," *Los Angeles Times*, November 30, 2003, http://www.latimes.com/news/printededition/front/la-na-justice30nov30,1,3885357.story?coll=la-headlines-frontpage.

666. Mintz, John, "Detainee to Get Hearing," *The Washington Post*, December 19, 2003, http://www.washingtonpost.com.

667. Savage, David G., "High Court Refuses to Take Up Case on Post-Sept. 11 Arrests," *Los Angeles Times*, January 13, 2004, p. A1.

668. Lichtblau, Eric, "FBI Scrutinizes Antiwar Rallies." *The New York Times*, November 22, 2003, www.commondreams.org/headlines03/1122-09.htm.

669. Lindorff, Dave, "The No-Fly List: Is a federal agency systematically harassing travelers for their political beliefs?" *In These Times*, November 22, 2002, www.inthesetimes.com/issue/27/02/feature3.shtml

670. Ibid.

671. Yant, Martin, "Enron played key role in events presaging war," *Columbus Free Press*, April 10, 2002, mywebpages.comcast.net/howardluken/enron%20Afganistan%20pipeline.html.

672. Mann, Martin, "Swiss Investigation Into Bush/Cheney Involvement In Oil Company Bribes To Kazakhstan," August 14, 2000, (www.whatreallyhappened.com/swiss.html); see also "If ExxonMobil Is Not Indicted for Payments in Kazakhstan, What Has This To Do With Iraq?" April 13, 2003, (ist.socrates.berkley.edu/~pdscott/qfmobil2.html).

673. "If ExxonMobil Is Not Indicted for Payments in Kazakhstan, What Has This To Do With Iraq?" April 13, 2003, ist.socrates.berkley.edu/~pdscott/qfmobil2.html.

674. Ruppert, Michael C., "The Elephant In The Living Room - Part I," *From The Wilderness Publications*, 2002, www.fromthewilderness.com/free/ww3/04_04_02_elephant.html.

675. Ibid.

676. Ibid.

677. Ivanovich, David, "Local Feds, Ashcroft Recused From Inquiry," *Houston Chronicle*, January 11, 2002, www.chron.com/cs/CDA/ story.hts/topstory2/1207236.

678. "If ExxonMobil Is Not Indicted for Payments in Kazakhstan, What Has This To Do With Iraq?" April 13, 2003, ist.socrates.berkley.edu/~pdscott/qfmobil2.html.

679. Yant, op cit.

680. Alterman and Green, op. cit., pp. 76, 77.

BUSH ON DRUGS

Senior citizens must often depend upon prescription drugs to stay alive. Although Bush tells them they have a drug benefit coming from Medicare, the overwhelming benefit will go to the hugely profitable pharmaceutical corporations who contribute so generously to politicians.

Harry Truman believed it was a tragedy we didn't take better care of the elderly in our society, and as soon as he became president, he called for a national system of compulsory health insurance, funded by payroll deductions, whereby all citizens would receive medical and hospital services irrespective of their ability to pay. Speaking at Oxford University on June 20, 1956, Truman stated "we must declare in a new Magna Carta, in a new Declaration of Independence, that henceforth economic well being and security, that health and education and decent living standards, are among our inalienable rights."[681]

Although Truman failed to secure national health insurance for all Americans, in the early 1950's an idea began to take hold that the Social Security system could never achieve its promise until it provided protection against the high cost of medical care for the elderly. Since insurance companies considered the elderly bad risks and declined to insure them, the burden of medical care stripped the elderly of their savings and reduced them to poverty, no matter how hard they had worked and saved.[682]

Although he had promised to help indigents meet the cost of medical care, President Eisenhower opposed the provision of health insurance through the Social Security system, and it was not until 1957 that government health insurance became the top priority for organized labor. Coincidentally, the American Hospital Association, whose members increasingly had to absorb the cost of providing care to elderly charity cases, began to favor the Social Security approach in 1958. However, the American Medical Association remained adamantly opposed.[683]

In 1960, Congress defeated both a Democratic Social Security Medicare plan and a Republican supported "subsidy" plan. Instead, it passed a compromise plan to increase medical vendor payments through the States in matters of "medical indigence."[684]

During the 1960 presidential campaign, John Kennedy proposed that the government provide medical care for the elderly through Social Security, and immediately following his inauguration, he sent a special message to Congress urging its adoption. Supported by organized labor, Medicare bills were introduced in the House and Senate, but the AMA attacked the legislation as "the most deadly challenge ever faced by the medical profession." Debate continued for a year, with amendments and compromises; however, when the bill finally came to a vote in the Senate, it was barely defeated by just two votes. President Kennedy vowed to take the matter to the voters.[685]

Following the assassination of President Kennedy, and along with the re-election of President Lyndon Johnson with the greatest plurality in history, the Democrats made major gains in Congress. President Johnson had vowed that Medicare was his top priority, and bills to enact it were the first ones introduced in both the House and Senate. Even though the AMA continued with a last-ditch fight, Congress passed bills making medical care an integral part of Social Security on July 9, 1965.[686]

On July 30, 1965, standing beside a beaming Harry Truman in Independence, Missouri, President Johnson signed the Medicare bill and established the principle that caring for the medical needs of our elderly is one of the duties of our "Great Society." President Johnson proclaimed, "No longer will older Americans be denied the healing miracle of modern medicine. No longer will illness crush and destroy the savings they have so carefully put away over a lifetime so that they might enjoy dignity in their later years."[687]

Medicare coverage was expanded to include disabled persons under age 65 in 1972 and to all federal civilian employees, including the judiciary, members of Congress and the president, in 1984. There was a major overhaul of Medicare in 1988 that included coverage for prescription drugs; however, the coverage was dropped the next year when seniors realized they would have to pay its full cost through increased fees and premiums.[688]

President Reagan believed that Medicare represented socialism at its worst and that, in the future, the elderly would tell "our children and our children's children what it was like in America when men were free." The attack against Medicare was carried on by Newt Gingrich, who compared it to "centralized command bureaucracies" in Moscow. Gingrich called for significant reductions in the cost of Medicare through free-market competition and private alternatives.[689]

With advances in pharmaceutical science, much of it conducted with government research grants, seniors became increasingly dependent upon a wide range of prescription medications for ailments such as arthritis, cardiovascular problems, osteoporosis, and Alzheimer's disease.[690] However, Medicare did not cover the costs of any of these drugs, if prescribed on an outpatient basis. Many seniors purchased Medigap insurance to help pay for essential prescriptions. These plans are regulated by the government, with coverages labeled from A to J, and premiums vary with the coverage and deductible. Plans H, I, and J cover prescription drugs, and after an annual deductible of $250, seniors pay one half of prescription costs up to $6,250 per year (under Plan J).[691]

Going into the 2000 presidential campaign, it was estimated that Medicare provided health insurance coverage for 39 million elderly and disabled Americans, about one out of every seven people. At least one third of the beneficiaries did not have any prescription drug coverage, requiring them to pay their outpatient prescription drug costs out of their own pockets or do without. With the senior population expected to double over the next 25 years, growing to 20 percent of the population, polls revealed that health care was the most important concern of Americans.[692]

Although both presidential candidates talked about health care and providing prescription drug coverage, there were differences in their positions. Gore stated that he would maintain the existing structure of Medicare but would add a limited prescription drug benefit for all beneficiaries, with deductibles and maximum limitations.[693]

Bush essentially proposed the elimination of Medicare under Social Security and urged its replacement with a "premium support" program similar to the "subsidy" plan originally supported by the Republicans in 1960. Instead of guaranteeing specific health benefits, he wanted to provide a limited payment to seniors in the form of a voucher to be used to purchase their own health plan. Any difference between the voucher amount and the cost of the plan would be paid by the senior."[694]

Bush promised "to have prescription drugs as an integral part of Medicare," but that was not exactly what he meant. What he meant was that he wanted to privatize the process by having seniors obtain prescription insurance offered by HMOs, Medigap, retiree health insurance, and special prescription plans. Under these plans, there would be no guarantee that specific medicines would be covered, as the "formulary" would be defined by each private plan.

Thar's Gold in Them Thar Pills!

There were two reasons why Bush began to support Medicare reform and prescription drug coverage for the elderly. One was to use "reform" as cover to get seniors out of traditional "fee for services" plans, where they chose their own hospitals and medical providers, and into lower cost HMO's. The second reason was money, lots of money, tons of money.

First the payout, then the prize. Between 1997 and 2001, the pharmaceutical industry spent at least $403 million on lobbying. During the presidential campaign of 2000, the drug industry spent at least $262 million on lobbying, direct campaign contributions and issue ads. The drug industry fielded a virtual army of lobbyists in Washington D.C. in 2001, with more than one for each member of Congress. In addition, the industry created two different tax-exempt groups (Citizens for Better

Medicare and United Seniors Association*) to avoid disclosing the $65 million these groups spent on issue ads. Some ads opposed Medicare drug coverage, but many managed to get messages out either supporting or opposing a candidate. Finally, the drug industry contributed $625,000 to help make Bush's inauguration party a smash.[695]

During the last midterm election cycle in 2001 and 2002, the drug industry gave a total of $12 million to federal candidates and their political parties, with 74 percent going to Republicans and 26 percent to Democrats.[696]

What prize did the drug companies expect to win in return for their political investment? Protection and cash, plenty of protection and lots of cash! The national expenditure for prescription drugs almost doubled in just four years, from $78.9 billion in 1997 to $154.5 billion in 2001.

The drug industry, by most measures, has been the most profitable industry in America for the past 10 years, and was one of the top two for the previous 20 years. In 2001, the 10 largest drug companies posted a gross profit of $37.3 billion in 2001, an increase of 33 percent. All of this money was made while most other Fortune 500 companies were reporting a downturn in profits consistent with the economic slowdown.[697]

One company, Pfizer, earned $7.8 billion in 2001, more than all of the Fortune 500 companies in the apparel, homebuilding, publishing and railroad industries put together. Merck, at $7.3 billion, earned more than all the companies combined in the

---

* The Center for the Study of Elections and Democracy at Brigham Young University was funded by the Pew Charitable Trusts to review the 2002 midterm elections. It found that the United Seniors Association was the most active issue advocacy group on television. The Center's survey also found that, by using such a nondescript name as United Seniors Association, the pharmaceutical industry was able to avoid being associated with its message inasmuch as 58 percent of seniors held an unfavorable impression of the industry. Following the industry's advertising blitz, seniors had a 95 percent favorable impression of the United Seniors Association. Talk about wrapping your message in the good old USA!

casino, crude oil production, food production, hotel, pipeline, resort, and semiconductor industries.[698]

The drug companies are able to make these obscene profits because the government allows them to market their products directly to consumers, provides them extended patent protections, provides generous tax breaks, helps fund their research, and prevents the imposition of price controls.[699]

Americans pay between 35 and 60 percent more for the identical medications than patients in most other industrialized countries, and the primary reason is that the United States does not impose any form of price control. One survey in 1994 found that the 77 most frequently dispensed drugs in America cost 60 percent more than in England. More recently, a Canadian survey of all patented drugs in 1999 found that Americans paid between 35 and 50 percent more than Canadians for identical medications. Because of this difference, the United States accounts for 60 percent of the profits earned by drug companies worldwide.[700]

Other governments use a variety of means to ensure that drug companies (many of the same companies that do business in the United States) receive a fair profit, and that consumers pay a fair price somewhat related to the cost of research and production. Many countries, including Germany, Belgium and the Netherlands, group drugs into clusters and establish a "reference" price for the cluster. Companies may charge more, but insurance companies will not pay the difference. France, Italy and Portugal negotiate directly with each company to determine a "fair" price for each medication after reviewing the company's justification and conducting price comparisons with other countries.

England directly controls manufacturers' profits by negotiating a target rate of return on sales to the National Health Service, currently between 17 and 21 percent. England pays the least for its prescription drugs. Canada regulates the entry price of newly patented drugs "to prevent brand name firms from abusing their monopoly position during the market exclusivity period." Canada has established a Patented Medicine Prices Review Board to establish pricing rules. Most companies comply voluntarily, and in only four cases has the government had to resort to legal action to compel price reductions.[701]

Drug companies have avoided the imposition of price controls in the United States by claiming that controls would reduce their incentive to research and develop (R&D) new drugs because they would not be able to recapture their investment costs. This representation is suspect for a number of reasons, not the least of which is the absolute refusal of drug companies to reveal their R&D data, even after nine years of effort by the General Accounting Office and a decision of the U.S. Supreme Court. One thing that might be revealed by such disclosure would be a significant portion of R&D devoted not to the development of new drugs but to the tweaking of existing, so called "me-too" drugs to extend their patent life.

Until 1992, the U.S. Food and Drug Administration ranked each new drug, 1A through 1C, by its ability to improve health. A drug ranked as 1A represented an important therapeutic breakthrough, and a 1C drug represented little or no therapeutic gain. President Bush Sr. eliminated these distinctions; however, the data show that between 1981 and 1991, more than half of the new drugs approved were in the "me-too" category. Only 16 percent were rated as 1A. Since 1992, 560 out of 730 "new" drugs approved by the FDA had therapeutic qualities similar to ones already sold.[702]

The National Institute of Health spent over $1 billion of our tax dollars on drug R&D in 1996. This was a windfall benefit for drug companies, but not for the rest of us. Between 1965 and 1992, publicly funded research helped develop 71 percent of the 21 most important drugs introduced during the period. Between 1992 and 1997, taxpayers spent at least $175 million for R&D of 45 of the 50 top-selling drugs during the period. Another study found that 11 of the 14 most medically significant drugs introduced in the last 25 years originated in government-funded studies. Finally, NIH-funded scientists conducted 55 percent of the research that resulted in the five top-selling drugs in 1995.[703]

These statistics tell us that government funding pays for the grunt work, and drug companies exploit it for free. A study by the National Science Foundation established that only 14 percent of the drug industry's R&D funds went to basic research; 38 percent went to applied research and 48 percent to product development. In other words, the drug companies don't usually start to work unless they believe they have a marketable product.[704]

Another benefit enjoyed by drug companies in the United States is the lack of government control over the direct marketing of drugs to citizens. Only the United States and New Zealand, among the industrialized nations, allow drug companies to directly create an individual's desire for particular prescription drugs, irrespective of the medical provider's advice.

In 1997, the FDA weakened its rules for television advertising of prescription drugs, and direct-to-consumer advertising rapidly increased. In 1996, drug companies only spent $220 million on TV ads. By 2000, they were spending $1.57 billion. By 2001, Fortune 500 drug companies were devoting almost three times as much of their cash flow to marketing and advertising (30.4 percent) as to R&D (12.5 percent). And it pays off. Nearly one in three adults has spoken to their doctor about a drug they have seen advertised, and one in eight has received a prescription as a result. The 50 most advertised drugs resulted in retail sales of $41.3 billion in 2000.[705]

Since the drug companies are making all this money, you would think that they are paying a bundle in taxes, right? Wrong. Between 1993 and 1996, the drug industry averaged an effective tax rate of 16 percent, compared to 27 percent for all other major industries. Between 1990 and 1996, the drug industry was able to use the tax credits provided by Congress to reduce its taxes by almost $28 billion.[706]

The Health Reform Program of Boston University has estimated that the drug industry will garner $139 billion in increased profit from the new prescription drug program's $400 billion cost over the next eight years. This windfall to the world's most profitable industry will provide it with a 38 percent profit increase.[707]

The profits will likely be even more obscene because Bush knowingly misled Congress as to the actual costs of the legislation. The government's chief Medicare actuary had estimated that the plan would cost $551 billion over 10 years; however, he was ordered to withhold the information from Congress and told that he would be fired for insubordination if he disobeyed.[708]

What is even more disgraceful, increases in profits by drug companies may personally and directly benefit the Bushes. The Bush family has been heavily invested in the prescription drug industry for years. In 1977, Bush Sr. was appointed to the board of directors of Eli Lilly, and he disclosed in 1979 that he was invested in Lilly, Abbott, Bristol and Pfizer. While he was Vice President, Bush Sr. lobbied to allow drug companies to dump obsolete drugs in the Third World and for special tax breaks for companies that manufactured drugs in Puerto Rico.[709]

Do your prescription drugs cost a fortune? Are you taken advantage of by the high price of prescription drugs? Have you been manipulated by drug company advertising? You're not stupid! Get the truth.

The Large Print Giveth and the Small Print Taketh Away

On November 26, 2003, Congress passed the Medicare Prescription Drug, Improvement and Modernization Act of 2003 that created a Medicare prescription drug benefit and gave private insurance companies $14 billion to lure elderly beneficiaries from "fee for service" plans into HMOs. Employers and unions received $71 billion in subsidies and $14 billion in tax breaks to encourage them to continue health insurance benefits for their employees and members. Nonetheless, it is estimated that approximately four million retirees will lose their employer-provided health benefits under the new prescription drug plan.[710]

The vote was close and largely split along party lines, with Republicans voting for the plan and Democrats against. The vote in the House was 220-215, and in the Senate it was 54-44. Primarily, the Democrats opposed the bill because they believed it undermined traditional Medicare, allowing younger and healthier retirees to abandon traditional Medicare for less expensive government-subsidized HMOs, leaving the older and more infirm to pay ever increasing premiums. The Alliance for Retired Americans accused Congress of having "failed older Americans."[711]

Seniors at the lowest income levels will receive an immediate $600 annual prescription drug subsidy. However, the only immediate benefit for most disabled and elderly beneficiaries is the availability of a $30 per year prescription drug card for use in 2004 and 2005, to obtain prescription price reductions of up to 15 percent.[712]

That portion of the Medicare bill that created the drug card program was crafted by David Halbert, one of Bush's friends, who just happens to be the CEO of AdvancePCS, a drug card company. Thus, is it any wonder that once seniors purchase a card, the provider can change prices on a weekly basis, providing no guarantee of continued savings? Rather than admit this deficiency, Bush spent tens of millions of dollars on television ads that misled seniors into believing the drug cards would save them money, and some ads used fake reporters to appear as serious news stories. The General Accounting Office reported the ads contained "notable omissions and errors."[713]

Commencing in 2006, seniors with individual incomes less than $14,505 will, after paying a deductible of up to $50, receive up to 85 percent of drug costs up to $5,100, with increased benefits after that point.[714]

The vast majority of seniors, those having incomes of more than $19,577, will pay a monthly premium of $35 and an annual deductible of $250. The plan will pay 75 percent of the next $2,000 in costs. Seniors will then have to pay 100 percent of the next $2,850 in annual drug costs, and after that the plan will pay 95 percent of costs over $5,100. Premiums and deductibles will increase annually to $58 per month and $445 per year in 2013.[715] Is this not a strange payment schedule? What happens to seniors on a fixed income?

The legislation prohibits the government from directly negotiating with drug manufacturers to obtain lower prices.

Instead, benefits will be administered regionally through private insurers or pharmacy benefit managers.[716]

At best, this is a ho-hum plan wherein most of the money flows to employers and the drug industry. Its primary consequence for retired individuals is to get them out of traditional Medicare into less expensive HMOs, at least until they get old enough and sick enough to be kicked out. However, it does help the elderly pay for their medications, right, at least after 2006?

There is a line in a song by poet-singer Tom Waits that goes, "The large print giveth, and the small print taketh away." Thus it is with Bush's prescription drug benefit. One of its provisions actually prohibits the sale of any Medigap policies after January 1, 2006 that would help seniors pay their drug costs. Now, why would Congress do away with the benefits of Medigap policies? They intentionally wanted the elderly to feel the pain of having to pay for a large portion of their prescriptions so they would be "sensitive" to the costs. In other words, seniors would not be allowed to obtain a policy to help them to bridge the $2,850 gap between the first $2,250 in costs and $5,100, where the benefit kicks in again.[717] Do you know any seniors who are *not* sensitive to costs? Do know any who will not still stop to pick up a penny?

Get out your magnifying glass; there's more small print. The new drug plans could, and probably will, establish lists of preferred medicines known as "formularies." While the lists will include drugs in each "therapeutic category and class," such as cholesterol-lowering drugs, Medicare would not have to pay for any prescription drug not listed in the formulary. Isn't this increasing the risk of favoritism and corruption?

In addition, beneficiaries will not be allowed to purchase Medigap insurance to cover unlisted drugs, nor will they be allowed to count the price of unlisted drugs in reaching the $5,100 level where the benefit kicks in again.[718] Remember, these are medications that have been prescribed by a medical doctor for a medical need.

There's even more small print. The 12 million retirees with employer-provided health care and prescription drug plans may sign up for the Medicare prescription drug benefit, but any contribution from their employer plan will not count toward reaching the $5,100 level.[719] Why do we want to punish our elderly like this?   What have they done to deserve this treatment?

Now, the print gets really tiny.   Those low-income beneficiaries who have been receiving prescription drugs under state-administered Medicaid programs are forced to move over to the Medicare program, even if they have been receiving medications no longer available under Medicare.   The Act prohibits state Medicaid programs from supplementing the Medicare prescription drug benefit. If a state wants to provide more than the Medicare benefits, they will have to pay the entire cost, and they will not be entitled to receive any of the discounts and rebates they now receive from drug companies.[720]

There's more.   A conference committee report that accompanied the bill's passage encouraged the revision of existing Medigap policies to require beneficiaries to pay increased deductibles and more of the initial costs of physician and hospital services. The justification according to the report is that "Numerous studies have demonstrated that covering deductibles and coinsurance has led to higher Medicare spending because beneficiaries become insensitive to costs."[721] What this means is that those members of Congress who voted for this Act and the president who signed it may pretend to feel the pain suffered by the elderly, but they just don't care.

Or perhaps they really are so self-absorbed and isolated from those who elect them that they really don't understand how ordinary hard-working people feel and what is important in their lives. Nearly half of the newly elected representatives and senators in the class of 2002 are millionaires, and many own stocks in the very drug companies receiving the primary benefits from the legislation.[722] These are the same caring congressmen who have given themselves $5,000 raises during four of the past five years. This $20,000 pay raise is almost double the $10,712 a minimum-wage worker earns for a full year's labor.[723]

There are some who believe that Bush Jr. will receive a political benefit from the enactment of his prescription drug benefit; however, that assumes that the elderly and their families who have the responsibility for their care and support can't read the fine print. We are smart enough to figure out where the money is really going, and why, and who is going to suffer even more as a result.

Who do you think benefited most from Bush's prescription drug bill, the elderly or the drug companies? You're not stupid! Get the truth.

681. McCullough, David, *Truman* (New York: Touchstone, 1992), p. 957.

682. Corning, Peter A. "The History of Medicare," 1969, http://www.ssa.gov/history/ Corning.html.

683. Ibid.

684. Ibid.

685. Ibid.

686. Ibid.

687. Ibid.

688. "Brief History of the Medicare Program," www.seniorjournal.com /NEWS/2000%20Files/Aug%2000/FTR-08-04-00MedCarHistry.htm.

689. Herbert, Bob, "The Downfall of Medicare," *Press-Telegram*, December 9, 2003, p. A17.

690. "Prescription Drugs," The Center For Responsive Politics, http://www.opensecrets.org/news/drug/.

691. "Medigap Plans: Medicare Supplemental Insurance Policies," http://www.aarp.org/Articles/a2003-06-03-medigapcharts2.html.

692. Pelosi, Nancy, "A Democratic Health Care Agenda," http://www.sfms.org/sfm/sfm400d.htm.

693. "Compare the Candidates on Medicare & Prescription Drugs," http://www.afscme.org/publications/political/pt00203.htm.

694. Ibid.

695. "America's Other Drug Problem: A Briefing Book On The Rx Drug Debate," Public Citizen's Congress Watch, 2002, http://www.citizen.org/publications/release.cfm?ID=7188.

696. Ibid.

697. Ibid.

698. Ibid.

699. Ibid.

700. Ibid.

701. Ibid.

702. Ibid.

703. Ibid.

704. Ibid.

705. Ibid.

706. Ibid.

707. "The Big Medicare Fix," *Public Campaign*, November 20, 2003, http://www.publicampaign.org/publications/ouch-cpi/121-140/ouch123.htm.

708. Pugh, Tony, "Bush administration ordered Medicare plan cost estimates withheld," *Knight Ridder Newspapers*, March 11, 2004, http://www.realcities.com/mld/krwashington/8164060.htm.

709. Bowen, op. cit., pp. 102, 103.

710. Kemper, Vicki, "Sweeping Medicare Changes Okd," *Los Angeles Times*, November 26, 2003, p. A1.

711. Kemper, Vicki, "Senate Poised to Pass Drug Plan That Would Overhaul Medicare," *Los Angeles Times*, November 25, 2003, p. A1.

712. Kemper, Vicki, "Sweeping Medicare Changes Okd," op. cit.

713. "Bush Misleads Seniors On New Drug Cards," *The Daily Mis-Lead*, April 27, 2004, daily.misleader.org/ctt.asp?u=2323986&1=31346.

714. Kemper, Vicki, "Sweeping Medicare Changes Okd," op. cit.

715. Ibid.

716. Ibid.

717. Pear, Robert, "Medicare Plan for Drug Costs Bars Insurance," *The New York Times*, December 6, 2003, http://www.startribune.com/stories/587/4253120.html.

718. Ibid.

719. Ibid.

720. Ibid.

721. Ibid.

722. Salant, Jonathan D., "A Richer Congress," December 25, 2002, http://www.commondreams.org/headlines02/1225-02.htm.

723. Hightower, op. cit., pp. xvi, xvii.

THE MEDIA ARE NOT LIBERAL,
AND THEY DO NOT TELL YOU THE TRUTH!

For the last 30 years, right-wing millionaires have funded and led an organized rout of liberal political expression while convincing us that the media are too liberal. In fact, they've tried to convince us that liberal is a dirty word.

Once upon a time "liberal" was not a naughty word; it was not a label to be avoided at all costs; in fact, it was a badge of honor. It did not denote cowardice; it was used to describe fighters. Liberals cared about you, your family, your community and your nation.[724] The 20th Century even started out with a liberal Republican president, Theodore Roosevelt, and he was followed throughout the century by other liberal presidents, no less effective and no less brave, but all were Democrats.

When Theodore Roosevelt became president in 1901, following the assassination of President McKinley, he brought energy and excitement to the office and led the government and the people towards progressive reforms. He believed that the president should be the "steward of the people," and to ensure their protection, he greatly expanded the power of the presidency. Roosevelt believed that government should arbitrate between the competing economic forces of business and labor, favoring neither and guaranteeing justice to both. He supported miners in their strike against the coal barons and convinced the owners to accept arbitration.

Roosevelt became known as the "trust buster" as he broke up the great railroad combinations and effectively made use of the Sherman Antitrust Act against businesses, when it had only been used to break up labor unions before. In pursuit of a "Square Deal" for Americans, T.R. succeeded in getting the Pure Food & Drug Act, a meat inspection bill, and an employer's liability law passed. He was one of the first conservationists, setting aside national forests and parks for public use and enjoyment.

Roosevelt was no coward; he served as the Secretary of Navy in preparing for the war against Spain, and he personally led the charge of his "Rough Riders" up Kettle Hill in the battle for San Juan[725].

Woodrow Wilson was elected president in 1912 in a three-way race against William Howard Taft, the Republican nominee, and Theodore Roosevelt, running as an independent. Wilson called for a "New Freedom" to energize the economy by reducing tariffs, reorganizing the banking and credit industries, and strengthening and enforcing anti-trust laws.[726]

Breaking with tradition, Wilson appeared personally in Congress and advocated his legislative agenda. He succeeded in pushing through the Underwood Act, which reduced tariffs generally and greatly increased the free list, against the opposition of manufacturing interests; the Federal Reserve Act, which established Federal Reserve Banks and the issuance of Federal Reserve notes and was opposed by banking interests; and the Federal Trade Commission Act, which outlawed unfair trade practices and empowered the Federal Trade Commission to issue "cease and desist" orders to prevent unfair competition. Wilson obtained legislation to outlaw child labor, and achieved an eight-hour workday for railroad workers.[727]

Wilson was no coward, and in 1917, when Germany declared unrestricted submarine warfare against all maritime commerce, including that of the nominally neutral United States, he asked for and Congress granted a declaration of war against Germany. Following the war, Wilson helped establish the League of Nations; however, the opposition of isolationist Republicans, led by Senator Henry Cabot Lodge, delayed its Senate ratification as Wilson became gravely ill. The opposition thereafter blocked ratification by adding amendments that essentially nullified the treaty, resulting in its defeat.[728]

Following 12 years of Republican administration, Franklin Roosevelt was elected president in 1932 in the depths of the Great Depression. Thirteen million Americans were unemployed, and virtually every bank was closed. In the first "hundred days" of his administration, Roosevelt proposed, and a Democratic-controlled Congress passed, a broad-based "New

Deal" to assist businesses and agriculture to recover and help the unemployed keep their homes. With the establishment of the Federal Deposit Insurance Corporation to guarantee bank deposits and the Security and Exchange Commission to regulate stock exchanges, a limited degree of recovery was achieved. In 1935, over the objection of business and banking interests, Roosevelt proposed and Congress passed legislation establishing Social Security, increasing taxes on the wealthy and large-scale work relief programs.[729]

This Roosevelt was no coward either. A former secretary of the Navy, he conceived of the Lend Lease Plan to assist England and Russia in holding out against German aggression, and following the attack on Pearl Harbor, he asked for and received a declaration of war against the Axis powers. In cooperation with the Allies, Roosevelt successfully worked until his death to prosecute the war almost until its conclusion.[730]

After Roosevelt's sudden death on April 12, 1945, Harry Truman became president. He, too, was no coward. He had fought in Europe during World War I as an artillery captain, and he was quickly required, as president, to make courageous decisions. The first was his decision to deploy atomic weapons against Japan after the nation refused to surrender. The second was his decision to deploy American forces in support of the United Nations' defense of South Korea after it was invaded by North Korea and later by China. He obtained aid for Greece and Turkey to avoid a Soviet takeover, and he arranged a massive airlift to supply Berlin when it was blockaded by Russian troops. Truman witnessed the signing of the United Nations Charter in June 1945, and he negotiated the North Atlantic Treaty Organization in 1949. Domestically, Truman introduced his own "Fair Deal" to expand Social Security, achieve full employment, establish a permanent Fair Employment Act, and engage in the building of public housing and slum clearance. By executive order, he desegregated the armed forces and he fought to maintain the bargaining power of unions.[731]

Following eight years of the Eisenhower administration, John Kennedy was elected president in 1960, the youngest ever to be elected, and when he died in 1963, he was the youngest to die in office. Kennedy was no coward. As a naval officer, when his PT boat was rammed and sunk by a Japanese destroyer, he repeatedly swam out in the surrounding dangerous waters to secure the rescue of his crew, despite serious injuries. During the Cuban missile crisis, he faced down Russia, securing the removal of nuclear missiles from the island and eliminating that threat of nuclear blackmail. Thereafter he achieved an agreement with Russia to ban above-ground testing of nuclear weapons.

Although President Kennedy sent measures to Congress to cut taxes to stimulate the economy and to protect civil rights, they were not enacted until after his assassination. Nonetheless, the programs he initiated commenced the longest period of sustained economic expansion since World War II.[732]

Lyndon Johnson succeeded to the presidency in 1963 and quickly moved to obtain passage of Kennedy's tax cut and civil rights plans. Reelected in 1964 by the largest margin in history, Johnson pushed his "Great Society" agenda through a Democrat-controlled Congress. Among the highlights were Medicare, urban renewal, aid to education, voting rights, conservation and the war against poverty. He fulfilled Kennedy's promise to put man on the moon, and he effectively ended hunger in the United States through a food-stamp program.[733]

Johnson was no coward. He fought in World War II and won a Silver Star for bravery, and he carried out the Vietnam War to support the commitments made by the United States, even though his efforts were unsuccessful.[734]

After eight years of Republican administration by Richard Nixon and Gerald Ford, Jimmy Carter was elected in 1976. Carter was a Naval Academy graduate who served on nuclear submarines. During his four years in office, in spite of high inflation and energy costs, eight million new jobs were created, and the budget deficit, as a percentage of the gross national product, was reduced. He commenced deregulation of the trucking and airline industries, expanded the national park system, and created the Department of Education. He was defeated for reelection by Ronald Reagan.[735]

When President Clinton took office in 1994, the national debt had quadrupled over the past 12 years of Republican administration. While the income of America's wealthiest families had increased by 67.3 percent thanks to Reagan's tax cuts for the wealthy, the average middle-class family's income had been reduced by 17 percent. President Clinton discovered that Bush Sr. had left him a government that was running an annual deficit estimated at $300 billion.

As a matter of fiscal urgency, Clinton managed to obtain a modest increase in the tax rate for the top 1.2 percent of the richest taxpayers. Senator Phil Gramm predicted that with adoption of the increase, "the economy is going to get weaker and not stronger, the deficit four years from today will be higher." What actually happened is that President Clinton presided over eight years of economic expansion, the longest in history. During his term, 22 million new jobs were created, the unemployment rate dropped to 4 percent, the median family income increased by almost $6,500, the poverty rate decreased, and between 1998 and 2000, the government paid off more than $360 billion of the national debt.[736]

Although the received wisdom is that Republicans are better at business, which may be true (for many of them seem to be living quite well), they do not appear to be better at running the federal government. Over the past century and using a variety of business measures, we find: (1) Democratic presidencies produced an average return of 12.3 percent on the Standard & Poor's 500 stock index, while Republican presidencies only produced 8 percent; (2) Democratic control over Congress produced stock returns of 10.7 percent, while Republican control only produced 8.7 percent; and (3) Democratic presidencies produced price gains of 13.4 percent on Dow Jones stocks, while Republican ones only produced increases of 8.1 percent.[737]

Overall, on average and by every measure, including economic growth, reduced inflation, increased wages, and lower government spending, Democratic presidents have done a better job of managing the economy than have Republican presidents.[738]

Thus, it appears that in the last century it has largely fallen upon the Democratic presidents to fight the wars, straighten out the economy, defend individual rights, and protect the environment. So, if all this is true, why have the liberals gained such a bad reputation? Why do the Republicans use "liberal" as a dirty name? Why are the Democrats afraid to identify themselves as liberals?

The Attack of the Killer Neocons

The modern political conservative movement may have begun with the *National Review* in the late 1950's and William F. Buckley Jr.'s editorializing about the civil rights movement. He opposed the Voting Rights Act and called for the maintenance of "states' rights" and Southern "civilized standards." In 1961, he stated, "I am not ready to abandon the ideal of local government in order to kill Jim Crow." He blamed the non-violent civil rights marchers for their own beatings and the 1965 Watts riots on Martin Luther King Jr.'s "anarchic teachings."[739]

During the 1960's, whenever journalists needed expert comment regarding political or foreign policy, they would contact members of academia or one of several research institutes such as the Council on Foreign Relations, the Carnegie Endowment for International Peace, or the Brookings Institution. Scholars and staff members of these organizations were, on average, probably a little left of center on most political and economic questions, and, collectively, their research and thoughts resulted in the "Establishment" opinion on most issues.[740]

The neo-conservative, or "neocon" movement arose in the mid-1970s in reaction to the Establishment's influence on political opinion. Irving Kristol, in cooperation with Robert Bartley of the *Wall Street Journal* editorial page, and a few others, set about creating a highly effective alternative to the Establishment. All it took was a little money; actually, it took a lot of money, but it was well targeted. Their success has been overwhelming.[741]

Much of the money came from family foundations, such as those established by Lynde and Harry Bradley, John Olin, Sarah

Scaife, and Smith Richardson.[742] Individual supporters included Bunker and Nelson Hunt, Joseph Coors, Richard Mellon Scaife,* and Korean minister Sun Myung Moon. Hundreds of new think tanks sprang up overnight, including The American Enterprise Institute, the Heritage Foundation, and the Center for Strategic and International Studies. Between 1992 and 1994, twelve foundations gave $210 million to these institutions to fund conservative agenda building. That is, the money was spent to formulate and market conservative opinions.[743]

These new organizations are far more proactive than the Establishment ever was, and the emphasis is more on marketing opinions than upon research. William Baroody, the former president of the American Enterprise Institute, said, "I make no bones about marketing. ... We pay as much attention to the dissemination of the product as we do the content. We're probably the first major think tank to get into the electronic media. We hire ghost writers for scholars to produce op-ed articles that are sent to the one hundred and one cooperating newspapers–three pieces every two weeks."[744]

In 1995, the Heritage Foundation's president, Edwin Feulner, stated, "We don't just stress credibility. We stress timeliness. We stress an efficient, effective delivery system. Production is one side; marketing is equally important." Heritage vice president Burton Pines states, "We're not here to be some kind of Ph.D. committee giving equal time. Our role is to provide conservative public-policymakers with arguments to bolster our side." He adds, "Our targets are the policymakers and the opinion-making elite. Not the public. The public gets it from them."[745] Ronald Reagan bought the Heritage Foundation's product wholeheartedly. At the Foundation's tenth-anniversary banquet, Reagan stated, "Historians who seek the real meaning

---

* In 1981, Karen Rothmyer of the *Columbia Journalism Review* asked Scaife about his financial backing of conservative groups. He answered, "You f***ing Communist c**t, get out of here." He warned her, "Don't look behind you." (Alterman Eric, *What Liberal Media?* page 245.)

of events in the latter part of the twentieth century must look back on gatherings such as this."

The Heritage Foundation's influence continues unabated under George W. Bush. The Foundation provided him with between 1,200 and 1,300 names and resumes, including the Secretary of Labor, Elaine Chao, a former Heritage Distinguished Fellow.[746] And if you recall, Bush addressed a gathering of the American Enterprise Institute on February 26, 2003, and told them that his administration had "borrowed" 20 of its members.

Fairness and Accuracy in Reporting conducted a study to determine the number of "expert" quotes found in the media from the various foundations, which were then ranked from conservative to centrist to progressive (liberal). Of 25,823 citations identified through Lexis, 48 percent of all mentions came from conservatives, 36 from centrists, and only 16 percent from progressives.

One of the most influential organizations funded by Richard Scaife is the Federalist Society for Law and Public Policy Studies, whose membership has grown to over 25,000. A legal society, the Federalist acts as a watchdog on the American Bar Association, publishing the *ABA Watch* to document the Association's allegedly liberal stands on abortion, the death penalty and gun control. The Federalists attack "judicial activism" and praise "strict construction."[747] The society includes some of the most influential judges in America, including four close affiliates* who sit on the U.S. Supreme Court.[748]

Justice Antonin Scalia, considered one of the founders of the society, declared in 2002 that "government ... derives its moral authority from God" and acts as the "minister of God." Scalia

---

* Chief Justice William H. Rehnquist and Justices Antonin Scalia, Anthony M. Kennedy, and Clarence Thomas. The Society was also instrumental in the selection and confirmation of Justice Sandra Day O'Connor. (Remember, these are the same five who gave the 2000 presidential election to Bush.) Other Federalist Society members are Attorney General John Ashcroft, Solicitor General Ted Olson, Secretary of Energy Spencer Abraham and Senator Orrin Hatch.

aggressively states, "The reaction of people of faith to this tendency of democracy to obscure the divine authority behind government should not be resignation to it, but the resolution to combat it as effectively as possible."[749] What! Believers should defeat democracy if necessary to avoid a separation of church and state? On March 18, 2003, Justice Scalia said, "The Constitution just sets minimums. Most of the rights that you enjoy go way beyond the Constitution."[750] Says who?

The primary target of the conservative opinion mills is the liberal enemy. Liberalism is painted as being illegitimate. The attack is unrelenting and it is dirty. The object is to associate liberalism with Democrats with socialism. Every opportunity is taken to disparage liberals and progressives. Taking a clue from Gingrich's game book, liberals are referred to as "elitist," "limousine liberals," "upper-class liberals," "Hollywood liberals," "liberal snobs," and "liberal eggheads."[751] Ann Coulter threatens them with execution to keep them from becoming "outright traitors." Andrew Sullivan warns of liberals "mounting a fifth column" against the war on terrorism. Steve Dunleavy denounces "liberals, whom I regard as traitors" for daring to quote the Constitution.[752]

Do you believe the neocons represent your point of view? Do you think they represent your best interests? You're not stupid! Get the truth.

Creating the Myth of the Liberal Media

Not only have the neocons spent millions to establish their superior position in rendering and controlling media opinions, they have worked equally hard to convey the false impression that liberals control the media. As far back as 1992, a former chairman of the Republican National Committee, Rich Bond, conceded that bashing the liberal media was just part of the game. He explained, "There is some strategy to it. I'm a coach of kids' basketball and Little League teams. If you watch any great coach, what they try to do is 'work the refs.'" Working "the ref" means to raise a stink about *every* adverse call the referee makes so that "Maybe the ref will cut you a little slack on the next one."[753]

Accusations that liberals control the media are both unfair and unfounded. In a moment of candor, the editor of the *Weekly Standard*, William Kristol, stated, "I admit it. The liberal media were never that powerful, and the whole thing was often used as an excuse by conservatives for conservative failures." Nevertheless, the truth doesn't stop him from complaining in print, "The trouble with politics and political coverage today is that there's too much liberal bias. ... There's too much tilt toward the left-wing agenda. Too much apology for liberal policy failures. Too much pandering to liberal candidates and causes."[754] It is doubtful that the neocons would be satisfied with the death of liberal thought; it's far more fun to kick the whimpering dog.

Even Patrick Buchanan, who ran for president as a reform candidate in the 2000 election, stated, "I've gotten balanced coverage, and broad coverage–all we could have asked. For heaven sakes, we kid about the 'liberal media,' but every Republican on earth does that."[755]

Nonetheless, the neo-conservative movement spends millions to ensure that the public continues to believe that the liberals have control of the media. Among the organizations funded to monitor radio and television broadcasting is the Media Research Center (MRC) chaired by William F. Buckley, Jr.'s nephew, L. Brent Bozell III. Operating with a $7.8 million annual budget, the MRC openly supports Republican and conservative campaigns and causes.[756]

MRC uses e-mail to alert its 11,000 followers on a daily basis to any liberal leanings it may detect in the media and encourages its members to send complaints.[757] Following 9/11, MRC appointed itself as America's "Patriotism Police" and sent out an e-mail threatening anyone who dared to oppose the Bush administration's policies. MRC promised to attack any journalist or media outlet that failed to support Bush.[758]

All this money is not wasted. In September 2002, a Gallup poll revealed that 47 percent of Americans believe the news media is "too liberal," while only 13 percent believe the media is biased toward conservatives.

How have we, average, hard-working people, allowed ourselves to believe that "liberal" is a bad word, when it stands for the social and economic progress that "We The People" have made under the Roosevelts, Wilson, Truman, Kennedy, Johnson, Carter and Clinton? Have you bought into the conservative agenda? Have you been manipulated by right-wing propaganda? You're not stupid! Get the truth.

In Fear of the Conservative Media

By every objective measure, the message one hears and reads in America's news media is conservative, unrelentingly conservative. One of the main reasons is that while most individual journalists would define their personal politics as centrists, their employers and managers (and advertisers) are conservative, and the managers are the ones who control content.

In the week before the 2000 election, *Editor & Publisher* commissioned a poll of newspaper executives. The magazine found that, by a wide margin, the executives were personally going to vote for Bush and that their newspapers had endorsed him by a 2-1 margin. The largest margin was with the smallest newspapers (3-1), but even the largest newspapers supported Bush by a 5-4 margin. Overall, 58 percent of the population read that Bush was the favored candidate of their local newspaper. *Editor & Publisher* wondered, "what ever happened to the so-called 'liberal press?'"[759]

Since these same newspaper executives decide who writes what and how it is presented in their papers, it shouldn't be a surprise to learn that conservatives control the op-ed pages. A 1990 independent study reviewed the writing of seven syndicated columnists who regularly appeared in more than a hundred newspapers with over ten million readers. Four were conservative and only one might be called liberal.[760]

Even the Heritage Foundation admits the shift to the right on newspaper opinion pages. According to Adam Meyerson, "Journalism today is very different from what it was ten or twenty years ago. Today, op-ed pages are dominated by conservatives." In 1999, *Editor & Publisher* found that the top four columnists were all on the right or extreme right and that they appeared in approximately 500 newspapers.

The choices made by newspaper executives on the op-ed pages are also displayed on the front pages. A survey by the Project for Excellence in Journalism of newspaper stories during the critical month between late September and October 2000, when Gore's solid lead in the polls dissolved, found twice as many stories favoring Bush as Gore.[761] Where did the stories appear in your local newspaper?

The Pew Charitable Trust's Project for Excellence in Journalism at the Columbia School of Journalism reviewed 1,149 stories from 17 leading news sources published during the 2000 presidential election. It found 24 percent of the stories were positive for Bush, while only 13 were positive for Gore; and that 56 percent of the stories were negative for Gore and 49 percent were negative for Bush. The remaining stories were neutral.

In one area of the media–AM talk radio–the love for Bush is never ending. Featuring personalities such as Rush Limbaugh, Sean Hannity, Dr. Laura Schlessinger, Michael Savage, Bob Grant, Howard Stern, G. Gordon Liddy and, more recently, Bill O'Reilly, AM talk radio reaches millions of Americans each day with a message that is exclusively right wing. Almost exclusively. Since the murder of Alan Berg by white supremacists in 1984, there has not been a single liberal AM radio talk show, until the recent advent of Air America Radio.[762]

Talk radio is an angry medium. The hosts yell at callers and cut them off. They loudly express their personal opinions and deride any opposition. Talk radio feeds upon the displaced anger in our society: anger over loss of employment or business opportunities, over our increasingly multi-cultural society, over changes in the role of women, over illegal immigration, and over perceived defeats or slights in daily life. Talk radio taps into the residual paranoia and anxiety left over from the Cold War and the threats posed by terrorism. It is a place where one can vicariously punch the boss or kick the dog, but it is not a very good place to obtain unbiased news or political opinion. It also functions to make liberal listeners feel they are a marginalized, small minority.

Clear Channel Communications (CCC) owns half of the radio outlets in America, more than 12,000 local stations. CCC exercises almost total control over local programming, including a ban on the Dixie Chicks band after one of its members (from Lubbock, Texas) told fans in England they were ashamed to be from the same state as Bush. CCC also provided financial sponsorship and aired promotions for pro-war "Rallies for America."[763]

One of America's most popular commentators, Howard Stern, has been suspended from appearing on CCC stations because he began to deviate from the company's pro-Bush line. Stern says, "I gotta tell you something, there's a lot of people saying that the second that I started saying 'I think we gotta get Bush out of the presidency,' that's when Clear Channel banged my a** outta here. Then I find out that Clear Channel is such a big contributor to President Bush, and in bed with the whole Bush administration, I'm going, 'Maybe that's why I was thrown off, because I don't like the way the country is leaning too much to the religious right.'"

CCC also fired two other commentators for their anti-war views. Roxanne Walker was discharged when she began to charge that Bush's War was not justified, "I was reprimanded by [Clear Channel] management that I need to tone that down. Basically I was told to shut up." Phoenix talk show host Charles Goyette was kicked off for "inviting administration critics like former weapons inspector Scott Ritter on his show, and discussing complaints from the intelligence community that the analysis on Iraq was being cooked to support the White House's pro-war agenda."[764]

Surveys establish that 22 percent of Americans listen to talk radio, up to as many as 40 percent in the major cities.[765] AM talk radio is not only conservative, it is hard-hitting, take-no-prisoners conservative. It is here, and not on the op-ed pages, that the opinion of working Americans is most influenced. There is no denial. Rush Limbaugh gloats, "There's been a massive change in media in this country over the last 15 years. ... Now it's 2002 and the traditional liberal media monopoly doesn't exist anymore."

Limbaugh has been credited with Bush's defeat of McCain in the 1999 presidential primaries and of Gore in the general election. William Kristol says that Limbaugh "helped make it the orthodox conservative position that McCain was utterly unacceptable and also that Bush was fine, neither of which were intuitively obvious if you're a conservative." Newt Gingrich's former press secretary Tom Blankley stated, "Given the closeness of the election, but for Rush Limbaugh's broadcasts, we would now be led by President Al Gore."[766]

Once upon a time, the Federal Communication Commission's Fairness Doctrine required broadcasters to provide a balance of political opinion in their programming, and the FCC would not have allowed the present monopoly of conservative opinion. However, the Reagan-appointed FCC repealed the doctrine in 1987, and Reagan vetoed attempts by Congress to reinstate it.

Now that they are in control, the same neocons who once relied upon the access doctrine believe that it would be an unwarranted imposition on the First Amendment to allow today's dissenters an equal opportunity to exercise *their* freedom of speech.[767] Given the power of the media to shape opinion, do you think we should allow it to be biased, without any opportunity for the other side to provide balance?

Following his election, Bush enjoyed an extraordinarily long honeymoon with the news media. On May 6, 2002, John Harris wrote in the *Washington Post*, "Are the national news media soft on Bush? ... The truth is, this new president has done things with relative impunity that would have been huge uproars if they had occurred under Clinton. Take it from someone who made a living writing about those uproars."[768]

The mainstream press is clearly intimidated by the conservative media. For example, following Bush's State of the Union address in January 2003, in which he repeatedly and demonstrably lied, the *New York Times* "found little that could lead to a conclusion that the president actually lied." Instead, it was possible that Bush may have been guilty of having "stepped over the line." Even the *Washington Post*, in a story entitled "Presidential Tradition of Embroidering Key Assertions

Continues," only found Bush's statements to be "dubious, if not wrong" and that they "outpaced the facts."⁷⁶⁹

Bush told a bald-faced lie in Africa on July 14, 2003, regarding Saddam: "We gave him a chance to allow the inspectors in, and he wouldn't let them in. And, therefore, after a reasonable request, we decided to remove him from power." In fact, the inspectors returned to Iraq and essentially determined that there was no current evidence of weapons of mass destruction, before they had to leave so Bush could start bombing Iraq. The *Washington Post* could only say that Bush's lie "appeared to contradict the events leading up to war this spring."⁷⁷⁰ A lie is a lie, except when one has newspapers to sell and one has come to live in fear of the truth.

The news media is big business, and journalists who rock the boat really don't get ahead, *All the President's Men* to the contrary notwithstanding. To get along, many journalists go along with self-censorship. Dan Rather, who has been labeled a liberal by the neocons, confesses, "There was a time in South Africa that people would put flaming tires around people's necks if they dissented. And in some ways the fear is that you will be 'necklaced' here, you will have a flaming tire of lack of patriotism put around your neck. Now it is the fear that keeps journalists from asking the toughest of the tough questions. ... I do not except myself from this criticism. What we are talking about here–whether one wants to recognize it or not, or call it by its proper name or not–is a form of self-censorship. I worry that patriotism run amok will trample the very values the country seeks to defend."⁷⁷¹

In *The Note*, ABC's Internet publication, journalists are warned, "Since the Republican party is the only one of our two major political parties in America who believes the press is routinely biased against them ... the press needs to be extra careful in making sure that perspective and fairness are maintained." In *What Liberal Media?*, Eric Alterman comments on ABC's warning: "Talk about 'working the refs.' Between the fear of appearing to tear down a national icon during wartime and the effect of decades of fielding attacks by politically minded conservatives drumming to a beat of their own invention, the elite media has so internalized the false message of their own 'liberalism' that they were openly holding back on the Republicans, as if in fear of where the truth might lead. The media's gentle treatment of George W. Bush and his administration was, in many ways, a tribute to decades of hard spadework by conservative activities undertaken specifically for this purpose. And given its effect across the broad swath of American politics in the late 1990's and early 2000's, they had every right to take pride in their work."[772]

Joe Conason concurs in *Big Lies*: "Conservatives enjoy their virtual monopoly over the nation's political conversation, of course. They paid a lot of money for it and they intend to keep it. They dominate the national debate not because their ideas are better (or more popular), but because they have more resources and a vast, coordinated infrastructure that has been built up during three decades. They also tend to dominate because– unlike the supposedly liberal mainstream media–conservatives are perfectly willing to stifle opposition. Liberal opinion is hard to find in conservative newspapers and liberal voices are rarely heard on conservative talk radio."[773]

Bush of course would not agree. He complains that the media "are biased against conservative thought." Yet another lie?

We all want an honest and truthful parent figure to lead us in times of adversity; however, when it turns out that our parent is repeatedly lying to us and deceiving us about the dangers we face, we must intervene and avoid becoming co-dependent enablers. The President desperately needs to be helped "out."

Do you want the truth? Do you want to hear both sides of a story, an issue, so you can make up your own mind and form your own opinion? Are you concerned that the conservative media is so willing to smother liberal thought? Is the conservative media treating you like you are stupid? You're not stupid! Get the truth.

724. Conason, op. cit., p. 3.

725. gi.grolier.com/presidents/ea/bios; see also www.whitehouse.gov/history/presidents.

726. Ibid.

727. Ibid.

728. Ibid.

729. Ibid.

730. Ibid.

731. Ibid.

732. Ibid.

733. Ibid.

734. Ibid.

735. Ibid.

736. Ibid.; see also Conason, op. cit., pp. 77-80.

737. Conason, op. cit., pp. 85, 86.

738. Ibid., p. 86.

739. Ibid., p. 135.

740. Alterman, Eric, *What Liberal Media? The Truth About Bias and the News*, (New York: Basic Books, 2003), p. 81.

741. Ibid., p. 81, 82.

742. Conason, op. cit., p. 35.

743. Alterman, op. cit., p. 82.

744. Ibid., p. 82.

745. Ibid., p. 83.

746. Ibid.

747. Ibid., pp. 249, 250.

748. "The Federalist Society: From Obscurity to Power," People For The American Way Foundation, August 2001, (www.pfaw.org/pfaw/general/default.aspx?oid=652); see also Swomley, John M., "The Network of Righteousness. (The Federalist Society)," *Humanist*, November 2000, (www.findarticles.com/cf_0/PI/search.jhtml?key=%john%20m.%20swomley%20).

749. Conason, op. cit., p. 99.

750. Ivins, op. cit., pp. 278, 279.

751. Conason, op. cit., p. 19.

752. Ibid., p. 55.

753. Ibid., p. 34, 35; see also Alterman, op. cit., p. 2.

754. Ibid.; see also Alterman, op. cit., p. 23.

755. Alterman, op. cit., p. 2.

756. Conason, op. cit., p. 36.

757. Rampton, op. cit., pp. 166, 167.

758. Kellner, op. cit., p. 167.

759. Conason, op. cit., pp. 39, 40.

760. Ibid., pp. 41, 42.

761. Ibid., p. 45.

762. Ibid., p. 47; see also Alterman, op. cit., p. 70.

763. Rampton, op. cit., p. 170.

764. Boehlert, Eric, "The passion of Howard Stern," *Salon*, March 4, 2004, www.salon.com/news/feature/2004/03/04/stern/pring.html.

765. Alterman, op. cit., p. 70.

766. Ibid., p. 75.

767. Ibid., p. 71; see also Conason, op. cit., p. 50.

768. Conason, op. cit., p. 46.

769. Alterman, op. cit., pp. 198, 199.

770. Corn, op. cit., p. 292.

771. Solomon, op. cit., p. 23.

772. Alterman, op. cit., p. 223.

773. Conason, op. cit., p. 1.

THE PREVARICATOR III:
THE CAMPAIGN FOR REELECTION

Get ready. In the next election, Bush will use every dirty trick in Rove's book to win. The ballyhoo of his nominating convention in September 2004 will be an insult to the thousands who died unnecessarily on September 11, 2001.

Hollywood is not necessarily known for its creativity, and once it gets a box-office hit, it keeps churning out sequels until the public gets sick and tired of seeing the same old formula. Running a negative attack campaign got Bush close enough to be given the presidency, even though he lost the election, and it got him control over Congress in the midterm elections, even though he had to beat up a disabled war hero to do it. Now, he's baaaack.

Bush has already exceeded his goal of raising $170 million in campaign funds, and is on his way to $200 to $250 million. Even though he has no opponent in the primaries, he decided to fire a shot at the Democrats, just to keep their heads down. Timed to coincide with a Democratic Primary Debate in Iowa during the last week of November 2003, Bush ran a classic Rove attack ad. Showing Bush presidentially delivering his State of the Union lines, "Our war against terror is a contest of will in which perseverance is power," the ominous screen line says, "Some are now attacking the President for attacking the terrorists." Then, as he says, "Some have said we must not act until the threat is imminent," the screen line runs, "Some call for us to retreat, putting our national security in the hands of others."[774] Bush "knows we know" that "some" are Democrats, but it's an "unknown unknown," whether he's going to get away with "waving the bloody shirt" this time.[775]

Prevaricator III will be loaded with symbolism. The White House has announced that it is delaying the Republican nominating convention, scheduled for New York City, until the first week in September 2004, the latest in the party's history. This will allow Bush's acceptance speech, slated for September 2, to coincide with the 9/11 commemoration events scheduled to occur in the city. A coincidence?

Samuel Johnson once said, "Patriotism is the last refuge of a scoundrel." Bush keeps running around the country posing for photo ops in military jackets and spending millions in scarce military funds so he can be photographed climbing out of an airplane in front of a phony "Mission Accomplished" sign, and holding up a fake Thanksgiving turkey in Baghdad. However, he's not risking his life; he's putting the lives and futures of our children at risk. And he is spending the capital of our youth recklessly and cynically in fighting the wrong war for the wrong reasons. We Americans are used to rallying around the flag, and we will continue to do so. But once we realize that our President has drenched our flag in the blood of our children and that he is dragging our flag and their blood through the dirt of his nasty lying politics, we will throw the scoundrel out of office.

No matter how much Bush and Ashcroft try to make it appear unpatriotic to oppose Bush's War, opposition is a healthy thing, and it is the American way. A few days after the attack on Pearl Harbor, Republican Senator Robert Taft stated, "As a matter of general principle, I believe there can be no doubt that criticism in time of war is essential to the maintenance of any kind of democratic government ... because the maintenance of the right of criticism in the long run will do the country maintaining it a great deal more good than it will do the enemy, and will prevent mistakes which might otherwise occur."[776]

Bush raised $100 million for the 2000 primaries and, even though he is unopposed this time around, he has already raised over $170 million in an attempt to bury the successful Democratic candidate. Political scientist Donald F. Kettl believes the Bush campaign is "lying in wait, hoping to kneecap a Democratic candidate likely to emerge from the primaries wobbly and out of cash. ... This could well be the most effective Rose Garden campaign in history, backed by a war chest the Democrats don't have a prayer of matching."[777]

Bush is expected to take in as much as $250 million before the election is over. As of March 14th, 187 "Rangers" have raised at least $200,000 each for Bush, and 455 "Pioneers" have raised at least $100,000. The campaign has banked approximately $590,000 per day since June 2003.[778]

But all that money really doesn't matter, Bush probably won't need to waste a dime of his hard-earned funds on attack ads. According to Pat Robertson, God has already picked the winner. "The Lord has just blessed him. I mean he could make terrible mistakes and come out of it. It doesn't make any difference what he does, good or bad; God picks him up because he's a man of prayer and God's blessing him."[779]

Do you have questions in your mind about voting for the re-election of Bush? Do you really want a president who cares nothing for you, your children, and your aging parents? Do you feel guilty, sinful or unpatriotic because of your thoughts? You're not stupid! Get the truth.

Wired to Win

If you recall, Republican Saxby Chambliss allegedly defeated Democrat Max Cleland in the 2002 senatorial race in Georgia. Although the Chambliss victory undoubtedly benefited from Bush's repeated personal attacks on Cleland and the "slime" television ads questioning Cleland's patriotism, not to mention the $14 million spent on the election by the Republicans, there may have been another and more sinister factor at play.

The last minute pre-election polls showed Cleland ahead by two to five points; however, Chambliss won 53 percent of the votes in the election, a difference of 12 points, far beyond the margin for statistical error. An analysis of the vote showed Chambliss exceeding Republican totals from the primary by as much as 22 points in the strongly Democratic regions of southern Georgia. Equally surprising, votes for Cleland went up 14 percent in the Republican areas of northern Georgia.

Amazingly, in the race for governor, the pre-election polls showed the Democratic incumbent ahead of the Republican challenger by 9 to 11 percent; however, the Republican candidate was elected by a margin of 51 to 46 percent, a statistical reversal of 16 percent. These bizarre results are strangely coincidental with the introduction of statewide computerized voting in Georgia.[780]

In 2002, Georgia became the first state to use electronic touch-screen voting in a statewide election as a result of the $3 billion Help American Vote Act signed by Bush following the 2000 election fiasco. Georgia paid Diebold Election Systems $54 million to install the secret computerized system, which leaves no paper trail and which cannot be audited, post election, for accuracy.[781]

According to Rob Behler, a Diebold contractor, there were constant problems with the touch-screen system that resulted in at least three "patches" or updates to the programming being installed at the last minute, after the equipment had been independently certified and without the knowledge of the secretary of state. Behler described the system as "JS equipment" or "Junk s**t, with error rates of up to 25 percent,[782] and said that votes "could have been manipulated."[783]

Behler reports that "the code for the patches was posted to an Internet FTP [file transfer protocol] site, along with all of the election software... However, even if the FTP site were password protected, experts said it would have been a relatively simple task to hack into the location and insert rogue code, which might be designed to affect election results."[784]

Diebold has refused to comment on its voting machines or the Georgia election, except to deny that there were any patches installed, claiming that to comment would place its proprietary, copyrighted information at risk. Surprisingly, Diebold doesn't have to discuss its system with anyone, including its own clients. Under the Digital Millennium Copyright Act, purchasers are not allowed access to information on how the results are recorded.[785]

In August 2003, Diebold's CEO, Walden O'Dell, attended a gathering of "Rangers and Pioneers" at Bush's ranch, where the attendees pledged to raise money in bundles of $100,000 and $200,000 for Bush's reelection. Eleven Diebold executives have given a total of $22,000, the legal maximum, to Bush in the current election cycle. O'Dell raised an additional $500,000 for the campaign at a fundraiser he hosted for Vice President Cheney at his home.[786]

Neither Diebold, its CEO, any of its executives, or any other manufacturer of voting systems have made campaign contributions to any Democratic candidates.[787]

Do you remember Florida Secretary of State Katherine Harris and the role she played in the 2000 presidential election? Although the current Secretary of State, Glenda Hood, has promised that Florida has "the very best" technology available, there were abundant problems in the March 2004 primary. "Voters were wrongly given computer cards that let them vote only on local issues, not in the presidential primary," and many machines did not work.

Since the Supreme Court ruling in *Bush v. Gore* requires states to use comparable recount methods from county to county, and since 15 Florida counties that use electronic voting machines do not produce paper records that can be recounted, a Florida congressman has filed a federal lawsuit to require paper audit trails.[788]

Do you trust election officials to remain nonpartisan in deciding whether secret voting machines are properly certified and operating as designed? In at least two swing states, Missouri and Michigan, the secretaries of state occupy top positions in their state's Bush-Cheney campaigns.[789]

In California, Secretary of State Kevin Shelley, a Democrat, withdrew his approval of electronic voting machines throughout the state after officials of Diebold Election Systems allegedly lied to state officials and used unapproved software in its equipment. Shelley said, "They broke the law. Their conduct was absolutely reprehensible." Ten counties that rely upon other electronic voting systems may be allowed to use the equipment if they certify that they meet 23 new requirements, including offering a paper ballot to any voter who requests it and releasing the software code to the secretary of state for evaluation.[790]

Should we trust Diebold or any other electronic voting company to secretly make changes to computerized voting machines after they have been certified, without notifying election officials of the changes, without allowing us to know how their systems operate, and without providing a paper audit trail?   If these practices disturb you, go to http://www. blackboxvoting.org to find like-minded patriots.

You're not stupid! Get the truth.

---

774. Saletan, William and Jacob Weisberg, "Treason's Greetings," *Slate,* November 25, 2003, http://slate.msn.com/id/2091666/.

775. "More Waving of the Bloody Shirt," October 14, 2003, http://www.discriminations.us/storage/002245.html.

776. *The Papers of Robert Taft* (Kent, 1997), p. 303, http://hnn.us/articles/631.

777. Simon, Richard, "In Race for Funds, Bush Is the Winner," *Los Angeles Times*, January 8, 2004, p. A8.

778. Justice, Glen, "Newcomers Provide Fuel for Bush Money Machine," *The New York Times*, March 14, 2004, www.nytimes.com/2004/03/14/politics/campaign/14MONE.html.

779. Scheer, Robert, "Lord Knows What Robertson Wants," *Los Angeles Times*, January 6, 2004, p. B13.

780. Moore, *Bush's War for Reelection*, op. cit., pp. 289-293.

781. Ibid., p. 293.

782. Ibid., p. 294.

783. Cohen, Adam, "The Results Are in and the Winner Is...or Maybe Not," *The New York Times*, February 29, 2004, www.nytimes.com/2004/02/29/opinion/29SUN3.html.

784. Moore, *Bush's War for Reelection*, op. cit., p. 295.

785. Ibid., p. 296.

786. Ibid., p. 305, 306.

787. Ibid., p. 306.

788. "Florida as the Next Florida," *The New York Times*, March 14, 2004, http://www.nytimes.com/2004/03/14/opinion/14SUN1.html.

789. "When the Umpires Take Sides," *The New York Times*, March 29, 2004, http://www.nytimes.com/2004/03/29/opinion/29MON1.html.

790. Pfeifer. Stuart, "State Blocks Digital Voting," *Los Angeles Times,* May 1, 2004, http://www.latimes.com/news/local/la-me-machines1may01,1,3927648.story?coll=la-home; see also Schwartz, John, "High-Tech Voting System Is Banned in California," *The New York Times*, May 1, 2004, http://www.nytimes.com/2004/05/01/national/01VOTE.html.

THE EMPEROR HAS NO CLOTHES

Who is the real George W. Bush? Is he the compassionate conservative, policy-involved politician, and world leader he plays on TV? Or behind the benevolent smile, is he an ignoramus just as cold-blooded, ruthless and paranoid as his personal political Machiavelli Karl Rove?

Bush is an illegitimate president. Although his father may acknowledge paternity, a majority of the American voters rejected him, and by his actions, he has proved our instincts were right. Although outwardly likeable, he is a deeply flawed individual, uncaring, devious, and lacking in moral character. But other presidents may have shared some of these traits. What is most troubling is that he just doesn't seem very smart, and worst of all, he tells lies constantly. This trait makes him doubly dangerous. To us, and to the world.

Bush makes poor decisions with little thought. He is easily manipulated by the mega-rich, who seek greater wealth, and by his own staff, who seek personal and political advantages. Worst of all, he uses lies as a weapon, easily and cunningly, with no regard for the truth or the irreparable harm he may cause, to us and to world civilization.

Although Bush has exhibited all the outward symptoms of alcoholism and other personality defects such as compulsive lying,* he has never, to public knowledge, sought professional

---

* In his book, *Lies! Lies!! Lies!!! The Psychology of Deceit*, Charles Ford, a professor of psychiatry, tells us that "words seem to flow out of [the] mouths [of pathological liars] without them thinking about it," and that they go from believing a falsehood could be true to believing that it is in fact true. Robert Reich, M.D., an expert in psychopathology, tells us that compulsive lying has no official diagnosis. It is associated with a number of different personality disorders. (Jozefowicz, Chris, "Understanding Compulsive Liars," *Psychology Today*, October 23, 2003, www.psychologytoday.com.) One writer suggested that Bush might suffer from a narcissistic personality disorder: arrogant, haughty behaviors or attitudes; inability to recognize or identify with feelings of

treatment. He views politics as a game to be played, with no real consequence for losing; however, the game he is playing involves millions of lives, perhaps even the future of humanity. We need to better understand what makes him tick so we can better evaluate his effectiveness as the leader of the most powerful nation on earth.

Bush can't remember any book that he ever read as a child.[791] He was a lazy student, preferring to collect baseball cards instead of reading and thinking about life and events beyond his comfortable surroundings.[792] It is not surprising that he has grown up to be intellectually lazy, refusing to read newspapers or briefing papers, or to spend more than 30 minutes considering any problem, irrespective of its complexity.[793]

Bush was a hyperactive child, throwing a football through his classroom window and riding around Midland, Texas, on his bicycle, stealing bags of drilling samples from the front porches of geologists to use in mock battles with playmates.[794] Is it any surprise that he spends hours each day jogging, working out and playing video games?[795]

Bush played cruel games as a child, blowing up frogs with firecrackers and shooting at his younger brothers with a BB gun as they ran away; he teased his mother about the death of her favorite dog, and he saw his father chastise his mother for allowing their African-American maid to get off work an hour early, even though she had nothing to do. Is it any surprise that he grew up to have little empathy for others?

Bush worked on his father's political campaigns as the "Roman candle," a temperamental "enforcer,"[796] and he saw Bush Sr. defeated for reelection because Bush *perceived* that his father was *perceived* as too wimpy and too preppy.[797] Is it any surprise that he grew up to be a governor who executed more prisoners than most of the rest of the other states combined, that he parodied one prisoner's plea for clemency as he was about to execute her, and chuckled when asked during a debate about

---

others; and exploitation of others. (Parry, Sam, "The Bush Exit Ramp, January 22, 2003, http://www.consortiumnews.com.)

lawyers sleeping during their client's death-penalty trials in his state?[798]

Although Bush challenged his own father to go "mano a mano," and although he is verbally nasty, it doesn't appear that he has ever actually been in a real fight; therefore is it any wonder that his challenge to the Iraqi resistance, "Bring 'em on," sounds more like an insecure cheerleader than a confident fighter?

Bush's world is a dark place, and he thinks dark thoughts. Although he professes a religion based upon the teachings of the Prince of Peace, his speeches are obsessed with evil and threats of danger. Rather than comfort us, he makes us fearful. Instead of creating hope, he drives us to despair. He feeds upon his own insecurities and strives to impose them on us. He cannot lead us to the mountaintop; he can only drive us into the pit.

Bush does not accept he can do wrong or that there are limits on his power, because he deeply believes "he was called by God to lead the nation" and that he is "an instrument of Providence." Bush says, "Events aren't moved by blind change and chance ... [but] by the hand of a just and faithful God." Bush believes that "heaven is open only to those who accept Jesus Christ."[799] There is no salvation for Jews, Muslims, or Buddhists. David Frum, his faithful former speechwriter reports that while he served in the White House "attendance at Bible study was, if not compulsory, not quite uncompulsory."

Another Bush admirer, Richard Brookhiser, believes that "Bush's faith means that he does not tolerate, or even recognize, ambiguity; there is an all-knowing God who decrees certain behaviors, and leaders must obey." Bush is reported to have told Palestinian Prime Minister Mahmoud Abbas, "God told me to strike at al Qaeda and I struck them, and then he instructed me to strike at Saddam, which I did."[800]

Perception is everything for George W. Bush. He once said, "I don't care what anyone says, politics is all about perception."[801] On becoming president, he said, "I hope I'm viewed as a humble person."[802] However, once he was in office, he said, "I'm the commander–see, I don't need to explain why I say things. That's the interesting thing about being the president. Maybe somebody needs to explain to me why they say something, but I don't feel like I owe anybody an explanation."[803] These are opposite attributes, and only an extremely arrogant or defective personality would fail to *perceive* the inconsistency—and the contradiction with America's Constitution and democratic way of life.

It is only important to Bush that he is *perceived* as having compassion or as being a leader, when in fact he has no feelings of truly caring for other people or any *vision* of what could be. Instead of imagining a rich scholarly educational environment for all of our children, he seeks to test and categorize them and to punish their teachers for failing to whip them into shape. Instead of imagining that it is the destiny of our children to fly to the stars, to carry forth a message of gentle cooperation and caring, he seeks to militarize space and the moon to benefit his wealthy corporate contributors. Instead of imagining new and innovative sources of energy and conservation programs, he seeks to conquer other nations and peoples to exploit the world's finite oil supplies for the benefit of his rich friends.

Bush once defined intelligence: "Intelligence is can you think logically. Intelligence is do you have a basis from which to make decisions. Intelligence in politics is do you have good instincts."[804] What more can be said? The leadership of the most powerful nation on earth requires a bit more insight than that.

Whether a consequence of having been a lazy student and/or because of excessive alcoholism or drug use into his 40s, Bush has made hundreds and hundreds of really stupid public statements. We keep overlooking them, hoping that he really doesn't mean it when he says things like, "We are resolved to rout out terror wherever it exists to save the world from freedom." Or, "We're freeing women and children from incredible impression!"[805] The frightening thing is that whenever he forcefully delivers one of these dumb lines during a speech, the audience applauds! It must be said. The Emperor has no clothes.

A Reflection of Our Self-Image?

Bush strives to create the *perception* that he is an ordinary guy, but no matter how hard he tries, he remains a rich spoiled brat at heart, one who has never earned anything on his own in his life, including the presidency. And when he's with his peers, he doesn't try to hide it.

On October 19, 2000, Bush addressed the Al Smith Memorial Dinner in New York City, and some of his remarks are telling: "This is an impressive crowd, the haves, and the have–mores. Some people call you the elite. I call you my base." [laughter] He joked, "[M]y opponent keeps saying I gave too much tax relief to the top one percent. But he hadn't heard my latest proposal. The bottom 99 percent will do well when they get to split Dick Cheney's stock options." [laughter][806] Not funny, at least not to the hard-working, ordinary people who carry the burden of supporting the government and economy that provide Bush and his base with the lifestyle of the rich and famous.

Immediately after taking office, Bush demonstrated his true sympathies. In March 2001, legislation written by bank and credit company lawyers and lobbyists was quickly enacted by his Republican-controlled Congress and was signed by Bush to make it difficult or impossible for working families to discharge their overwhelming personal debts in bankruptcy and to get a "fresh start."

The biggest beneficiary of the legislation was MBNA Corporation of Delaware, the world's largest independent credit card company. Unsurprisingly, ranked by employee donations, MBNA was the greatest corporate contributor to the Bush campaign, having handed him $240,000, plus $100,000 for his inaugural parties.[807]

In April 2001, Bush visited the Wilmington, Delaware, Boys and Girls Club to show off his gift of royalties from his book, *A Charge to Keep*, to the Boys and Girls Clubs of America. He said he was making the gift because "I believe so profoundly, I believe so strongly in mentoring. And I believe so strongly in helping children understand somebody loves them." What he did not reveal during the photo opportunity was that the budget he had already submitted entirely eliminated the government's $60 million in funding for the organization.[808]

Needless to say, his royalties did not make up the deficit in funding. If Bush had truly loved poor children and cared about keeping the Boys and Girls Clubs open, he would have ensured adequate funding. What he cared about most was creating a *perception* that he cared, therefore the photo op and chump change.

During his State of the Union address in January 2002, Bush asked for an increase in the AmeriCorps program, saying, "Americans are doing the work of compassion every day–visiting prisoners, providing shelter for battered women, bringing companionship to lonely seniors, ... These good works deserve our praise; they deserve our personal support; and when appropriate, they deserve the assistance of the federal government." Are you surprised that a year later he proposed an 80 percent cut in the program?[809] Were you one of the 50 million Americans who viewed his well-scripted performance that evening? Did you form a perception that he cared about battered women or lonely seniors? Listen not to what Bush says! Rather, look to his deeds to measure his compassion.

In April 2002, Bush traveled to Albuquerque for a photo op with Lucy Salazar, who collects books for Project Even Start and tutors pre-kindergarten children in reading. Bush praised Salazar; but failed to mention that his 2003 budget effectively cut the Project's funding by 20 percent.[810] That night on the evening news, it probably appeared that Bush cared about giving poor children an even start in reading skills, but do you believe it? Would it make you nervous to have the President praise something you believed in, and which required his budgetary support?

A few days after the 9/11 attacks, Bush went to Ground Zero in New York City. As the workers cheered him, Bush yelled, "I can hear you, and the rest of the world hears you, and the people who–and the people [who] knocked these buildings down will hear all of us soon." Bush wanted to project a perception of strength and comradeship with the brave firefighters. However, after he rejected a bill that contained $340 million to fund fire departments, the International Association of Fire Fighters boycotted a national tribute to firefighters who died on 9/11, and its general president, Harold Schaitberger, told Bush, "Don't lionize our fallen brothers in one breath and then stab us in the back."[811]

Moreover, Bush exposed the rescue workers and others employed in lower Manhattan to dangerous health risks when the White House instructed the EPA to say it was safe to return to work and breathe the air, a deliberate misrepresentation.[812]

On August 5, 2002, Bush went to Somerset County, Pennsylvania, to be photographed with nine coal miners who had escaped after being trapped for three days in a flooded coal mine. Bush threw his arms around them, smiled for the cameras, and praised them and their rescuers for "showing our fellow citizens that by serving something greater than yourself is an important part of being an American." He said their ordeal and rescue "really defines kind of a new spirit that's prevalent in our country, that when one of us suffer, all of us suffer."

The miners' rescue had depended upon technical assistance provided by the federal Mine Safety and Health Administration; however, Bush had already proposed a cut in the agency's existing inadequate budget, and he had appointed an administrator, dedicated to reducing or eliminating mine safety regulations, to emasculate the agency. Bush had proposed a six-percent reduction in the agency's budget, even though 42 miners had been killed on the job during 2001, up from 29 in 2000.

If Bush had truly cared about miners and the dangers under which they earn a living, he would not have cut the budget of the agency that protects their safety, nor would he have appointed someone dedicated to the elimination of mine safety regulations.[813] Rather, he cared only for the *perception* of concern, thus the photo op and his somewhat mangled words of cheer.

On December 19, 2002, Bush visited the Capitol Area Food Bank in Washington, D.C. for another staged event. He said, "Those who are poor, those who suffer, those who have lost hope are not strangers in our midst; they're our fellow citizens. ... And in this time of joy, in the time of blessing, we've got to remember that. To make the season complete and the season whole, we must help those who are in need." A *perception* of caring? Just words. Only days before Bush had proposed elimination of meal assistance for 36,000 seniors, after-school program slots for 50,000 children, child care benefits for 33,000 families, and the termination of heating assistance for 532,000 families during the winter Christmas season.[814]

On February 17, 2004, Bush addressed military personnel and their families at Fort Polk, Louisiana. He stated, "In the war, America depends on our military to meet the dangers abroad and to keep our country safe. The American people appreciate this sacrifice."[815] Bush wanted to create a *perception* that he cared about the soldiers he was sending off to be killed in his war; however, Bush doesn't appreciate their sacrifice enough to adequately fund programs that benefit them and their families. He has attempted to "roll back recent modest increase" in combat imminent-danger pay, and refused to extend the child tax credit to one million poor children living in military and veteran families as a part of his tax cut package for the wealthy.[816] In reviewing Bush's 2005 budget, The Veterans of Foreign Wars stated, "This funding package is a disgrace and a sham."[817]

Any doubts as to Bush's empathy or lack thereof for those who serve and who are dying in his war were laid to rest by his performance at the Radio and Television Correspondents' Association Dinner on March 24, 2004. Although in these appearances the president is expected to be funny in his remarks, Bush choose to narrate a slide show of himself on the telephone with a finger in his ear while listening to his European allies and searching under his office furniture for missing weapons of mass destruction. Bush sought to convey a *perception* that he is just a regular guy, without understanding that his antics made fun of his justification for sending over 750 of our sons and daughters to their deaths in Iraq.[818]

Bush says that he cares for the poor, those who suffer, and those who have lost hope, but does he really do anything about it? In 2002, the number of people living in poverty rose by 1.7

million to a total of 34.6 million.[819] What did he do? Bush cut taxes on the wealthy and axed benefits for the poor.

Do you believe that Bush feels your pain and shares your losses? Does he really care what happens to the rest of us? You're not stupid! Get the truth.

The Image We Present to the World

Bush is the President of the United States of America. As such, he is the political image we project to the rest of the world. He is our most visible representative. Knowing what you know now, would you buy a used car from him? Perhaps a better question is, would you choose this man as your lawyer to represent you in court and present your case to the jury, particularly if you were falsely accused of murder and the consequences were truly life or death? Would you trust his devotion to your welfare, his intellect, his knowledge of the law, his intuitive grasp of issues, his ability to formulate and ask logical questions? Do you believe he could draw out favorable testimony, ascertain subtle distinctions and explain them plainly to the jury? Could he sense your motivations and fears, and could he sympathetically convey them to the jury? Would you trust him to stay awake and focused during your trial? Would you trust him with your life, or the life of someone you love? Aren't these the very questions we should be asking about our president?

At his inauguration, Bush was introduced to teenage soprano Charlotte Church, who had sung in the ceremony. Bush asked "where does this lovely lil' lady hail from?" She answered, "I'm from Wales." He asked, "What state is that in?" She replied, "It's in Great Britain." Bush paused and a crease of perplexity appeared on his presidential brow. He said, "Oh really? I'll have my people look into that." Church said she found him "kind of stupid."[820]

In March 2001, shortly after taking office, Bush embarrassed both South Korean president (and Nobel laureate) Kim Dae Jung, who had been promoting a "sunshine" policy toward North Korea, and Secretary of State Powell, who had just endorsed the effort. Bush publicly repudiated the negotiations and declared, "We're not certain as to whether or not they're keeping all terms of all agreements." His own aides were unable to find any evidence to support his public accusation. Bush later launched into an embarrassing tirade to a group of U.S. senators about Kim Jong II, calling him a "pygmy."[821]

On September 5, 2001, at an informal press conference prior to his first state dinner in honor of Mexican president Vincente Fox, Bush told reporters to "shut up" in broken Spanish, and then cut off inconvenient questions by saying, *"No puedo oirle"* (Spanish–"I can't hear you").[822]

During another joint press conference a year later in Los Cabos, Mexico, Bush, who was upset with Fox's failure to support his invasion of Iraq, "glowered during Fox's windup and looked annoyed at the unruliness of the camera crews." According to the *Washington Post*, "The last straw was when a cell phone went off, which infuriates Bush. ... In a breach of protocol, Bush cut off the translator before Fox's answers could be rendered into English" and walked out.[823]

On the occasion of a joint press conference with British Prime Minister Blair, Bush was asked what they had in common. He answered, "We both use Colgate toothpaste."[824] Insipid, asinine, or just ignorant?

In February 2002, Bush gave a speech to the Japanese Parliament that stunned its members. Bush said, "My trip to Asia begins here in Japan for an important reason. (applause.) It begins here because for *a century and a half* now (emphasis added), America and Japan have formed one of the great and enduring alliances of modern times." (silence.)[825] The man was either hung over, slept through, or just ditched his history classes. Our alliance with Japan began a *half century* ago, following our use of atomic weapons for the only time in history to force its surrender in a war in which millions died.

In May 2002, Bush set off on a world tour to meet with other leaders and to encourage the *perception* that he is presidential. In Russia, he met with Prime Minister Vladimir Putin, to whom Bush had publicly given the insulting nickname "Pootie Poo." Russian television repeatedly showed a video clip of Bush chewing gum as he entered a meeting with Putin, and then spitting it into his hand before the press conference.[826]

In Germany, Bush was greeted by massive demonstrations against him and his plans to attack Iraq, and when he spoke in the German parliament, members held up a peace flag and walked out. The German magazine *Der Spiegel* held Bush up for ridicule when it reported that he had embarrassingly asked Brazilian President Fernando Enrique Cardozo, "Do you have blacks, too?" And it told how National Security Advisor Condoleezza Rice had to inform Bush that Brazil was populated with more citizens of African descent than was the United States.[827]

Bush met with French President Jacques Chirac for two hours and then participated in a lengthy joint press conference. When asked a question, Bush verbally wandered around the syntactical landscape until he was forced to admit that he had forgotten the question, saying, "That's what happens when you get past 55." Bush twice referred to President Chirac as "President Jacques," and pronounced his last name throughout as "shrak."[828]

NBC reporter David Gregory asked Bush, "I wonder why it is you think there are such strong sentiments in Europe against you and against this administration? Why, particularly, there's a view that you and your administration are trying to impose America's will on the rest of the world, particularly when it comes to the Middle East and where the war on terrorism goes next?" Then, speaking in French, Gregory asked President Chirac, "And, Mr. President, would you maybe comment on that?" Bush retorted, "Very good. The guy memorizes four words, and he plays like he's intercontinental." Gregory said, "I can go on." Bush replied, "I'm impressed–*que bueno* (Spanish– "how wonderful"). Now, I'm literate in two languages." He then accused Gregory of "showing off as soon as you get in front of a camera."[829] For Bush, it is all a matter of *perception*. But who was showing off, and who came off as being both ignorant and arrogant?

On March 18, 2003, the Pew Research Center for the People and the Press released a survey of the changes in world opinion about the United States between January 2002 and March 2003, following the commencement of Bush's War. In France, the percentage holding a favorable view plummeted from 63 to 31; in Italy, from 70 to 34; in Russia, from 61 to 28; and in Turkey, from 30 to 12. Even the citizens of our closest ally, England, lost respect for America, from 75 to 48 percent.[830] Overall, America's popularity roughly dropped 50 percent or more.

Does Bush represent the image of America you want to be projected to the rest of the world? You're not stupid! Get the truth.

The Stealth Co-President

Political consultant Karl Rove did the field research and taught the classes on political dirty tricks. Starting as a paid staffer for the Republican National Committee, he evolved an anything-goes approach to political campaigning in which winning becomes everything. Among his creations was the phony "push poll," in which potential voters are called and asked provocative questions, such as those asked in the 1999 primary campaign against McCain and in the midterm 2002 elections in Florida and Texas. More often, he relies upon the false whisper campaign, such as his rumors of Governor Ann Richard's appointment of gays and lesbians to state commissions and McCain's fathering of an illegitimate black child.

Rove taught classes on negative political campaigning at the University of Texas, relying upon the doctrine of war taught by Sun-Tzu, "All we need to do is throw something odd and unaccountable at the enemy." He taught that "Radio is really good for a negative attack, because it's tough to figure what the opposition is doing." He said, "The only thing worse to face is mail." Because direct mail "is immune from press coverage."[831]

When Bush Sr. was the chairman of the Republican National Committee in 1973, the *Washington Post* ran a story entitled, "GOP Probes Official as Teacher of Tricks." The teacher was Karl Rove, and although Bush Sr. promised to "get to the bottom" of the allegations that Rove was using dirty political tricks, he later promoted Rove to be his special assistant.[832]

One of Rove's jobs was to make sure that Bush Jr. got the keys to the family car whenever he came to visit in Washington.[833] Rove served as Bush Jr.'s political advisor in his failed run for Congress in 1978. It is unknown whether Rove had anything to do with Bush's television ads showing him jogging through West Texas,* a scene which is downright ridiculous.[834]

Karl Rove created George W. Bush, the politician. In 1990, Bush hired Rove to do a makeover from being a failed featherweight businessman into a heavyweight political contender. Rove arranged tutoring sessions with experts in juvenile justice, corrections, state government, school finance and education issues, welfare, and social services. Bush was not a quick study. For example, he had difficulty grasping the difference between federal Medicare for the elderly and disabled and state Medicaid for the indigent. He was better at business issues. Whatever was good for the corporations had to be good for the citizens of Texas; the issue just had to be properly packaged and marketed.

Once Bush graduated from political kindergarten, Rove enrolled him in public policy elementary school by creating policy teams to formulate positions for Bush on education, welfare, crime, and business issues, including "tort reform."[835] Rove would take the policy issues, place a political spin on them, and reduce them to one or two simple themes for Bush to memorize.

This approach worked well as the campaign for governor commenced in 1993, unless Bush was questioned too closely, which Rove normally would not allow. Once, however, after Bush gave a prepared speech on education, a reporter approached him and asked him about his plan to reform education. After repeating a couple of his staple lines, Bush was unable to answer basic questions about the workings of the state education agency, how his plan would change the school-finance formula, how much it would cost, and finally, if the voters

---

* Bush's opponent joked that in Muleshoe, Texas, the only people who jogged were running away from something or somebody.

would know how much it would cost before the election. His answer, "Probably not."[836]

Bush was elected governor and settled into a job often described as the fourth or fifth most powerful political office in Texas, following even the lieutenant governor in authority. According to his political ally Representative Paul Sadler, Bush delegated responsibility to top aides to study issues and to report back with recommended solutions for snap decisions. Bush had a limited attention span and was uninterested in discussing the philosophy of an issue. Sadler said, "I have absolutely no question in his ability to make the right decision if he's presented with the facts from all sides. I have watched him do it. Where I found he gets off track is if he only has one voice in the room. There's what's always bothered me. ... It's about the need to have different viewpoints in the room. Part of my training as a lawyer is trying to understand what the other side thinks. He comes from an MBA background. He doesn't have that training. I want to know why I think the way I do, but I always want to know why the other side thinks the way they do. He doesn't go through that thought process as often. To me, it makes it more important to make sure the counselors around him come from different viewpoints."[837] Do you think Bush is exposed to differing viewpoints?

Bush concedes that he only "glance[s] at the headlines just to [get a] kind of a flavor for what's moving. I rarely read the stories." He says "the most objective sources I have are people on my staff who tell me what's happening in the world."[838] Do you believe Bush's "people" are objective enough to tell him what he needs to know to make critical decisions?

Rove agrees that Bush "doesn't make decisions alone. That is to say, you know, you get a sense of some people. They are self-contained. They are totally self-contained so they need nothing in order to arrive at a decision. He respects, he honors the process that gives information." Bush honors Rove by giving Rove control over the information that is provided to him, and by accepting Rove's interpretation of that information, especially as it relates to its political implications.[839]

Bush repeatedly lies and says he does not govern by polls. The truth is that Rove conducts the polls, discerns political trends, and then advocates for policies that will move Bush in the same direction.[840] Rove identifies the opponent's weaknesses, designs the attack, and releases the attack dogs. For Rove and Bush, the true course of a political campaign is attack, attack, and attack.[841]

For Rove and Bush, *perception is reality*. They engage in the politics of pretense.[842] For Rove and Bush, it does not matter if the President is in fact compassionate, it matters only that he is *perceived* as being compassionate. In many respects, their belief appears pathological in that they seem to really believe that the rest of us will never catch on to their deceptions, or that if we do, they will be able to convincingly lie their way out of it.

When Bush was asked about meeting with Log Cabin Republicans, an affluent gay lobbying group, he said he probably wouldn't meet with them. Why? "Well, because it creates a huge political scene."[843]

Message. For Bush to follow the program, Rove's themes and messages have to be simple and repetitious. It does not matter what the question is, the answer must always be the same. Rove is proud of developing the theme and articulating the message, and Bush is proud to deliver it. However, a part of the scheme is to always give Bush credit for the thinking of others. An internal memorandum instructs government spokespersons to refer to Bush's "leadership" in all media contacts. His staff constantly refers to "the president's position," and what "President Bush believes" about different issues.

Writing in *From 9/11 to Terror War*, Douglas Kellner concludes, "In fact, the pro-corporate, unilateralist, and militarist hard-right corps of his administration formulates the plans, makes the decisions, and carries out the policies, with Bush serving as a mere figurehead and cheerleader. Bush's role is to provide sound bites to the public when his handlers have agreed on specific policies and to raise funds for the Republican Party."[844]

Bush says, "The important question is, How many hands have I shaked [sic]?" and "I don't want to win? If that were the case, why the heck am I on the bus 16 hours a day, shaking thousands of hands, giving hundreds of speeches, getting pillared [sic] in the press and cartoons and still staying on message to win?"[845]

Rove and his relationship with Bush were described by a well-connected business and political consultant: "Rove is Nixonian in his cynicism and manipulation of patriotic themes. The irony is that W., in many ways, is the anti-Nixon. Nixon was brilliant but self-destructive. W. is dull but, in Rove's hands, maniacally disciplined. It's like Rove is Nixon's heir. Cold-blooded. Ruthless. Paranoid. But unlike Nixon, Rove has figured out how to mask it all behind Bush's smile."[846] A smile, or a smirk?

Is Rove the kind of guy you want making policy for America? Pulitzer Prize-winning author Ron Suskind was once waiting outside Rove's office and overheard him yelling, "We will f**k him. Do you hear me? We will *f**k* him. We will ruin him. Like no one has ever f**ked him." A real Christian gentleman, right?[847]

Since 1990, Bush and Rove have entered into a continuing political marriage of convenience in which their thoughts and actions have become inseparable.[848] Clinton openly said that, if elected, he and Hillary would give us two for the price of one. In contrast, Bush's political twin is kept out of view in a backroom at the White House. But he's there, ruling the roost, our unelected stealth co-president.

Do you trust Rove more than Bush? Did you vote for Karl Rove? Did anyone? Does it bother you that Rove has so much power and control over the president? You're not stupid! Get the truth.

The Mayberry Machiavellis

It is not often that we are able to obtain inside information about the high-level decision-making that takes place inside the White House while the administration is still in power. Luckily, John DiIulio, a former Assistant to the President, sent a lengthy

"For/On the Record" letter to journalist Ron Suskind that sheds light on Bush's policy-making process. DiIulio, an author, historian and professor at the University of Pennsylvania, was appointed by Bush to create the Office of Faith-Based and Community Initiatives, which Bush called the Cornerstone of his "compassionate conservatism."

Once Suskind published an article in *Esquire* magazine, based upon DiIulio's letter, that was critical of Karl Rove and Bush's policy-making apparatus,[849] Bush's press secretary Ari Fleischer labeled the charges "groundless and baseless." However, DiIulio stood by his assertions, at least initially, before issuing an "apology."[850]

DiIulio's insights, based upon his 20 years of studying American government and public policy formulation and his personal observations made during numerous senior staff meetings within the White House, are quoted here at some length.

As of the date of the letter, October 24, 2002, DiIulio did not believe the administration had done much, "either in absolute terms, or in comparison to previous administrations at this stage, on domestic policy. There is a virtual absence as yet of any policy accomplishments that might, to a fair-minded non-partisan, count as the flesh on the bones of so-called compassionate conservatism."

DiIulio advised, "they could stand to find ways of inserting more serious policy fiber into the West Wing diet, and engage much less in on-the-fly policy-making by speech-making." He believed that "what they needed ... was more policy-relevant information, discussion, and deliberation." During all the meetings attended by DiIulio, he heard perhaps three "meaningful, substantive policy discussions. There were no actual policy white papers on domestic issues. There were, truth be told, only a couple of people in the West Wing who worried at all about policy substance and analysis."[851]

DiIulio found that "on social policy and related issues, the lack of even basic policy knowledge, and the only casual interest in knowing more, was somewhat breathtaking–discussions by fairly senior people who meant Medicaid but were talking Medicare; near-instant shifts from discussing any actual policy pros and cons to discussing political communications, media strategy, et cetera. Even quite junior staff would sometimes hear quite senior staff pooh-pooh any need to dig deeper for pertinent information on a given issue."[852]

DiIulio continues, "This gave rise to what you might call Mayberry* Machiavellis† –staff, senior and junior, who consistently talked and acted as if the height of political sophistication consisted in reducing every issue to its simplest, black-and-white terms for public consumption, then steering legislative initiatives or policy proposals as far right as possible. ... Like college students who fall for the colorful, opinionated, but intellectually third-rate professor, you could see these 20- and 30-something junior White House staff falling for the Mayberry Machiavellis."[853]

DiIulio offers his insights regarding Rove: "Some are inclined to blame the high political-to-policy ratios of this administration on Karl Rove. Some in the press view Karl as some sort of prince of darkness; actually, he is basically a nice and good-humored man. And some staff members, senior and junior, are awed and cowed by Karl's real or perceived powers. They self-censor lots for fear of upsetting him, and, in turn, few

---

* The Andy Griffith Show was a highly successful sitcom that ran on television from 1960 to 1968 featuring a small-town sheriff in Mayberry, North Carolina who spent more time fishing and discussing philosophy than fighting crime.
† Writing in *The Prince*, Niccolò Machiavelli discussed the use of deception by leaders: "the experience of our own time shows that those princes who had little regard for their word and had the craftiness to turn men's minds have accomplished great things and, in the end, have overcome those who governed their actions by their pledges." Machiavelli believed that "Men are so simple and so much inclined to obey immediate needs that a deceiver will never lack victims for his deceptions." The advantage goes to those "who broke faith"; however, the prince "must know how to mask this nature skillfully and be a great dissembler." (Corn, David, *The Lies of George W. Bush*, p. 6)

of the president's top people routinely tell the president what they really think if they think that Karl will be brought up short in the bargain. Karl is enormously powerful, maybe the single most powerful person in the modern, post-Hoover era ever to occupy a political advisor post near the Oval Office. The Republican base constituencies, including beltway libertarian policy elites and religious right leaders, trust him to keep Bush '43' [Jr.] from behaving like Bush '41' [Sr.] and moving too far to the center or inching at all center-left. ... Little happens on any issue without Karl's okay, and, often, he supplies such policy substance as the administration puts out."854

DiIulio wonders, "A year after 9/11 and with a White House that can find time enough to raise $140 million for campaigns, it's becoming fair to ask, on domestic policy and compassionate conservatism, 'where's the beef?'"855

DiIulio was not alone in his questions. In his *Esquire* article, "Why Are These Men Laughing?" Suskind quoted several other senior White House officials, one of whom confided, "Many of us feel it's our duty–our obligation as Americans–to get the word out that, certainly in domestic policy, there has been almost no meaningful consideration of any real issues. It's just kids on Big Wheels, who talk politics and know nothing. It's depressing. DPC [Domestic Policy Council] meetings are a farce."856

Bush's former speech writer, David Frum, wrote a generally favorable book about Bush, *The Right Man*, after he left the White House, in which he describes Bush as "impatient and quick to anger; sometimes glib, even dogmatic; often uncurious and as a result ill informed." Frum said that Bush's staff has a "dearth of really high-powered brains," and that one seldom "met someone who possessed unusual knowledge."857

Bush fired his first Treasury Secretary, Paul O'Neill, because he publicly questioned the wisdom of Bush's second round of tax cuts. In a recent book, *The Price of Loyalty*, by Ron Suskind, O'Neill described a lack of real dialogue in the Cabinet meetings he attended, saying that Bush "was like a blind man in a roomful of deaf people." According to O'Neill, Bush is a disengaged president, who doesn't encourage debate either at Cabinet meetings or in one-on-one meetings with his Cabinet secretaries.[858] So, who does Bush listen to?

Are you satisfied that Bush receives adequate advice on alternatives before making policy decisions? Is Bush creating sensible policies or is he pandering to political perceptions? You're not stupid! Get the truth.

The Disappointment of Diogenes

In around 400 B.C., the Cynic philosopher Diogenes is said to have walked through Athens in broad daylight carrying a lighted lamp, hoping that its light might reflect upon a man of virtue.

A person of virtue conforms to a standard of right, exhibits a particular moral excellence, and displays courage. Would Diogenes be disappointed, should the light of his lantern shine in the direction of our president?

During the third presidential debate at Washington University in St. Louis, Mo., the candidates were asked about the "apathy amongst young people who feel there are no issues directed to them and they don't plan to vote." Bush answered, "I don't think it's the issues that turn kids off. I think it's the tone. I think it's the attitude. I think it's a cynicism in Washington and it doesn't have to be that way." He concluded, "And finally, sir, to answer your question, it needs somebody in office who'll tell the truth. That's the best way to get people back in the system."[859] Bush's approach to truth-telling may be getting people back into the system, not as he expected, but in revolt against his lies and where they have taken us.

If nothing else, this book has shown that Bush does not tell the truth and that he may be incapable of knowing or recognizing the truth. Bush lies about the most serious and life-threatening matters facing our country and its government. His continued inability to tell even basic truths reflects no virtue.

On taking his oath of office, Bush placed his hand on the Bible and swore to protect and defend the Constitution of the United States. His willful refusal to defend America against the 9/11 terrorist attacks, although he was repeatedly given specific advance warnings, his subsequent abrogation of our freedoms for no just cause, and his engaging us in an illegal war are all violations of his Constitutional duties. There is no virtue in his performance.

As this effort is being concluded, we learn that Saddam has been finally captured in Iraq.[860] As an old cop, I cannot help but feel excitement at the arrest of a mass murderer. But as an old prosecutor, I have yet to identify any offense in America's criminal codes for which Saddam could be indicted and successfully tried in any court in this country. Certainly, the people of Iraq have the right to draft a new constitution and to form a lawful government, which would then have the authority to try Saddam for his crimes against the people of Iraq. Even though I generally believe the death penalty does little to deter crime, I believe I could present the case against Saddam and argue for the ultimate penalty if the evidence supported it, but not here, and not now.

The facts that Iraq was invaded and conquered using the military forces that Bush inherited from Clinton, and that the military was successful in finally locating Saddam's hiding place, reflects no virtue upon Bush. His secret trip to Baghdad and his photo op with a phony Thanksgiving turkey contributed nothing to the search. No, nothing about Bush's War and the capture of Saddam reflects any virtue on the part of Bush.

His creation of endless preemptive war is not a virtue; indeed it is a scandal. No, more than that, it is a crime, a war crime that has made our world a less safe place to live in. In Bush's dark world, our freedoms are continually at risk and our peace is forever threatened.

Bush's War threatens the safety of ordinary people everywhere, and they live in fear of his aggressive, never-ending preemptive war. A survey was conducted of the European Union public to identify the countries that currently present the greatest threat to world peace. Fifty-three percent of those surveyed believed that the United States threatened their security, a distinction we shared with the "axis of evil," Iran, North Korea, and Iraq.[861]

Has Bush's War made you feel safer? If not, you're not alone. An NBC/*Wall Street Journal* poll found that 79 percent of Americans did not believe that Bush's War has made them feel safer from terrorism.[862]

Do you believe that Bush is telling you the truth about weapons of mass destruction in Iraq? If not, you're not alone. A CBS poll has revealed that 53 percent of Americans believe that Bush "either was hiding important elements of what he knew about WMDs in Iraq (37 percent) or was mostly lying about what he knew (16 percent). Another poll released by the Program on International Policy Attitudes reveals that a majority of Americans no longer see Bush as "honest and frank" (56 percent).[863]

In his State of the Union address delivered on January 22, 2004, Bush stated, "Last March, Khalid Shaikh Mohammed, a mastermind of September 11th, awoke to find himself in the custody of U.S. and Pakistani authorities."[864] What he did not tell the American people is that Khalid Shaikh Mohammed has told his American "interrogators that al Qaeda rejected the idea of any working relationship with Iraq, which was seen by the terrorist network as a corrupt, secular regime. When Hussein was captured, he was found with a document warning his supporters to be wary of working with foreign fighters."[865]

In his address to Congress, Bush stated, "We are seeking all the facts–already the Kay Report identified dozens of weapons of mass destruction-related program activities and significant amounts of equipment that Iraq concealed from the United Nations. Had we failed to act, the dictator's weapons of mass destruction programs would continue to this day."[866] A lie. David Kay revealed the truth the very next day when he resigned as the chief U.S. arms hunter in Iraq. In fact Kay had concluded that the stockpiles of biological and chemical weapons that everyone expected to find in Iraq never existed because they were eliminated by "a combination of U.N. inspectors and unilateral Iraqi action."* Kay reported that Iraq's

---

* Bush's doctrine of preemptive war has been dealt a severe blow by his inability to find any weapons of mass destruction in Iraq. David Kay

nuclear program was only "rudimentary." He said, "It really wasn't dormant because there were a few little things going on, but it had not resumed in anything meaningful."[867]

On February 8, 2004, Bush appeared on NBC's "Face the Nation" and repeatedly lied about the justification for his war. While he conceded the error of his pre-war statement that "the intelligence ... left no doubt that the Iraq regime continues to possess and conceal some of the most lethal weapons ever devised," he attempted to cover up by lamely suggesting that Saddam may have hidden the weapons or moved them out of the country.[868]

Even if it was true that Saddam did not have any weapons of mass destruction, Bush said that inspector "David Kay did report to the American people that Saddam Hussein ... was dangerous with the ability to make weapons." Another lie (see above). According to a *New York Times* editorial, "Kay said that Iraq's weapons program seemed to have ground to a halt under the pressure of the United Nations inspections and sanctions that Mr. Bush and his staff disdained last year. Mr. Kay said Saddam Hussein retained only the basic ability to restart weapons programs if that pressure was removed."[869]

Bush argued that the war was necessary so people don't "look at us and say, they don't mean what they say, they are not willing to follow through." Bush warned, "In my judgment, when the United States says there will be serious consequences, and if there isn't [sic] serious consequences, it creates adverse consequences."[870] However, it was the United Nations, not the United States, that had threatened "serious consequences" in Resolution 1441, and it was the United Nations inspectors who had reported there was no evidence of an imminent threat from

states, "If you cannot rely on good, accurate intelligence that is credible to the American people and others abroad, you certainly can't have a policy of preemption. ... Pristine intelligence–good, accurate intelligence – is a fundamental bench stone of any sort of preemption to be even thought about." (Savage, David G., "Failed Arms Search Called Blow to Strike-First Policy," *Los Angeles Times*, February 2, 2004, p. A9.)

Iraq. Bush insisted, "We had run the diplomatic string in Iraq;" however, in truth, Bush rejected all diplomatic alternatives.

Perhaps the most chilling thing Bush said in the interview was, "I believe it is essential that when we see a threat, we deal with those threats before they become imminent. It's too late if they become imminent."[871] Thus, in his arrogant aggrandizement of power, Bush is now convinced he can launch an immoral war without the legal justification required by international law.

Bush stated, "I'm a war president. I make decisions ... with war on my mind. ... And the American people need to know they got a president who sees the world the way it is." Does he? He went on to say, "I'm not going to change, see? I'm not trying to accommodate. I won't change my philosophy or my point of view."[872] That much is certainly true. Since he won't or can't change, we must. We have no choice. We must have a leader who forms opinions based upon an informed reality, rather than one who attempts to manipulate reality to conform to his ignorant beliefs.

Increasingly, Bush is finding himself without official support for his lies. CIA Director George J. Tenet stated on February 6, 2004, that his agency never warned Bush that Saddam's government posed an "imminent threat." Tenet confirmed that the CIA had allowed "fabricated" information from an "unreliable" Iraqi defector about suspected mobile germ-weapon labs to be used in its October 2002 National Intelligence Estimate provided to Congress, just before it voted to approve the use of force in Iraq, and later used by Secretary of State Powell in his pre-war address to the United Nations.[873]

Bush is without virtue as he continues to lie to Congress and to the American people. As we learned earlier, Section 1001 of Title 18 of the United States Code, prohibits anyone (including the President of the United States) from "knowingly and willfully" making "any materially false, fictitious, or fraudulent statement or representation to Congress. Bush continues to commit high crimes and misdemeanors with impunity, and he will do so until he is removed from office.

Some day, when our children's grandchildren look back at this moment, they will see the world we live in as it is, not the imaginary perceptions our president and his gang of zealots have attempted to pass off as the truth. History will judge us, not by what we believe, but by what we do. Awareness will be presumed, and ignorance will be no defense. If we continue to allow the commission of horrible crimes against others on our behalf, without protest, our names shall be joined in the indictment engraved upon the monument of our civilization. Will it be with pride that our descendants read the chronicle of our lives or will they be filled with shame?

You're not stupid! Get the truth. Act upon it!

791. Miller, op. cit., p. 12.

792. Minutaglio, op. cit., p. 51.

793. Alterman and Green, op. cit., p.3.

794. Ibid., p. 50.

795. Ibid., p. 334.

796. Ibid., pp. 222, 225.

797. Ibid., p. 263.

798. Begala, op. cit., pp. 89-91.

799. Kinsley, Michael, "Go to Hell: The Gospel according to George W.," July 4, 1999, *Slate,* http://slate.msn.com/id/32438/.

800. Alterman and Green, op. cit., pp. 189, 190, 301.

801. Minutaglio, op. cit., p. 330.

802. Huffington, Arianna, "White House Chutzpah," December 12, 2002, www.salon.com/news/col/huff/2002/12/12/bush/print.html.

803. "Bush's Vision Through a Veil Darkly," November 8, 2003, http://www.theleftcoaster.com/archives/000772.html.

804. Miller, op. cit., p. 132.

805. Ibid., pp. 278, 280.

806. Ibid., pp. 166, 217.

807. Ibid., p. 218.

808. Conason, op. cit., p. 174.

809. Alterman and Green, op. cit., p. 172.

810. Ibid., p 49.

811. Alterman op. cit., p. 208.

812. Alterman and Green, op. cit., p. 251.

813. Conason, op. cit., pp. 14, 15.

814. Alterman and Green, op. cit., p. 166.

815. www.whitehouse.gov/news/releases/2004/02/20040217-5.html.

816. "Nothing but lip service," *Army Times*, June 30, 2003,
http://www.armytimes.com/archivepaper.php?f=0-ARMYPAPER-
1954515.php; see also "12 Million Children Denied Child Tax Credit
Help: 1 Million Are Children in Military Families," June 6, 2003,
www.childrensdefense.org.

817. "VFW Terms President's VA Budget Proposal Harmful to
Veterans," February 2, 2004, http://www.vfw.org/
index.cfm?fa=news.newsDtl&did=1576.

818. Corn, David, "MIA WMD—For Bush, It's a Joke," *The Nation*,
March 25, 2004, www.veteransforcommonsense.org/
newsArticle.asp?id=1650

819. Alterman and Green, op. cit., p. 166.

820. Miller, op. cit., p. 301.

821. Parry, Sam, "The Bush Exit Ramp," January 22, 2003,
http://www.consortiumnews.com/2003/012203a.html.

822. Miller, op. cit., p. 318.

823. Alterman and Green, op. cit., p. 191.

824. Miller, op. cit., p. 201.

825. "Remarks by the President to the Diet, Tokyo, Japan," February 18,
2002, http://www.usembassy-china.org.cn/press/release/2002/0902-
gwbjapan1.html.

826. Kellner, op. cit., pp. 240, 242.

827. Ibid., pp. 241, 242.

828. Ibid., p. 241.

829. Ibid., pp. 241, 242.

830. Rampton, op. cit., p. 6.

831. Moore, op. cit., pp. 257, 258.

832. Minutaglio, op. cit., pp. 166, 167.

833. Ibid., p. 332.

834. Ibid., pp. 179, 188.

835. Moore, op. cit., pp. 163, 167.

836. Ibid., p. 171.

837. Ibid., p. 232.

838. Alterman and Green, op. cit., p. 338.

839. Moore, op. cit., p. 337.

840. Ibid., p. 10.

841. Ibid., p. 205.

842. Ibid., p. 296.

843. Miller, op. cit., p. 144.

844. Kellner, op. cit., p. 243.

845. Miller, op. cit., pp. 246, 247.

846. Moore, op. cit., p. 298.

847. Franken, op. cit., p. 159.

848. Moore, op. cit., p. 11.

849. Suskind, Ron, "Why Are These Men Laughing," *Esquire*, www.esquire.com/features/articles/2002/021202_mfe_rove.html.

850. Conason, op. cit., pp. 187-189.

851. "The DiIulio Letter," www.esquire.com/features/articles/2002/021202_mfe_diiulio_1.html.

852. Ibid.

853. Ibid.

854. Ibid.

855. Ibid.

856. Suskind, op cit. (n. 724).

857. Parry, op. cit.

858. Crutsinger, Martin, "O/Neill Calls Bush a Disengaged President," *Associated Press*, January 9, 2004, http://story.news.yahoo.com/news?tmpl=story&u=/ap/20040109/ap_on_go_ca_st_pe/bush_o_neill_1.

859. "The Third 2000 Gore-Bush Presidential Debate: October 17, 2000," Commission on Presidential Debates, http://www.debates.org/pages/trans2000c.html, p.18.

860. Hendawi, Hamza, "Saddam Captured," *York Sunday News*, December 14, 2003, www.yorksundaynews.com/Stories/0,1413,137~10047~1830740,00.html.

861. Kohut, Andrew, "Anti-Americanism: Causes and Characteristics," The Pew Research Center For the People and the Press, December 10, 2003, people-press.org/commentary/display.php3?AnalysisID=77.

862. Teixeira, Ruy, "Worth The Cost?" *TomPaine.common sense*, http://www.tompaine.com/feature2.cfm/ID/9447.

863. Ibid.

864. "Text of President Bush's State of the Union speech," http://www.csmonitor.com/2004/0122/p25s02-uspo.html.

865. Miller, Greg, "Cheney Is Adamant on Iraq 'Evidence,'" *Los Angeles Times*, January 23, 2004, p. A1

866. "Text of President Bush's State of the Union speech," op. cit.

867. Zakaria, Tabassum, "U.S. arms hunter says no Iraq WMD," *Reuters*, January 24, 2004, www.reuters.co.uk/newsPackageArticle. jhtml?type=topNews&storyID=444547&section=news.

868. "Interview With President George W. Bush," *NBC News*, "Meet the Press With Tim Russert," February 8, 2004, http://www.msnbc.msn.com/id/4179618/.

869. "Mr. Bush's Version," Editorial, *The New York Times*, February 9, 2004, http://www.commondreams.org/views04/0209-04.htm.

870. "Interview With President George W. Bush," *NBC News*, "Meet the Press With Tim Russert," February 8, 2004, http://www.msnbc.msn.com/id/4179618/.

871. Ibid.

872. Ibid.; see also Saletan, William, "You Can Make It With Plato: Bush's difficult relationship with reality," *Slate*, February 8, 2004, http://slate.msn.com/id/2095160/.

873. Drogin, Bob and Greg Miller, "CIA Chief Saw No Imminent Threat in Iraq," *Los Angeles Times*, February 6, 2004, p. A1.

NO END IN SIGHT

The Iraqi resistance to our occupation is intensifying, we are losing control of the cities and supply lines, more soldiers are dying every day, and our allies are abandoning us. What happened?

On April 1, 2004, the front page of my daily newspaper carried a large color photograph of a jubilant mob of Iraqis in the city of Falluja dancing around and upon the smoldering wrecks of two automobiles following the ambush and killing of four U.S. civilian security guards.

That evening, television news showed the partial remains of one of them thrown over a telephone line, another was dragged down the street tied to a car, and the burned corpses of the other two were hung from a nearby bridge. Although there are a number of police stations and a military base of more than 4,000 marines nearby, the desecration and demonstration continued for hours as the crowd chanted, "Viva Mujahideen!" (Long live the resistance!)

Al Qaeda did not kill these brave Americans; Iraqis who consider us to be invaders of their country killed them. Bush uses the euphemism "insurgents" and labels them as "cowards," but no matter what you and I may think about their motives, the truth is that these cheering Iraqis are celebrating a victory in their resistance to our occupation.[874]

What happened? Just days before President Bush ordered the invasion of Iraq a year ago, Vice President Cheney was asked if Americans were prepared for a "long, costly and bloody battle?" He replied, "The read we get on the people of Iraq is there is no question but what they want is to get rid of Saddam Hussein and they will welcome as liberators the United States when we come to do that." Deputy Secretary of Defense Wolfowitz stated, "Like the people of France in the 1940s, they view us as their hoped-for liberator."

A year ago, on April 30, 2003, Secretary of Defense Rumsfeld told the U.S. troops in Iraq, "You came not to conquer, not to occupy, but to liberate, and the Iraqi people know this." Only a few days before Rumsfeld spoke, American troops had shot down 13 Iraqi civilians during a pro-Saddam march in Falluja. Rumsfeld promised that he would be able to reduce the number of troops in Iraq to 30,000 by September.[875]

What happened? Either Bush and his gang of zealots really think we are stupid and that they can get away with lying to us, or, they are really stupid and they believed their own lies.

In the week before April 1st, recently deployed American marines conducting roadblocks and armed searches in Falluja fought a street battle resulting in the deaths of a marine, 18 members of the resistance and other innocent bystanders, including an 11-year-old boy and an ABC cameraman.

A local teacher said, "They are always provoking the people, blocking the streets, detaining the civilians, under the pretext of searching for weaponry and insurgents. If they continue to behave like this, the response of the people will be more tough." City walls in Falluja are covered with graffiti that say it is "halal" (clean) to kill Americans.[876]

The sad truth is that the American people want to believe we are liberators, and we are spending a billion dollars and the lives of a dozen soldiers every week to prove it, but to the Iraqi people, we are just the latest conquerors to occupy their homeland.

The carnage in Falluja was no April Fool's joke, yet Osama bin Laden surely laughed. Bush and his flock of Chicken Hawks have swallowed bin Laden's bait, and they have dragged the rest of us into the trap. Al Qaeda is stronger than ever.

Throughout the Middle East, thousands of young men and women are proudly lining up to surrender their lives in suicide attacks to expel the modern infidel crusaders. Richard Clarke wrote in *Against All Enemies*, "It was as if Usama bin Laden, hidden in some high mountain redoubt, were engaging in long-range mind control of George Bush, chanting "invade Iraq, you must invade Iraq."[877]

Whether it is bin Laden, Cheney, Karl Rove or the other neocon zealots who control Bush's mind, it is up to us to end this tragedy. It is all but certain that al Qaeda will launch another terrorist attack on America, and the next time Bush and his zealots are likely to suspend the Constitution.[878]

Then it will be too late. The torch of freedom will be extinguished, and the voice of democracy will be silenced.

It has proven difficult to end this book. Every day there's more death and destruction, and the entire nature of Bush's War changed during the month of April. Most obviously, it is clear that a year after Bush announced "Mission Accomplished," his war is far from over. The mission has again shifted. It is no longer the "insurgents" or terrorists who are threatening U.S. troops; it is simply the Iraqis who must be defeated.

The Iraqi resistance repelled an assault by American marines to regain control of Falluja. Not only did the Iraqi security forces we have trained to take over policing in Iraq refuse to assist the marines, many joined with the resistance. Now, we have made a deal with one of Saddam's former generals to raise an army and take over the task of pacifying the city as the marines withdraw from their siege of the city.

The Shiite "Mahdi Army" has denied American troops entry into the holy city of Najaf and has established occupation-free zones in Kufa and Karbala. There are increasingly violent attacks in the usually peaceful areas in southern Iraq, including Basra.

Spain has withdrawn its troops, and Honduras is posed to follow "in the shortest time possible." The Dominican Republic, Nicaragua and Kazakhstan are withdrawing their forces, and it appears that El Salvador, Norway, the Netherlands and Thailand will be next. New Zealand is withdrawing its engineers, and South Korea and Bulgaria have pulled their troops back to their bases.[879]

The resistance has begun to take and hold hostages, and a strange videotape of the beheading of an American visitor has shocked the world. The main highways through Iraq are no longer under the control of American forces. Money budgeted to rebuild Iraq is being diverted to pay for private security forces, which operate outside the control of American commanders. Two major contractors, General Electric and

Siemens have suspended operations with the Iraqi Ministry of Electricity and the Coalition Provisional Authority.[880]

Finally, the world has been outraged in the last month by the publication of dozens of photographs depicting widespread torture and sexual abuse of Iraqi prisoners by American soldiers. Although the Pentagon attempted to suppress its own report on the outrage, it was quickly revealed that the International Red Cross had notified American authorities of the prisoner abuse months before the photographs were taken. We also learned that Paul Bremer repeatedly raised the issue of prison conditions with Rumsfeld and other top officials last year, yet nothing was done.

More troubling was the revelation that Major General Geoffrey Miller, the commander of the Guantanamo Bay prison, visited Iraq last year and advised Iraqi military jailers to follow his Guantanamo model. Specifically, military guards should soften up prisoners to improve the conditions for interrogations by intelligence officers.

It was no surprise that Bush defended Rumsfeld and the top military commanders or that he blamed the torture and abuse on a few bad apples at the bottom of the barrel; however, he demonstrated his absolute arrogance and total lack of remorse by reassigning General Miller to take over and run the Iraqi prisons.

In spite of all of this, Bush says, "We will stay the course in Iraq. We're not going to be intimidated by thugs or assassins. We're not going to cut and run from the people who long for freedom. Because, you know what? We understand a free Iraq is an historic opportunity to help change the world to be more peaceful."[881] In announcing that he was delaying bringing home as many as 25,000 troops as scheduled, Rumsfeld said, "We're facing a test of will, and we will meet that test.[882]

The widespread Iraqi uprising caused April to be the bloodiest month since the war began, including the initial invasion. 140 American soldiers were killed and 1,073 were wounded. Since the war started, 777 American soldiers have lost their lives, and 4,327 have been wounded in action. 109 soldiers from other countries have been killed, for a total of 886, an average of almost three a day. [883] They each have a name and a family. They each had a future. Has it been worth the price? What happened?

This must end...

874. Sanders, Edmund, "Iraqi Mob Kills 4 Americans: Civilians' Bodies Are Mutilated by a Cheering Crowd in Falluja," *Los Angeles Times*, April 1, 2004, p. A1.

875. Sheer, op. cit., pp. 123, 129, 132.

876. "Marines engage in deadly battle," March 27, 2004, *Los Angeles Times*, http://www.magicvalley.com/news/ worldnation/index.asp?StoryID=8258.

877. Clarke, op. cit., p.246.

878. "General Franks Doubts Constitution Will Survive WMD Attack," November 21, 2003, www.newsmax.com/archives/articles/ 2003/11/20/185048.shtml.

879. Klein, Naomi, "Mutiny is the only way out of Iraq's Inferno," *The Guardian*, May 1, 2004, www.guardian.co.uk/Iraq/Story/ 0,2763,1207504,00.html.

880. Glanz, James, "Violence in Iraq Forces 2 Big Contractors to Curb Work," *The New York Times*, April 22, 2004, www.nytimes. com/2004/04/22/international/middleeast/22REBU.html.

881. Gettleman, Jeffrey and Douglas Jehl, "Fierce Fighting With Sunnis and Shiites Spreads to 6 Iraqi Cities, *The New York Times*, April 7, 2004, www.nytimes.com/2004/04/07/international/middleeast/ 07IRAQ.html.

882. Hauser, Christine, "Iraq Uprising Spreads; Rumsfeld Sees It as 'Test of Will,'" *The New York Times*, April 8, 2004, www.nytimes.com/ 2004/04/08/international/middleeast/08IRAQ.html.

883. "Iraq Coalition Casualty Count," http://www.lunaville.org/warcasualties/Summary.aspx.

BIBLIOGRAPHY

(*Primary Sources)

Abraham, Rick. *The Dirty Truth, The Oil and Chemical Dependency of George W. Bush.* Houston, Texas: Mainstream Publishers, 2000.

*Ahmed, Nafeez Mosaddeq and John Leonard. *The War on Freedom: How and Why America was Attacked, September 11, 2001.* Joshua Tree, California: Tree of Life Publications. 2002.

*Alterman, Eric. *What Liberal Media? The Truth About Bias and the News.* New York: Basic Books, 2003.

*–, and Mark Green. *The Book on Bush: How George W. (Mis)leads America.* New York: Viking, 2004.

*Begala, Paul. *Is Our Children Learning?: The Case Against George W. Bush.* New York: Simon & Schuster, 2000.

Benjamin, Dan. *The Age of Sacred Terror: Radical Islam's War Against America.* New York: Random House Trade Paperbacks, 2003.

Bergen, Peter I. *Holy War, Inc: Inside the Secret World of Osama bin Laden.* New York: Free Press, 2002.

Blix, Hans. *Disarming Iraq.* New York: Pantheon Books, 2004.

Blumenthal, Sidney. *The Clinton Wars.* New York: Farrar Straus & Giroux, 2003.

Bok, Sissela. *Lying: Moral Choice in Public and Private Life.* New York: Vintage Books, 1999.

Bonifaz, John C. *Warrior King: The Case for Impeaching George Bush.* New York: Thunder's Mouth Press, 2003.

Borjesson, Kristina, editor, *Into the Buzzsaw: Leading Journalists Expose the Myth of a Free Press.* Amherst, New York: Prometheus Books, 2002.

Bowen, Russell S. *The Immaculate Deception: The Bush Crime Family Exposed.* Carson City, Nevada: American West Publishers, 2001.

Brewton, Pete. *The Mafia, the CIA, and George Bush.* New York: SPI Press, 1992.

Brisard, Jean-Charles, et al. *Forbidden Truth: U.S.-Taliban Secret Oil Diplomacy, Saudi Arabia and the Failed Search for bin Laden.* New York: Thunder's Mouth Press/Nation Books, 2002.

Brock, David. *Blinded by the Right: The Conscience of an Ex-Conservative.* New York: Crown Publishing Group, 2002.

Bryce, Robert and Molly Ivins. *Pipe Dreams: Greed, Ego, and The Death of Enron.* New York: Public Affairs, 2002.

Bugliosi, Vincent, et al. *The Betrayal of America: How The Supreme Court Undermined the Constitution and Chose Our President.* New York: Thunder's Mouth Press/Nation Books, 2001.

Bush, George W. and Karen Hughes. *A Charge to Keep.* New York: William Morrow, 1999.

* Chomsky, Noam. *9-11,* New York: Seven Stories Press, 2001.

—, *Hegemony or Survival: America's Quest for Global Dominance [The American Empire Project]* New York: Metropolitan Books, 2003.

Cirincione, Joseph, et. al. *WMD in Iraq: Evidence and Implications.* Washington, D.C.: Carnegie Endowment for World Peace, January 2004.

*Clarke, Richard A. *Against All Enemies: Inside America's War on Terror.* New York: Free Press, 2004.

*Conason, Joe. *Big Lies: The Right-Wing Propaganda Machine and How It Distorts the Truth.* New York: Thomas Dunne Books, 2003.

*Corn, David. *The Lies of George W. Bush: Mastering The Politics of Deception.* New York: Crown Publishers, 2003.

Dean, John W. *Worse than Watergate: The Secret Presidency of George W. Bush.* New York: Little Brown & Company, 2004.

Dubose, Lou, et al. *Boy Genius: Karl Rove, the Brains Behind the Remarkable Political Triumph of George W. Bush.* New York: Public Affairs, 2003.

Flanders, Laura. *Bushwomen: Tales of a Cynical Species.*

New York: Verso, 2004.

Ford, Charles V. *Lies! Lies!! Lies!!!: The Psychology of Deceit.* Arlington, Virginia: America Psychiatric Press, 1999.

Fox, Loren. *Enron: The Rise and Fall.* Hoboken, New Jersey: John Wiley & Sons, 2002.

Frank, Thomas. *One Market Under God: Extreme Capitalism, Market Populism, and the End of Economic Democracy.* New York: Anchor, 2001.

*Franken, Al. *Lies and The Lying Liars Who Tell Them: A Fair and Balanced Look at The Right.* New York: Dutton, Penguin Group, 2003.

Fromkin, David. *A Peace to End All Peace: The Fall of the Ottoman Empire and The Creation of The Modern Middle East.* New York: Henry Holt and Company, 1998

Frum, David. *The Right Man: The Surprise Presidency of George W. Bush.* New York: Random House, 2003.

Garrison, Jim. *America as Empire: Global Leader or Rogue Power?* San Francisco: Berrett-Koehler Publishers, Inc., 2004.

Halberstam, David. *War in a Time of Peace: Bush, Clinton, and the Generals.* New York: Scribner, 2001.

Halstead, Ted, and Michael Lind. *The Radical Center: The Future of American Politics.* New York: Anchor, 2002.

Hartung, William D. *How Much Money Did You Make on the War, Daddy: A Quick and Dirty Guide to War Profiteering in the Bush Administration.* New York: Thunder's Mouth Press, 2004.

Hatfield, J. H. *Fortunate Son: George W. Bush and the Making of an American President.* Brooklyn, New York: Soft Skull Press, 2002.

Hertz, Noreena. *The Silent Takeover: Global Capitalism and the Death of Democracy.* New York: Harper Business, 2003.

*Hightower, Jim. *Thieves in High Places: They've Stolen Our Country–And It's Time To Take It Back.* New York: Viking Press, 2003.

Huffington, Arianna. *Fanatics and Fools: The Game Plan*

for Winning Back America. New York: Miramax, 2004.

*Ivins, Molly and Lou Dubose. *Bushwhacked: Life in George W. Bush's America.* New York: Random House, 2003.

—, and Lou Dubose. *Shrub: The Short but Happy Political Life of George W. Bush.* New York: Vintage Books, 2000.

Johnson, Chambers. *The Sorrows of Empire: Militarism, Secrecy and the End of the Republic.* New York: Metropolitan Books, Henry Holt and Company, 2004.

Johnson, David Cay. *Perfectly Legal: The Covert Campaign to Rig Our Tax System to Benefit the Super Rich–And Cheat Everybody Else.* New York: Portfolio, 2003.

Kagan, Robert. *Of Paradise and Power: America and Europe in the New World Order.* New York: Knopf, 2003.

Kaplan, David A. *The Accidental President: How 413 Lawyers, 9 Supreme Court Justices, and 5,963,110 Floridians (Give or Take a Few) Landed George W. Bush in the White House.* New York: William Morrow, 2001.

*Kellner, Douglas. *From 9/11 to Terror War: The Dangers of the Bush Legacy.* Lanham, Maryland: Rowman & Littlefield, 2003.

—, *Grand Theft 2000: Media Spectacle and a Stolen Election.* Lanham, Maryland: Rowman & Littlefield, 2001.

Kleveman, Lutz. *The New Great Game: Blood and Oil in Central Asia.* New York: Atlantic Monthly Press, 2003.

Krugman, Paul. *The Great Unraveling: Losing Our Way in the New Century.* New York: W.W. Norton & Company, 2003.

Korten, David C. *When Corporations Rule the World.* San Francisco: Kumarian Press and Berrett–Koehler Publishers, 1995, 1996, 2001.

Lance, Peter. *1000 Years for Revenge: International Terrorism and the FBI.* New York: Regan Books, 2003.

Landau, Saul *The Pre-Emptive Empire: A Guide to Bush's Kingdom.* London: Pluto Press, 2003.

Lewis, Charles and Center for Public Integrity. *The*

Buying of the President 2000. New York: Avon, 1999.

___, and Center for Public Integrity. *The Buying of the President 2004.* New York: Perennial, 2004.

___, and Bill Allison. *The Cheating of America.* New York: William Morrow, 2001.

Leone, Richard C. and Greg Anrig, Jr., editors, *The War on Our Freedoms: Civil Liberties in an Age of Terrorism.* New York: Public Affairs, 2003,

Lind, Michael. *Made in Texas: George W. Bush and The Southern Takeover of American Politics.* New York: Basic Books, 2002.

Longman, Jere. *Among the Heroes: United Flight 93 & the Passengers & Crew Who Fought Back.* New York: Perennial, 2002.

Mann, James. *The Rise of the Vulcans: The History of Bush's War Cabinet.* New York: Viking, 2004.

Mann, Michael. *Incoherent Empire.* New York: Verso, 2003.

McCain, John S. and Mark Salter. *Faith of My Fathers.* New York: Random House, 1999.

Miller, John, et al. *The Cell: Inside the 9/11 Plot, and Why the FBI and CIA Failed to Stop It.* New York: Hyperion, 2002.

*Miller, Mark Crispin. *The Bush Dyslexicon: Observations on a National Disorder.* New York: W.W. Norton & Company, 2002.

*Minutaglio, Bill *First Son: George W. Bush and the Bush Family Dynasty.* New York: Three Rivers Press, 2001.

*Moore, James. *Bush's War for Reelection: Iraq, The White House, and the People.* Hoboken, New Jersey: John Wiley & Sons, 2004

*Moore, James and Wayne Slater. *Bush's Brain: How Karl Rove Made George W. Bush Presidential.* Hoboken, New Jersey: John Wiley & Sons, 2003.

Moore, Michael. *Dude, Where's My Country?* New York: Warner Books, 2003.

Murray, Williamson and Robert H. Scales Jr. *The Iraq War: A Military History.* Cambridge: Harvard University Press, 2003.

*Palast, Greg. *The Best Democracy Money Can Buy: The Truth About Corporate Cons, Globalization, and High-Finance Fraudsters.* New York: Plume, Penguin Group, 2002.

*Phillips, Kevin *American Dynasty: Aristocracy, Fortune, and the Politics of Deceit in the House of Bush.* New York: Viking, 2004.

*Pitt, William Rivers and Scott Ritter. *War on Iraq: What Team Bush Doesn't Want You to Know.* New York: Context Books, 2002.

Prestowitz, Clyde. *Rogue Nation: American Unilateralism and the Failure of Good Intentions.* New York: Basic Books, 2003.

*Public Citizen, "America's Other Drug Problem: A Briefing Book On The Rx Drug Debate," Public Citizen's Congress Watch, 2002, (http://www.citizen.org/publications/release.cfm?ID=7188).

*Rampton, Sheldon and John C. Stauber *Weapons of Mass Deception: The Uses of Propaganda in Bush's War on Iraq.* New York: J.P. Tarcher, 2003.

Rea, Milan and Noam Chomsky. *War Plan Iraq: Ten Reasons Against War with Iraq.* New York: Verso Books, 2002.

Rees, David and Colson Whitehead. *Get Your War On.* New York: Soft Skull Press, 2002.

*Scheer, Christopher, et al. *The Five Biggest Lies Bush Told Us About Iraq.* New York: Seven Stories Press and Akashic Books, 2003.

Shipler, David K. *The Working Poor: Invisible in America.* New York: Knopf, 2003.

*Solomon, Norman and Reese Erlich. *Target Iraq: What the News Media Didn't Tell You.* New York: Context Books, 2003.

Sperry, Paul. *Crude Politics: How Bush's Oil Cronies Hijacked the War on Terrorism.* Nashville, Tennessee: WND

Books, 2003.

Suskind, Ron. *The Price of Loyalty: George W. Bush, the White House, and the Education of Paul O'Neill.* New York: Simon & Schuster, 2004

Tapper, Jake. *Down and Dirty: The Plot to Steal the Presidency.* New York: Little Brown & Company, 2001.

Toobin, Jeffrey. *Too Close to Call: The Thirty-Six-Day Battle to Decide the 2000 Election.* New York: Random House Trade Paperbacks, 2002.

Unger, Craig. *House of Bush, House of Saud: The Secret Relationship Between the World's Two Most Powerful Dynasties.* New York: Scribner, 2004.

*Van Bergen, Jennifer. "Repeal the USA Patriot Act." 2002, (http://truthout.com/docs).

Vidal, Gore. *Dreaming War: Blood for Oil and the Cheney-Bush Junta.* New York: Thunder's Mouth Press, 2002.

Waldman, Paul. *Fraud: The Strategy Behind The Bush Lies And Why The Media Didn't Tell You.* Naperville, Illinois: Sourcebooks, Inc., 2004.

Woodward, Bob. *Bush at War.* New York: Simon & Schuster, 2002.

___ , *Plan of Attack.* New York: Simon & Schuster, 2004.

Wright, Micah Ian, et al. *You Back the Attack, We'll Bomb Who We Want.* New York: Seven Stories Press, 2003.

INDEX

quote, on media slant, 264
Kurdistan, 141, 170
Kurds, 146, 156, 170
Kuwait, 141, 143-145, 147
Kwasniewski, Aleksander, 206
Kyrgyzstan, 122
Lay, Ken, 49, 50, 53, 54
League of Conservation Voters, 137
League of Nations, 141
Leahy, Patrick, 189
Lebanon, 85, 153
Levin, Carl, 102
Liddy, G. Gordon, 266
Limbaugh, Rush, 266, 268
    quote, on media slant, 267
Los Angeles Times, 158, 168
Luntz, Frank, 2
Madison, James, 224
MaGuire, William, 80
Mann, Horace, 58
Maresca, John J., 124
Massoud, Ahmed Shah, 102
Mathis, William J., 68
MBNA Corporation, 217., 283
McCain, John, 23-25, 268, 290
McClellan, Scott, 205
McGraw-Hill, 59
media
    AM talk radio, 266, 267
    bias, 265, 266
    myth of liberal bias, 263, 264
    perceptions of, 264
Media Research Center, 264
    suppressed dissent, 264
Mehalba, Ahmed, 209
Merck, 245
Meyerson, Adam, 265
Microsoft, 73
middle class, 44, 75
Mine Safety and Health Administration, 285

Mirant Corporation, 50
Mitchell, Larry, 98
Mohammed, Khalid Shaikh, 300
Moon, Sun Myung, 261
Morocco, 181
Moussaoui, Zacharias, 100, 112, 226, 227
Mubarak, Hosni, 181
Mueller, Robert, 111, 236
Musharraf, Pervez, 126
Nader, Ralph, 31
Nairobi, 90
National Commission on Terrorist Attacks upon the United States, 114, 117, 118
National Energy Policy Development Group, 49
National Institute of Health, 247
National Review, 260
National Security Council, 152
Nazis, 219
NBC, 299
neocon movement, 149, 150, 159, 260-264
Netanyahu, Benjamin, 149
Netherlands, 246
New York Times, 8, 160, 268
New Zealand, 248
Nicaragua, 84, 143
Niederer, Sue, 191
Niemöller, Martin, 219
    quote, unchecked power, 219
Nixon, Richard M., 5, 6, 142
Niyazov, Saparmurat, 126
North American Aerospace Defense Command, NORAD, 105-107, 116
North Korea, 159, 171, 287, 299
Norton, Gale, 48
O'Dell, Walden, 276
O'Neill, John, 119
O'Neill, Paul, 54